Portraits of Peer Violence in Public Space

Experiences from Young People in Four Localities in Europe

Austrian Institute of Youth Research

Vienna, 2009

Contributions to Youth Research, Volume 11

Edited by the Austrian Institute of Youth Research

Barbara Riepl and Howard Williamson (Eds.)

Portraits of Peer Violence in Public Space

Experiences from Young People in Four Localities in Europe

Austrian Institute of Youth Research

Vienna, 2009

Published by:

Österreichisches Institut für Jugendforschung
Austrian Institute of Youth Research
Maria-Theresienstraße 24/10
A - 1010 Vienna, Austria
www.oeij.at

Funded by the European Commission, DG Justice, Freedom and Security, in the Daphne Programme II and by the Austrian Federal Ministry for Health, Family and Youth Affairs.

ISBN: 978-3-9502020-2-1

Photo: sxc.hu
Layout: Verlag des Österreichischen Gewerkschaftsbundes GmbH, A - 1230 Vienna
Print: REMAprint Druck- und Verlagsges.m.b.H., A - 1160 Vienna

Printed on white chlorine-free paper.

Contents

Preface

Peer violence in public space is a topic that has generally not been much in the focus of recent European comparative research – some national or local, commissioned or graduate studies may exist, but largely the subject is conspicuous by its absence. Yet it is an important political issue, not least because of those rare, tragic and sometimes fatal incidents that inevitably attract huge attention in the media.

To remedy the absence of profound and detailed information on the prevalence and nature of more 'routine' and 'ordinary' violence between young people in public settings, an international research project designed to explore and analyse experiences of peer violence in four different countries was funded by the European Commission, DG Justice, Freedom and Security. The co-funding was secured through the Austrian Federal Ministry for Health, Family and Youth Affairs.

The study was part of the Daphne Programme II of the European Commission, which aims to prevent and combat violence against children, young people and women and to protect victims and groups at risk. Dealing with a better understanding of violence against young people by young people, this study belonged to priority 1 of the call for 2006: Peer violence and peer protection mechanisms.

Focussing on disadvantaged neighbourhoods, the study is furthermore of particular relevance to those policies currently addressing the Europe-wide challenges of segregation in urban areas. Moreover, this project speaks to the concerns of European institutions "to be accountable for the particular needs of youth from disadvantaged social areas" (Decision on Social Integration and Youth 2004). The EU German Presidency in 2007 was concerned with 'new cohesion strategies' for children and young people in disadvantaged neighbourhoods. The 'Berlin process' of the Council of Europe has demonstrated a commitment to constructing the 'social city', in which the safety of young people is one component. All this, of course, both flows from and contributes to municipal agendas that are concerned with making the streets safe *for*, and safe *from*, young people. For these and other reasons, the research reported in this book could not be more topical.

This publication is the final step in a long process, starting with securing funding, establishing a network and building a team, developing a methodology, implementing the fieldwork, and constructing the analysis. We would like to thank the European Commission as well as the Austrian Ministry for recognising the importance of the study and providing the necessary budget. In particular, we also wish to thank all the interviewed young people, youth workers and other experts for their contribution to the study.

We hope that this publication, which will be distributed to experts from NGOs and representatives from public authorities, will fulfil its aim and responsibility to disseminate the research results across both national and international levels. If it provides a baseline for reflection and consideration of a hitherto relatively invisible but increasingly topical issue in policy and practice, then it will have served its purpose.

Barbara Riepl and Howard Williamson (editors)

Introduction

Barbara Riepl and Howard Williamson

1 Presentation of the Study in this Book

This book reports on an empirical research study of peer violence in public space in and across four different European localities: a small town in eastern Finland, a suburb of a city in southern Estonia, a town in the valleys of south Wales in the United Kingdom, and a district in the capital city of Austria. Following this introduction, which provides an underpinning theoretical context, and describes the common methodological framework that shaped the study design, each of the four 'case studies' is presented in the next four chapters.

These locality studies all follow the same structure with same section headings. In 'Introduction: Setting the Scene', they report on research findings and public debate on young people's violence in their country. In 'Locality in Focus' some background information on the locality is given. This is followed by 'The Approach Adopted' which provides information on how the overarching research design was adopted and adapted by the research team according to the specific challenges in each of the localities, as well as problems encountered during fieldwork. In the next two sections 'Models of Peer Violence' and 'The Character of Violent Encounters', the results of the analysis of the data are presented. 'Feedback and Consultation' then reports on the workshop with experts and the workshop with young people that was held in each locality to reflect the research findings and to develop recommendations. Finally, each of the locality reports concludes with 'Some Final Reflections'.

In the presentation of the study results, the original names of the localities were replaced by pseudonyms. In addition, all other names of places and people were changed to provide anonymity and ensure confidentiality. Examples from the interviews - either as quotations or as summarising descriptions - were put into cameos. Each of these cameos provides as much information on the interviewee(s) as seemed to be useful or necessary to connect the cameo to the text. This means that information on age, gender, ethnic background or youth culture group was given only where it was relevant to the arguments or ideas being advanced. Information on the interview situation is always provided, using the following three categories: individual interview, mixed sex group interview and single sex group interview.

After the locality reports, the publication continues with a comparative chapter written by the whole research team. 'Looking Across the Localities: Commonalities and Differences in Peer Violence' aims to highlight what is common and what is distinctive in the local studies. In the section 'Towards a Typology of Peer Violence in Public Space' the information from the local studies was clustered into joint models that cover all the forms of peer violence that were reported by young people. The next section 'The General Characteristics of Violent Encounters' provides more in-depth information on the key dimensions of peer violence in public space. The section 'The Role of Age, Gender and Ethnicity' finally describes the relevance of age, gender and the ethnic dimension for the description and interpretation of violent encounters and their impact. The book ends with 'Conclusions: Reflections and Recommendations', a consideration of theory and methods and of implications for policy and practice.

2 Concepts and Definitions on Violence in Literature and Research

In a document on violence and health, the *World Health Organization* defines violence as *"the intentional use of physical force or power, threatened or actual, against oneself, another person, or against a group or community, that either results in or has a high likelihood of resulting in injury, death, psychological harm, maldevelopment or deprivation"* (WHO 1996 cited by Krug *et al.* 2002: 5). The definition encompasses interpersonal violence as well as suicidal behaviour and armed conflict. It also covers a wide range of acts, going beyond physical acts to include threats and intimidation. Besides death and injury, the definition also includes the myriad and often less obvious consequences of violent behaviour that compromise the well-being of individuals, families and communities. Similarly, the European Monitoring Centre on Racism and Xenophobia (2005) states that violence encompasses a range of behaviours that are not limited to physical acts against people and property, and which can incorporate words, harassment and threats.

The *World Report on violence and health* (Krug *et al.* 2002) furthermore uses a typology of violence that divides violent behaviour into categories according to who has committed the act, who the victims are, and to what kind of violence they have been subjected.

- Interpersonal violence

- Suicide and self-harm

- Collective violence

Suicide and self-harm are clearly forms of physical violence against the self, though they may also cause psychological harm to others. Collective violence is considered to be the instrumental use of violence by a group (or a group member) in order to achieve political, economic or social objectives. Both may have some bearing on peer violence, but it is *interpersonal violence* that would appear to be the most pertinent aspect of violence referred to and represented in this study.

Interpersonal violence – violence inflicted by an individual or a small group of individuals – includes youth violence, violence between intimate partners, other forms of family violence such as abuse of children and the elderly, rape and sexual assault by strangers, and violence in institutional settings such as schools, workplaces, nursing homes and prisons. Interpersonal violence covers a wide range of acts and behaviours from physical, sexual and psychological violence to deprivation and neglect. While violence in the community, particularly youth violence, is highly visible and generally labelled as 'criminal', violence within the family is more hidden from public view. Weist and Cooley-Quille (2001) differentiate between (a) family violence and (b) community violence as types of interpersonal violence.

One manifestation of interpersonal violence is individual violence. *Individual violence* is exercised by individual perpetrators (or by individuals in peer groups) against strangers in the street, in public spaces or public institutions, and also exercised in the private sphere against friends and relatives (Imbusch 2003). Imbusch further distinguishes between the concepts of direct physical violence and psychological violence in the context of interpersonal violence:

(a) Direct physical violence is aimed at harming, injuring, or killing other people, and stands unequivocally at the centre of the whole issue of violence. This form of violence is always exercised in a manifest manner and is mostly intentional.

(b) Psychological violence is aimed at the mind, the soul, and the psyche of a person and is based on words, gestures, pictures, symbols, or deprivation of the necessities of life.

Tolan and Guerra (1994), through an analysis of the apparent causes of violence, the segments of the population most at risk from violence, and the type of interventions, distinguish four types of adolescent violence. These have been labelled situational, predatory, psychopathological, and relationship. They can be considered as existing on a multidimensional continuum within a bio-psychosocial model of causation. The continuum shows differences in (a) the proportion of the population likely to show each type, (b) the likely causes, (c) the synergy of risk factors, and (d) the likely age of onset.

Situational catalysts can lead both to the initiation of violence and to an increase in the seriousness of the violent act. Police records, emergency room surveys, and other archival sources show increases in violence rates during extreme heat, on weekends, and during times of social stress independent of individual characteristics. Similarly, frustration in pursuing planned events and the occurrence of unavoidable accidents or events increase the likelihood of aggressive behaviour. Social factors such as poverty relate to a greater likelihood of violence perpetration and victimisation. Presumably, the higher rates of violence perpetration and victimisation among minority youth reflect social discrimination and oppression. The availability of weapons and alcohol and drug use also represent powerful catalysts for adolescent violence. The occurrence of violence is not attributable simply to individual tendency or relationship difficulties; situational influences may exacerbate an individual's predisposition toward violence or increase the seriousness of the violence that occurs.

Predatory violence is perpetrated intentionally to obtain some gain or as part of a pattern of criminal or antisocial behaviour. Muggings, robbery, and gang assaults are common forms of this type of violence. Much predatory violence is part of a pattern of serious chronic antisocial behaviour that includes this type of violence. This pattern represents the most studied and the best understood type of adolescent violence. It seems to be predictable, develops slowly over time with onset in early adolescence, lasts long after adolescence, is dependent on multiple risk factors, and seems to require intensive and early prevention and treatment intervention methods.

Psychopathological violence is rare in prevalence but represents a particularly virulent form. The violence tends to be more repetitive and extreme than other types of violence. Of the four types, it represents the clearest example of individual pathology. Research suggests that such behaviour is related to the neural system and severe psychological trauma. Apparently, the violent behaviour represents a by-product of the pathology rather than situational provocation or an aspect of a developing criminal career.

Relationship violence encompasses a significant proportion of violence for all age-groups, including adolescents. It arises from interpersonal disputes between persons with ongoing relationships, in particular among friends and family members. In some cases the violence erupts as an unusual incident, in other cases it occurs routinely. In many cases, it appears that relationship violence is a familial habit, with the occurrence of violence between parents related to violence towards and among the children. For adolescents, dating violence is another example of relationship violence. Relationship violence seems to affect a large proportion of the adolescent population and seems to have its basis in both social and psychological characteristics.

The period of *adolescence and young adulthood* is a time when violence, as well as other types of behaviour, is often given heightened expression. Youth violence can develop in different ways. Some children exhibit problem behaviour in early childhood that gradually escalates to more severe forms of aggression before and during adolescence. Longitudinal studies have examined in what ways aggression can continue from childhood to adolescence and from adolescence to adulthood to create a pattern of persistent offensive behaviour throughout a person's life. Several studies have shown that childhood aggression is a good predictor of violence in adolescence and early adulthood. Most violent young people, however, depicted as 'adolescence-limited offenders' by Krug *et al.* (2002), engage in violent behaviour over much shorter periods.

Retrospective reports in the particular context of *bullying* have found that children who are bullies tend to be bullies as adults and to have children who are bullies; similarly, children who are victimised tend to have children who are victimised. Longitudinal research also indicates that childhood bullying is associated with antisocial behaviour and criminality in adulthood, and with limited opportunities to attain socially desired objectives, such as stable employment and long-term relationships (Farrington 2002 cited by Craig and Harel 2004).

With regard to *age*, it is obvious that younger children are more likely to be victims of violence from parents or other caretakers, whereas for youth over 12 the perpetrator-victim dichotomy *and* relationship varies more widely. A larger proportion of violence then is youth-to-youth, whether it is predatory violence that is part of criminal behaviour 'on the street', partner violence that is part of intimate relationships, or intra-familial violence (Tolan 2001). In the research of Díaz-Aguado, Martínez Arias and Martín Seoane (2004 cited by Díaz-Aguado 2006) it was found that the risk of peer aggression is greatest in early adolescence (13-15 years of age).

Youth involvement in violence is a *global problem*, yet research and interventions tend to be dedicated to specific events and circumstances, such as the participation of children in war, inter-group tensions in the aftermath of war, street living, intergroup fighting, and interpersonal aggression or exclusion (Daiute 2006).

Acosta *et al.* (2001) present the results of a systematic literature review of abstracts on *studies related to violence and young people*. A total of 1,168 empirical articles on violence-related problems connected to youth were identified by a *PsycINFO* (American Psychological Association, 1980-1999) search and then classified in a multidimensional grid. The major findings from this review indicate that between 1980 and 1999 (a) significantly fewer articles were published on treatment or prevention than on the description/assessment of violence-related problems relating to young people, (b) a greater number of articles were published on the description/assessment, treatment and prevention of direct forms of violence exposure (by being a victim or perpetrator) than on less direct forms of violence (witnessing violence, knowing about violence, or media exposure to violence), (c) most articles on assessment and treatment of violence were about violence occurring in the home, followed by violence occurring in the school setting, and most articles on prevention were about preventing violence in schools, with fewer about preventing violence in the home, (d) fewer empirical articles were about violence in the community, particularly when the focus was on dating violence, and (e) from 1980 to 1999, while significant research attention on the description/assessment of violence-related problems and young people has been maintained relative to the other approaches, the focus on treatment has decreased and the focus on prevention has increased.

The majority of studies carried out over the last two decades *on peer violence* amongst young people have focused on the violence found in schools, and on one of its principal forms, commonly termed bullying, highlighting that a) it includes a range of behaviours (making fun of others, threats, intimidation, physical abuse, systematic isolation, insults), b) it tends to cause problems that are repeated and prolonged over time, c) it involves an abuse of power, with one pupil, who has the general support of a group, bullying another who is defenceless and cannot escape from the situation alone, and d) it is maintained due to the ignorance or passivity of those around both bully and victim, who do not involve themselves directly. Most research on school bullying has been carried out from a descriptive perspective, trying to discover the prevalence of the problem and the characteristics of those involved, both bullies and victims (Diaz-Aguado 2006).

Poor emotional adjustment, school adjustment, and high-risk health behaviours among those involved with bullying are remarkably consistent elements within findings from international comparisons. A large cross-national study demonstrated that the adverse relationship between bullying involvement – as a victim, bully, or bully-victim – and psychosocial adjustment is similar across young people in 25 countries (Eisenberg and Aalsma 2005).

3 Theoretical Background of the Study

Currently there is a broad range of approaches in violence research as these depend very much on the professional background of the researchers. Violence research conducted by psychologists, pedagogues, sociologists or criminologists often reflects different interests and uses different methods. Yet what is common to most studies is that the theoretical concept is developed by adult researchers. Based on scientific literature, the researchers start with a specific theory that is then tested with empirical data. Often these studies are quantitative and aim to measure the spread of specific types of violence or identify predictive factors. What Kovacheva (2005) states for the research on political participation of youth seems also to be true for other topics: Inadequate designs of comparative multi-country surveys often miss young people's own interpretations and impose researchers' conceptions upon respondents.

To contribute to a better understanding of the meaning of peer violence to young people and to be sensitive to unknown phenomena, another methodology needs to be applied. For this reason we decided to use qualitative methods in this study in order to explore the perspective of the young people. This approach was influenced by current developments in childhood and youth research that promote the active role of young people (Alanen 2007; Fraser *et al.* 2004; Lewis *et al.* 2004). The study further refers to the social constructionist point of view according to which people reconstruct the social reality around them by interpreting the experienced phenomena (Burr 2003; Gergen 1999). Corsaro (2005) uses the term 'interpretive reproduction' to stress that children are on the one hand not simply internalising society and culture but they actively contribute to cultural production. On the other hand, children and young people are of course constrained by the existing social structure. Their navigation (or pathways, niches or trajectories – see Evans and Furlong 1997) between constraint and choice, or structure and agency, as it is more routinely depicted, has been and remains a central locus of theoretical assertion, contention and debate. Nevertheless, there has to be a *prima facie* case for bringing their accounts of their experiences and their perspectives into that debate and to accommodate it within any wider data collection and analysis.

The collection of good quality data for comparative analysis acknowledges variations across the different contexts in Europe. Studying everyday peer violence in disadvantaged neighbourhoods means to study an international phenomenon that is not restricted to particular countries. According to the relevant theories on cross-national research, our methodological approach was to see the nation with its specific dimensions as one relevant component but not as the object of the study (see for example Kohn 1989). The idea was to select four 'disadvantaged' localities that are very different yet simultaneously reflect the great variety of disadvantaged areas in the European cultural context. These localities may not be seen as typical for the country in which they are situated and they certainly cannot be held to typify or represent that country. Nevertheless each country does in some respects set some of the context that may be relevant to explain certain findings, just as more local specificities, such as particular cultural traditions or contemporary aspects of social and economic infrastructure, are also part of that context. The idea of using such diverse localities was to optimise the possibility of producing a variety of findings. This variety could then be analysed and used to work towards an inclusive and, arguably, more universally applicable typology of peer violence in public space.

4 Aims, Objectives and Implementation of the Study

Aims and Research Questions

The study aimed to draw a picture of the different types of everyday violence amongst 13 to 16 year olds in disadvantaged neighbourhoods in Austria, Estonia, Finland and the United Kingdom. Beyond the school gate, this age group and their behaviour remains largely a hidden phenomenon, in terms of both research knowledge and local policy provision.

The following objectives were therefore defined: to draw attention to everyday peer violence in this age group, to look at the phenomenon from the young people's point of view, to develop recommendations which seek to empower young people in dealing with peer violence in public space, to enable experts from NGOs and public authorities at national and international level to develop appropriate and complementary measures, and to contribute to international networking and information exchange on youth and violence research.

By raising awareness and developing recommendations for meaningful measures of intervention the project was designed to benefit young people who are victims of everyday peer violence. It should further indirectly benefit other young people who are witnesses to peer violence or feel restricted in their daily routine because they fear becoming victims. Finally, reduced peer violence in public space could also benefit all other population groups as it improves the general atmosphere of a neighbourhood and enhances community safety and that elusive concept of 'the quality of life'.

The main research questions were:

- What different types of violent interactions and engagement amongst 13 to 16 year olds can be found in public space?

- How do young people describe these violent encounters?

- How do they experience and interpret these violent encounters?

- What is the impact of direct or indirect involvement in these violent encounters?

- In which ways do gender and ethnicity mediate experiences and understanding of such violent encounters?

Definitions in the Project

The team of researchers involved in the project discussed the conceptualisation of peer violence that should be applied to this study and arrived at the following definition: *Peer violence is the range of physical and non-physical behaviours which – whether by intent or effect – causes physiological and/or psychological hurt to other young people.*

Furthermore, for the choice of the locality the team agreed to define disadvantaged neighbourhoods as *areas of social, professional and political disinterest*. It was determined that the localities selected should *not* be places that are routinely mentioned (in the media, political debate or policy attention) as epitomising neighbourhoods with high levels of violence. Instead, the localities chosen should be areas that are not part of the political dialogue because the problems of violence are not considered to be significant or severe enough to merit dedicated attention. They should, however, be areas where young people feel somewhat disillusioned about their likely futures, on account of local learning and labour market opportunities, and where significant numbers of young people visibly spend much of their time in public space.

With regard to the definition of public space, we decided to look at peer violence in *publicly accessible space*, which largely meant streets or parks but could also include shopping malls or other similar public spaces. For clarification it should further be said that by 'publicly accessible space' we did not mean indoor settings such as sports halls, schools or youth centres (which usually are publicly accessible) and we did not mean the Internet. Our aim was to learn about the young people's life outside of organised activity. However, as we were also interested in the description of the 'journey' of conflicts and violent encounters, we decided to include information on where conflicts had started (which could have been at school or some other more 'organised' setting) and where it has travelled to (which could be back to school, another 'organised' context, or perhaps on to the Internet). But whatever the origins or destinations, it had to have been on the streets or in the parks of the chosen disadvantaged area at least once during its particular 'journey'.

Methodological Approach and Ethics

The study used a qualitative approach which seemed to be appropriate for a number of reasons beyond the theoretical rationale outlined above. First, it is a preferred method in violence research where little is known about a topic, for it can 'illuminate' emergent issues and help to formulate and frame tentative typologies and structures. Second, qualitative methods of observation and interviewing are favoured where the phenomenon in focus (whether the topic or the human subjects) is rather complex and unlikely to yield useful data through alternative methodologies such as a questionnaire. Third, qualitative methods hold more promise if the aim is to understand subjective experiences (Böttger and Strobl 2003).

The study design determined that in each of the four localities approximately 25 young people would be interviewed. The interviews should be open ended and flexible in order to elicit and facilitate the narratives of the young people. During the common development of the interview guidelines by the research team, five topics to be dealt with in each of the interviews were identified.

Figure 1: Topics in the interviews with the young people

Personal details: Age, ethnicity, gender, living area and other relevant personal data

Activities in public space: How do you spend time in public space? What do you do? On your own or with friends? What other young people do you come across out here? Are there places/ people you fear or avoid?

Conflicts between young people in public space: When you had a conflict/ an aggressive encounter with other young people in public space, what happened exactly? When and where was it? How did it start? Who started what? How did it go on? Who else was involved? How and why did it end?

What other experiences with conflict or aggression between you and other young people in public space do you remember? When and where was it?

Coping strategies: How did you feel? What did you do? What did other young people do? Were any adults involved? Did you tell anybody afterwards? Were you happy that you did? Did you ask anybody for help? Do you think the same will happen again?

Definition of violence and attitudes towards: What you told me about conflicts and aggression between young people in public space, would you call it violence? If yes, why? If yes, would you call it severe violence? If no, how is it different from 'real' violence?

The questions listed above are illustrative and neither complete nor is the wording exact as this could be varied according to the course of the interview and the style of the interviewer.

For the analysis of the interviews, relevant *dimensions* of peer violence in public space were identified. These were based on the following question: What, who, where, when, how often, why, under which conditions, with what consequences and how was it perceived?

Each team, therefore, was asked to look for information on the following dimensions:

- Type of behaviour (physical/non-physical)

- Combatants (number, characteristics, roles, relationships)

- Time (moments, duration, frequency)

- Place (such as hot-spots, movement of location)

- Conditions (situational and individual)

- Intentions, motivations and justifications

- Consequences (harm, hurt and other impact)

- Interpretations by the young people

All interviews were transcribed and all research teams used computer programmes for the analysis. In the interpretation process, particular attention was paid to gender and ethnicity as relevant categories for the understanding of the researched phenomenon.

Instead of the more common and rather simple presentation of differences between the answers of boys and girls or young people from different ethnic backgrounds, our analysis tried to explore the relevance of the concepts of gender and ethnicity for the understanding of the different types of peer violence as well as for the variation in coping strategies under similar conditions.

In addition, the study design also included *two workshops* in each country: one with young people and one with adult experts. The invited young people had not necessarily been participants in the interviews but they needed to come from the chosen locality. The aims of these workshops were to consult on the research findings and to develop recommendations for policy and practice together with those who are dealing with peer violence in their daily routine. To involve not only experts but also young people in the development of the recommendations towards preventive measures meant to credit them with a positive and proactive role. It also ensured that the recommendations were not elaborated exclusively from an adult-centred perspective.

With regard to ethics, the following 'best practice' principles were adhered to in all four local studies: informed consent, confidentiality and anonymity in data storage and presentation, the well-being of the interviewed young people and the well-being of the researchers in the field.

Finally, external assessment from a consultant evaluator already during the research process aimed to optimise the project outcome.

Study Implementation

The study duration was two years, from March 2007 to February 2009. It was coordinated by the Austrian Institute for Youth Research and carried out by four research teams in the countries involved. Each of these teams consisted of a coordinator and one research associate. The team of researchers involved overall brought to the project a rich variety of professional backgrounds and experience.

The project started with a short period of desk research on similar research projects within each of the countries. As a next step, in each country the research team identified an appropriate locality for the study. Expert interviews were carried out to gain information on the area and relevant regional or local statistics were examined. The aim was not only to identify disadvantaged areas but also to ensure considerable variation between the four localities on a number of social and economic criteria.

The following four anonymised localities were eventually identified and chosen: *Urbanitz* is part of two outer districts of Vienna, Austria's capital and biggest city; *Perkova* is an old working class area in Tartu, the second largest city in Estonia; *Järvikaupunki* is a medium sized town (population 50,000) in the Province of Eastern Finland; and *Trewaun*, a relatively small post-industrial community of 15,000 people, is situated in a South Wales valley in the United Kingdom.

In addition to the selection of the localities, a common setting for the interviews with the young people needed to be developed during the first months. The main outcomes were:

- Young people were informed that the study was about young people and their interactions in public space. During the interview, the interviewer explained the project's special interest in conflicts between young people.

- Young people were asked for conflicts or aggressive encounters rather than for violent encounters because it was assumed that the term violence would depend too much on the understanding of violence and could possibly restrict the thinking of the young people in an unwanted way.

- During the general introduction to the interview, it was pointed out to the participants that they could refuse to answer a question whenever they wanted. In addition they were informed on their rights to anonymity and the researchers' commitment to confidentiality.

- Each research team designed a leaflet with information on services where young people could access help. This could be handed out to the interviewed young people if they seemed to need, or requested, support.

- All young people received contact information about the interviewer.

- The interviews were conducted mainly during the afternoon and evenings, to reach the younger as well as the older young people.

Due to the time consuming process of developing a common framework as well as common interview guidelines (see section 'Methodological Approach and Ethics' above), the interviews with the young people did not start until September 2007. This meant that the interviews took place during autumn and winter. In all countries, the researchers discovered that it was often difficult to meet young people in public during cold (and particularly wet) weather. Furthermore, though they spent considerable time making direct contact with young people in the streets, they sometimes needed to get support from youth workers as gatekeepers to facilitate such contact. It also quickly became apparent (and perhaps should have been anticipated) that many young people preferred to be interviewed in a group, when the original research aspiration had been to conduct individual interviews. However, as the rather open qualitative approach of the study was seeking to give young people a chance to shape the research process, it was decided to be responsive to the circumstances encountered and to use a mixture of single and group interviews in all countries, according to the wishes of the young people who were willing to engage with the research. The analysis of the interviews mainly took place in spring 2008. The data were organised to promote the understanding of *the meaning of peer violence from the perspectives of young people*. The findings of the analysis were therefore described in two ways. On the one hand, they were used to develop *models* of peer violence to give an insight into the different constellations and sometimes dynamics of violent encounters. On the other hand, each research team highlighted the most important findings in each of the *dimensions* delineated above. In summer 2008, towards the end of the study, the *workshops* with young people and with experts were organised in each country. Though a commendable idea as a policy-oriented mechanism within the research process, it met with mixed success, on account of the availability and interest both of young people and local experts. Further information on how the research design was adapted by each research team can be found in the different locality accounts (see chapters 2-5).

The last step in the project was to design a *common publication* in order to present the findings and conclusions on a trans-national level. Therefore, all the research teams not only wrote their own locality reports but also contributed to the comparative analysis as well as to the development of the recommendations.

For the external assessment, Youra Petrova agreed to be the project evaluator. She was recommended and asked to take on this role on account of her reputation in the field of youth cultural and youth violence research. The evaluator was involved twice: once to read the first draft of the locality reports and once to read the entire text before it was finalised for publication. On both occasions, her thorough and committed commentary and suggestions led to a considerable number of revisions and additions to the text. Her contribution to the quality of the analysis and to the presentation of the results needs to be fully acknowledged: the whole research team is very grateful for her diligence and detailed response.

References

Acosta, O. M., Albus, K. E., Reynolds, M. W., Spriggs, D. and Weist, M. D., (2001). Assessing the Status of Research on Violence-Related Problems Among Youth. *Journal of Clinical Child Psychology*, 30 (1), 152-160.

Alanen, L., (2007). Theorizing Children's Welfare. *In:* Wintersberger, H., Alanen, L., Olk, T. and Qvortrup, J., eds., *Childhood, Generational Order and the Welfare State: Exploring Children's Social and Economic Welfare*. Odense: University Press of Southern Denmark, 27-44.

Böttger, A. and Strobl, R., (2003). Potentials and Limits of Qualitative Methods for Research on Violence. *In:* Heitmeyer, W. and Hagan, J., eds., *International Handbook of Violence Research*. Dordrecht, Boston, London: Kluwer Academic Publ., 1203-1217.

Burr, V., (2003). *Social Constructionism*. London and New York: Routledge.

Corsaro, W. A., (2005). *The Sociology of Childhood*. London: Thousand Oaks, New Delhi: Sage Publications.

Craig, W.M. and Harel, Y., (2004). Bullying, physical fighting, and victimisation. *In:* Currie, C., Roberts, C., Morgan, A., Smith, R., Settertobulte, W., Samdal, O. and Rasmussen V.B., eds., *Young people's health in context – Health Behaviour in School-aged Children (HBSC) study: International report from the 2001/2002 survey*. Copenhagen: World Health Organization Regional Office for Europe, 133-144.

Daiute, C., (2006). General indroduction: The Problem of Society in Youth Conflict. *In:* Daiute C. ed. *International perspectives on youth conflict and development*. Oxford [u.a.]: Oxford Univ. Pr., 3-19.

Díaz-Aguado, M. J., (2006). Peer Violence in Adolescents and its prevention from the school. *Psychology in Spain,* 10 (1), 75-87.

Eisenberg, M. E. and Aalsma, M. C., (2005). Bullying and peer victimisation: Position paper of the Society of Adolescent Medicine. *Journal of Adolescent Health,* 36, 88-91.

European Monitoring Centre on Racism and Xenophobia, (2005). *Racist Violence in 15 EU Member States. A Comparative Overview of Findings from the RAXEN National Focal Points Reports 2001-2004.* Vienna: EUMC. Available from: http://eumc.eu.int/eumc/material/pub/comparativestudy/CS-RV-main.pdf [Accessed 20 February 2007].

Evans, K. and Furlong, A., (1997). Metaphors of youth transitions: niches, pathways, trajectories or navigations. *In:* Bynner, J., Chisholm, L. and Furlong, A., eds., *Youth, Citizenship and Social Change in a European Context.* Aldershot: Ashgate.

Fraser, S., Lewis, V., Ding, S., Kellett, M. and Robinson, C., (2004). *Doing Research with Children and Young People.* London: Sage.

Gergen, K. J., (1999). *An Invitation to Social Construction.* London: Thousand Oaks, New Delhi: Sage.

Imbusch, P., (2003). The Concept of Violence. In: Heitmeyer, W. and Hagan, J., eds., *International Handbook of Violence Research.* Dordrecht, Boston, London: Kluwer Academic Publ., 13-39.

Kohn, M. L., ed., (1989). *Cross national research in Sociology.* Newbury Park: Sage.

Kovacheva, S., (2005): Will youth rejuvenate the patterns of political participation? *In:* Forbrig, J., ed. *Revisiting youth political participation: challenges for research and democratic practice in Europe.* Strasbourg: Council of Europe Publ., 19-28.

Krug, E. G., Dahlberg, L. L., Mercy, J. A., Zwi, A. B. and Lozano, R., eds., (2002). *World report on violence and health.* Geneva: World Health Organization. Available from: http://www.who.int/violence_injury_prevention/violence/world_report/wrvh1/en [Accessed 20 February 2007].

Lewis, V., Kellett, M., Robinson, C., Fraser, S. and Ding, S., (2004). *The Reality of Research with Children and Young People.* London: Sage.

Tolan, P. H., (2001). Emerging Themes and Challenges in Understanding Youth Violence Involvement. *Journal of Clinical Child Psychology,* 30 (1), 233-239.

Tolan, B. and Guerra, N., (1994). *What Works in Reducing Adolescent Violence: An Empirical Review of the Field. Boulder.* CO: Center for the Study and Prevention of Violence.

Weist, M. D. and Cooley-Quille, M., (2001). Advancing Efforts to Address Youth Violence Involvement. *Journal of Clinical Child Psychology,* 30 (1), 147-151.

Gender Roles, Immigrant Victimisation and the Ambiguous Boundaries of Violence among Small Town Teenagers: Järvikaupunki, Finland

Veli Liikanen and Helena Helve

1 Introduction: Setting the Scene

Public concern about youth violence in Finland has primarily been related to high profile cases of homicides committed by underage young people. Among these are cases of manslaughter between peer teenagers (Reinboth 2004), premeditated murder of an adult couple by a group of young teenagers (Harju 2003) and two recent cases of school shooting in Jokela and Kauhajoki (committed by 18 and 22 year old males, respectively), which received worldwide attention (Helsinki Times 2008; Width 2008). These cases, and less conspicuous ones, have contributed to increasing discussion about the communal life and mental state of Finnish youth and the possible polarisation in both well-being and life styles of young people.

The trends in juvenile crime in general and youth violence in particular have been analysed (Kivivuori 2006; Kuure 2001), and some results support the hypothesis of polarisation of criminal violent behaviour among young people. The trends in juvenile violence have not been as positive as they have been in relation to many other crimes (e.g. against property), which appear to have decreased during the last decade (Kivivuori 2006). While the proportion of young people who refrain from delinquency has steadily increased and the attitudes of juveniles toward crime have become more condemnatory, recorded assaults by under 15 year old children have continued to grow during the 21st century. This is partly due to more efficient social control, but it might indicate an *increasing* trend in youth violence.

Violence related to ethnicity came to the centre of focus in Finland during the 1990s. As the number of foreign citizens in the country started to rise rapidly, ethnical conflicts and racist attitudes began to receive more attention in public. In some localities, prominent *racist* youth groups and *subcultures* emerged. Today, the number of foreign-born inhabitants is about 4% of the population. The biggest groups are Swedish and Estonian, followed by Russian and Somali. Finnish Swedes and the Sami and Romani peoples are prominent domestic minorities. Despite the relatively low foreign population, immigration continues to divide opinions in public debate. Especially the perceived misuse and costs of asylum-seeking has been targeted in public critique. Although most young Finns have a positive outlook on multi-culturalism, attitudes towards increasing immigration are much less favourable and only a minority of young people have concrete contacts with immigrants (Harinen 2005). Young people in rural communes are less sympathetic towards multi-culturalism and immigration than those dwelling in more urban areas.

Research on youth violence related to racism concentrated on the middle-sized town of Joensuu, in Eastern Finland. Studies of Joensuu Skinhead groups in the 1990s are a classic example of Finnish youth gang research (Hilden-Paajanen 2005). The youth cultural aspects of the racist youth milieu have also been studied. According to Perho (2005), the participants of the racist youth culture in Joensuu defined their position by distancing themselves from 'unordinary' subcultures and 'nerdiness'. Informants saw themselves as 'normal' and defined intolerance and 'toughness' as an ordinary feature of normal character. Members of recognised youth subcultures (e.g. punks, hip-hoppers) or ethnically different people were regarded as 'unordinary'. Suurpää (2002) shows that young people's own interpretations of racism link racist behaviour to people's fear of strangers, Finnish national character and ignorance towards the world outside.

According to annual reports surveying recorded racist offences, published by the Finnish Police College since 1998, the number of reported assaults has been on an increasing trend. For young immigrants themselves, the tendency to be convicted for violent crimes is more than twice the corresponding tendency for young Finns, and the difference has been growing (Iivari 2006).

Studies by Näre (2000) and Honkatukia (2001) have provided information about sexual violence against *girls* and young women. Among different age classes, women and girls under 21 years old are the most likely victims in situations where the perpetrator is previously unknown to the victim or during the 'getting-to-know' phase (Honkatukia 2001). On the other hand, the largest proportion of sexual violence against girls and women between 10-20 years of age seems to take place inside the family (Näre 2000).

Honkatukia's survey (2000) of sexual harassment experiences by 15 year old girls reveals a continuum of sexual abuse: 41% of the respondents admitted having been targets of unwanted advances and 5% of the girls admitted having been victims of sexual violence. Unknown, foreign or adult perpetrators were easily condemned, but the most common forms of harassment coming from familiar boys tended to be seen as non-serious. By speaking about coping strategies girls resist harassment, but also reproduce the cultural view of the 'strong Finnish woman'. On the other hand, victims of sexual violence did not reveal much about the experiences. Expectation to cope may be one factor silencing some of the girls' experiences.

According to Aaltonen (2006), interpretations of sex-based harassment incidents are justified and negotiated by referring to features of the target, the scene or the perpetrator. By situating incidents in different spaces and places, young people contrast their experiences with ordinary and predictable non-harassment and unusual and unexpected harassment. The city by night is considered to be a scene where harassment

Gender Roles, Immigrant Victimisation and the Ambiguous Boundaries
of Violence among Small Town Teenagers: Järvikaupunki, Finland

25

by drunken men routinely occurs and girls are afraid of violence from strangers, and house parties are often cited as scenes of coercive physical abuse.

Gender roles affecting approaches to violence were also present in the aforementioned study by Perho (2005). Both boys and girls saw the 'real members' of subcultures to be boys. Being tough and intolerant is more expected of boys than girls. For boys, being tough also meant a readiness to use physical violence in certain situations. Girls had more power to decide individually about their own participation in the racist youth milieu than boys, but at the same time they had less power to become members of the inner circles of the racist or Skinhead youth cultural group.

Bullying among young people has also been analysed in Finnish studies (Salmivalli 1998). It is worth pointing out here that some Finnish experts on youth violence have been outspoken about the importance of keeping bullying separate from assaults and other forms of violence explicitly covered in criminal law (Purjo 2006).

Honkatukia, Nyqvist and Pösö (2006) have recently examined young people's talk of violence to highlight the multiple meanings of violence. Their interviews in Finnish reform schools revealed several narrative means used by the young residents to describe violence. Violence had instrumental uses in belonging and sharing, creating social order and problem solving. Violence was also seen as an expression of madness and emotions, and used in fiction and fantasy.

The study presented in this chapter focuses on 13-16 year old young people's everyday experiences of peer violence in the Eastern Finnish town of Järvikaupunki. The locality is a population centre in an area suffering from detrimental structural change in economy and population during the last two decades. The target group of the study is the general youth population present in the public space of the town, including young people belonging to ethnic minorities. By gathering and analysing data on everyday experiences, this study adds to our understanding of different forms, interpretations and approaches of Finnish *small town* youth violence, the polarisation of violent experiences and the role of ethnicity and gender in everyday violence.

2 Locality in Focus

The town of Järvikaupunki is located in the Province of Eastern Finland, in a landscape rich with forests, lakes and both cultivated and abandoned farm land. The distance to the flourishing economical centres of Helsinki and the capital area in the south is some hundred kilometres.

Eastern Finland is very sparsely populated and the poorest NUTS 2 region in Finland (Eurostat 2007). Eastern Finland was deemed an "area whose development is lagging behind" (Objective 1) by the European Regional Development Fund (European Commission 2007). Unemployment in the area is higher and economic growth is lower than the national average. The economy is heavily dependant on public sector activity, such as agriculture and forestry, and small business and enterprise development is weak. Young people and women actively emigrate from the region, and the flight from the land still continues, crowding urban areas and weakening basic services in rural areas. Education levels are below the national average despite several good higher level educational establishments.

Järvikaupunki was established in the mid-19th century and developed as an administrative and military centre of the region. The town grew steadily in inhabitants and area, with the population rising from the few thousand in the beginning of 20th century to over 20,000 in the 1960s, and reaching the level of around 32,000 halfway through 1980s. Since then, the population size of the town itself has changed little. However, the consolidation of municipalities during this decade has again rapidly increased the administrative area, as two neighbouring municipalities have been joined to Järvikaupunki. As a result, the official number of inhabitants in Järvikaupunki is now almost 50,000, ranking the town in the top 20 of biggest cities in Finland.

The town centre is surrounded by a large sparsely populated rural area, continuing for roughly 50 kilometres in all directions, and consisting of woods, lakes, small farms, villages and, further away, neighbouring small towns. Jobs, education and other public services are provided in Järvikaupunki town for much of the population in the surrounding area.

In Järvikaupunki the age structure of the population is distinctly skewed towards the older cohorts. The proportion of elders (over 65 years) is greater and proportions of children and young people (under 20 years) lower than the national average (Tilastokeskus 2007a). The statistical forecast for 2025 sees Järvikaupunki losing 8 % of its young (under 20 years) inhabitants in the next 20 years (Tilastokeskus 2007b).

The number of young people aged 10 to 19 is about 6,000 in the whole municipality (Tilastokeskus 2007a). Of these, only about 250 live in the town centre area, which houses the most popular public gathering places for young people. Most of the young people live in different residential areas around, though relatively close to the town centre. Most of these residential areas house between 50-300 young people. The biggest suburb has around 600 young inhabitants. Of the main interview sites for this study, Tukkula has around 350 young inhabitants and Lampela a little over 150.

The economy in Järvikaupunki is dominated by the public sector and services, and characterised by large proportion of jobs in agriculture and forestry (Tilastokeskus 2007c). The proportion of industrial jobs is well below the national average. Most enterprises in Järvikaupunki are small or medium-sized. In 2007, the unemployment rate in Järvikaupunki was 9.7%, clearly higher than the national 8.2%. The number

Gender Roles, Immigrant Victimisation and the Ambiguous Boundaries
of Violence among Small Town Teenagers: Järvikaupunki, Finland

27

of unemployed youth (under 25 years) was about 300 in 2006 (Tilastokeskus 2007d). Educational indicators rank Järvikaupunki close to the national average.

Since 1990, the number of foreign inhabitants has increased by eight times in the Järvikaupunki area (Etelä-Savon TE-keskus 2006). The foundation of a refugee centre in 1990 facilitated the reception of around 200 refugees and a sharp doubling of the foreign population in Järvikaupunki. Since then, immigration has continued to increase the number of foreigners. Currently, there are around 800 foreign citizens in Järvikaupunki, with Russians (248), Afghans (129) and Sudanese (68) being the largest groups (Tilastokeskus 2007a). The city's Finnish-Swedish minority is practically non-existent, so the 'native' Finns are almost all unilingually Finnish.

In the summer Järvikaupunki and its surroundings attract a considerable number of tourists, both domestic and foreign. Around 5,000 holiday houses are situated in the Järvikaupunki region, making it one of Finland's most popular areas for summer houses and other forms of recreational dwelling. The city has a distinct 'summer buzz', with several nationally attractive summer happenings (music festivals, horse races, markets), and summer inhabitants and tourists. The city is much less lively during the long wintertime.

For many teenagers living in different parts of the Järvikaupunki town or its surroundings, the town centre acts as a nodal point of leisure time, where young people meet each other after school and on weekends. Especially on Friday and Saturday nights these gatherings often involve drinking alcohol. Weekend nights also gather adult bar clientele to the town centre, and therefore the central city blocks are the liveliest area in town both day and night.

Activities for teenagers are provided mainly by different hobby organisations (most importantly sports clubs) and the city youth service, which maintains a youth café in the centre and several youth centres in different residential areas and occasionally organises gigs and events for teenagers. However, the majority of the concert and night life in town takes place in bars and clubs with age limits that exclude under 18 year olds. Some seasonal festivals, such as the first of May celebrations, school's out parties and the New Year's Eve celebrations, trigger significant teenage partying outdoors. These parties are also focused in and around town centre.

There seems to be few obvious sub-cultural elements affecting or organising group formation by young people in Järvikaupunki. The most apparent sub-cultural references expressed by teenagers are the popular 'heavy metal' style, utilised especially by boys and the somewhat less common fashions such as Goth, Hip-hop, Skater and Punk. Most young people express less clear cut styles, avoiding obvious and explicit sub-cultural affiliations. Local sport clubs, even though somewhat popular, have not generated significant youth supporter groups around them. However, during the 1990s there was a period of an active racist youth subculture in Järvikaupunki. A local youth group of the time was involved in several violent crimes targeting both immigrants and some native peer teenagers.

3 The Approach Adopted

Choice of the Interview Sites

For defining the areas for field work several experts on youth violence in Järvikaupunki town were interviewed: a city youth worker, assistant chief of police, two NGO anti-violence youth workers, a worker for a Finnish mediation association (victim-offender mediation for young underage offenders) and two workers for an anti-violence organisation specialising in family violence. The experts were asked about the areas and locations where peer violence among young people takes place in Järvikaupunki. They were also asked to name the areas in Järvikaupunki they considered socio-economically 'disadvantaged'. The question of the social background characteristics of young violent offenders was also addressed.

Three main criteria were used in choosing the areas, based on the background information and these interviews. First, *hot spots* of youth gathering and recorded peer violence were identified. This was especially important, because the number of young people in Järvikaupunki is relatively low, and decreasing. Although there are many places where young people spend their leisure time hanging around with friends, there are not too many sites where several different groups of young people gather at the same time. These kinds of sites enable encounters between 'unfamiliar' youths and are of specific relevance to this study.

Secondly, the *social* and *ethnic diversity* of the population was considered. It seemed that the hot spots in the town centre attract outgoing young people from all parts of the city and its surroundings. The municipal and congregational youth facilities in different parts of the city also serve as focal points for young people, but the social structure of the participating young people was anticipated to be differently composed. Ethnic minority groups seemed to avoid the major youth gathering sites of the town centre, regardless of the 'outgoingness' of the individual member.

Lastly, areas were assessed in terms of *socio-economic disadvantage*. In Järvikaupunki, the low socio-economic status of inhabitants can be associated with the cheap rented flats owned and provided by the city. However, these blocks of flats are scattered around in different areas of the city and rarely form larger disadvantaged neighbourhoods. Often more middle class housing areas are situated nearby. Young people from these disadvantaged households apparently spend much of their time away from their local neighbourhoods, in city centre along with other young people. Teenagers travel around on foot, on bicycles, mopeds, scooters, buses and in cars to meet their friends.

Gender Roles, Immigrant Victimisation and the Ambiguous Boundaries
of Violence among Small Town Teenagers: Järvikaupunki, Finland

29

Based on these criteria, the Järvikaupunki city centre was identified as the main area for the fieldwork. Major youth hot spots in the centre are the marketplace, the promenade beside it and a park nearby. According to the police and other experts, the vast majority of violent offences by teenagers take place in these locations.

Additional fieldwork was done in the residential areas of Lampela and Tukkula. Looking at the population, unemployment and housing type figures by city districts, these two districts seemed to have both relatively low socio-economic status and a significant number of young inhabitants. These areas also housed local municipal youth centres, which were used for the interviews. In order to include immigrant teenagers in the sample, the local multicultural centre was also contacted to find interviewees with different ethnic backgrounds.

Conducting the Interviews

The interviews were conducted between from October 2007 to April 2008 at various sites in Järvikaupunki: at cafes in the town centre, at the local multicultural centre, at the town library and at three youth centres located in the town centre and two other neighbourhoods. In the town centre and in the youth centres the interviewees were contacted by the researcher. The staff at the multicultural centre assisted in finding young immigrants and made the initial contact with these interviewees. Half of the interviewees were contacted and interviewed at the town centre and the other half in the different youth centres.

At the beginning of the interview, interviewees were given a simple brochure about the study. They were told that the interview was part of an international Daphne study and was about teenagers' leisure time, their use of public space and their encounters with other teenagers. Violence was not mentioned at the beginning. Rather it was presented as a study question later on, when incidents of peer violence had come up during the interview. While there was some concern about the ethics of this approach before the interviews, the interviewees seemed not be disturbed about the subject. A leaflet about support services was available, in case discussing violence produced any distress in the respondents.

The length of the actual interviews (not including introductory remarks) varied from 15 to 70 minutes. In the group interviews, the group was formed by the teenagers themselves. This led to two cases where some participants in a group were 12 years old. In one other group interview a 19 year old friend of the interviewees joined the group. These overage and underage interviewees are not included in the sample.

For the most part, there were no clear indications of exaggeration, deceit or evasion in the narratives of the Interviewees. At some points in the analysis, however, the credibility of the interviewees raised new questions. Since there are no ways to validate these suspicions, the analysis treated the interviewees' narratives to be illustrations and illuminations of young people's discourses relating to their experiences, as much as 'factual' descriptions of events. No clear tendency of under or over reporting violent experiences during the interviews could be perceived.

Sample

In Järvikaupunki *32* young people between the ages of 13 and 16 were interviewed for the study. Nineteen interviews were conducted, including eight group and eleven individual interviews. There were three pair interviews, three interviews in groups of three and two interviews in larger groups of four and five persons (these groups did involve some teenagers that were outside the 13-16 age range).

In all, 17 girls and 15 boys were interviewed. Three 13 year olds, fourteen 14-15 year olds and fifteen 16 year olds are included. The number of 16 year olds is quite large because the young people encountered in the town centre were mostly these older young people, especially during wintertime. The sample includes five *immigrant* teenagers with a foreign appearance (black skin and/or darker curly hair in addition to a noticeable accent), who had lived in Järvikaupunki and Finland for 2-5 years. In addition to these, there was one individual with a similarly recent immigrant background who spoke fluent Finnish and had no foreign appearance. Two interviewees (one with a clearly foreign appearance) born in Järvikaupunki had one ethnically foreign and one native Finnish parent. Unfortunately, no first generation immigrant girls were interviewed, as none were recruited by the multicultural centre or encountered during the interviews conducted elsewhere. It seems that immigrant *boys* are more outgoing than girls, almost certainly on account of their cultural background. It may also be that the interview theme led to a male bias in the interviewee recruitment by the multicultural centre staff. The fact the interviewer was male might also have had an effect.

The home neighbourhood of the interviewees varied considerably. Only eleven interviewees actually had a home in the neighbourhoods where the interviews took place (town centre, Lampela and Tukkula). Five more resided in other areas of similar socio-economical profile. Many lived outside the town, coming into the town to see their friends.

26 interviewees (all except the first two groups) were also asked about their *housing* type to gather some further information about their socio-economic circumstances. Approximately half of the interviewees who gave information on this lived in blocks of flats. Most of the other half resided in single family houses, and the remaining three interviewees in row houses.

The groups of young people in which the interviewees spent their leisure time were described to be *friendship* or *hobby* groups. The relationships between the teenagers

Gender Roles, Immigrant Victimisation and the Ambiguous Boundaries
of Violence among Small Town Teenagers: Järvikaupunki, Finland

31

in a group were mostly based on the context of school, hobbies and neighbourhood. The groups described by the young people were almost always loose and undefined. These characteristics applied to both the interviewed groups and other youth groups the interviewees reported being part of.

Methodology and Analysis

The interviews were transcribed and the subject matters related to the study questions and themes were coded by hand using an open coding method. As an analytic tool, content analysis was used to determine the presence of words and concepts within transcribed texts quantifying and analysing the presence, meanings, relationships and forms of peer violence among young people in Järvikaupunki. A *classification* of violent encounters was constructed by describing eight models of violence that commonly came up in the interviews. These models aim not only to describe and typify the kind of violent behaviour but also the participants, conditions and stances of violent interactions.

Certain key dimensions were instrumental in defining the models of violent encounters. When interpreting violent incidents, the interviewees reflected on the seriousness of intention: young people distinguished serious or hostile interactions from playful or benevolent ones. Another important distinction regarded the severity of violence. Differences between physical and non-physical violence and presence of weapons were important in assessing severity. Gender and ethnicity affected young people's experiences and interpretations, and special attention was paid to these factors in the construction of the models. The number of individuals involved was also considered. The reported cases were classified as collective or individual, based on the number of combatants directly involved. Finally, the personal approaches of different combatants in the reported violent encounters were noted. The significance of active, aggressive conflict-seeking was more important in some models than in others.

4 Models of Peer Violence

The models of peer violence presented below represent the major *forms* of peer violence experiences among the interviewed teenagers. Most models were typified by many individual, exemplary cases, and they are considered to be widespread amongst the teenagers in Järvikaupunki. Some models, especially the ones relating to the experiences of immigrant young people, are based on fewer *incidents*. Nevertheless, these models are very important qualitatively, as they differ from the more frequent types of violence in some significant aspects.

It Might Get Messy: Weapons and Collective Conflicts

Conflicts, where prepared weapons had been used, were viewed to be the most serious form of violence by most interviewees. However, no interviewees reported using weapons themselves or being injured by a weapon. The personal experiences of interviewees were restricted to *witnessing* the use of weapons and being threatened with them.

Most of the prepared weapons mentioned were *knives*. Several interviewees had stories to tell about incidents where knives had been used. There were incidents that had happened to a friend or acquaintances in Järvikaupunki, and the informants brought up the cases as examples of serious violence between young people. The details or credibility of these stories were unclear because the interviewees themselves had not been involved directly. However, one 15 year old boy had been threatened with a knife. The narratives of these serious incidents helped the informants to lay down the boundaries and definitions for extremely, explicitly and unquestionably violent acts. Stabbings seemed to be a prototype of the kind of violence that was "worth being worried about".

In addition to knives, informants had heard of the use of club-like weapons such as baseball bats. One informant had witnessed an assault by a chain, targeting an immigrant in the town centre at night. But in this case the participants had been closer to 20 years of age. All interviewees who reported witnessing or being threatened by violence with weapons were 15-16 year old boys. Girls only talked about cases they had second hand information about. It seems that violence by prepared weapons directly involving 13-16 year old teenagers is not widespread in the study area. Since there were only few references to incidental weapons-use, the same seems to apply to these weapons, too.

There were few cases of planned collective violent behaviour reported in Järvikaupunki. Most of these were related to *racist* attacks on immigrant young people. The majority of the reported collective violence took place as a result of the escalation of conflicts that started as fights between individuals. Reportedly, these incidental clashes involving groups of teenagers could lead to over-exaggerated use of force and caused concern amongst some of the interviewees involved. Others considered them less severe. Some interviewees saw these seemingly incidental cases of collective violence to be results of people or groups looking for a fight or easy victims. In some cases it remains unclear whether conflicts were deliberately or accidentally escalated into collective violence.

Jarmo (16 yrs, mixed sex group interview) describes the development of a group fight. He says that he is involved in fights among young people every once in a while. It always starts with insults. Somebody taunts Jarmo and he responds in a similar manner, and so the incentive for a fight develops.

Gender Roles, Immigrant Victimisation and the Ambiguous Boundaries
of Violence among Small Town Teenagers: Järvikaupunki, Finland

33

It usually starts with only two persons. But if someone steps in to defend a friend, then more people might get involved and it might turn into a group fight. The fight can be called off when enough people are involved, but sometimes it might end up messy. It's mostly punches and some kicking. No prepared weapons are involved, but occasionally someone might grab a bottle. Jarmo says he's never been badly injured – at least never seriously enough to make him go see a doctor. Alcohol is heavily involved. Jarmo says that if you hang out on town and are drunk like everybody else, you can quite easily get yourself in a fight. And when alcohol is involved, the details are sometimes a bit unclear afterwards. Jarmo says he's not sure if he personally has started any fights. But he's been involved as a perpetrator in a police case that was settled by a mediation process.

Not one of the girls reported involvement in serious fights between groups or a group and an individual.

Punch in the Face: Serious Individual Physical Violence

Most of the boys interviewed reported being involved in serious individual physical violence with other boys. These fights were sometimes viewed as harmless, but they were not interpreted as humorous or playful. Often the interviewees reported that there were no injuries or other consequences worth mentioning, but the nature the clash was still adversarial. The range of violent behaviour used in these conflicts was extensive. Although reporting injuries warranting *medical* care was not very common, the consequences of these incidents were at times quite serious.

There was one reported incident of serious physical violence by a girl towards a boy. In this case, the form of violent behaviour was described to be quite similar to all-boy conflicts, but the punch used was seen to be relatively non-severe. However, the most commonly reported experience among girls was witnessing violence occurring between boys. In all fights between girls the forms of violent behaviour differed from the cases of this model and is described below in another model (see section 'Catfights: Girls' Physical Conflicts').

In the single reported case of serious physical violence by boy on girl, the consequences were rather severe. It is probable that physical peer violence by boys on girls is underreported in this study, probably due to the intimate, personal or sexual nature of these cases and the method of data collection. The same could apply to non-physical violence, sexual or otherwise, violence of a very intimate nature, and to violence by girls on boys in dating relationships. But it seems safe to assume that conflicts arising from public relationships and incidents involving violence between girls and boys are well represented here.

Serious fights most commonly took place between strangers or acquaintances, not friends. Of the two cases where girls were involved, one was between friends (or more specifically, relatives) and one between strangers. Alcohol was often involved. In most cases physical violence was preceded by verbal confrontation.

Sami (15 yrs, in an individual interview) mentions insults or badmouthing as a trigger for fights. He tells that he has been involved in a couple of fights that have taken place outdoors, for example in the town centre. According to him the fights start quite often when someone has been saying something negative behind one's back. When asked about initiators, Sami says that he tries not to start fights but sometimes fails. On the other hand, he says that one or the other always strikes first. Hitting has been a part of his fights. He says that the fights usually end when he strikes hard enough. Sami thinks his fights haven't been too serious - for example there hasn't been need for the police to intervene.

Racist Teenagers: Immigrant Victimisation in Ethnic Physical Conflicts

Immigrant teenagers' experiences of physical conflicts clearly differed from the general models of peer physical violence among young people in Järvikaupunki. Physical conflicts triggered by ethnic differences form a distinctive model of physical violence. The immigrant interviewees described these conflicts as racist, initiated by racist Finnish peers. The Finnish teenagers reported to have participated in racist attacks were mostly *older* teenagers, often between 16 and 20 years of age.

Peter (16 yrs, black immigrant, in an individual interview) says that typically the racist teenagers start by taunting the ethnically different young people. Last year Peter and his two friends had been hanging out near the town centre, by the multicultural centre, around 2000 hours. Two Finnish teenagers drove by with mopeds and started yelling, 'Negro! Negro!' Peter and his friends had given them the finger, and the moped boys had turned around and come back. Peter noticed that they were drunk. The boys told Peter that, 'negroes have to get away from our country, there should be no negroes here'. Peter and his friends had tried to talk to them, but the moped boys wanted to fight and attacked. Peter said that they had to fight back and protect themselves. The moped boys hit Peter's 18 year old friend with a motorcycle helmet. One of Peter's friends called the police. The fight ended when the police – after some time – arrived and apprehended the moped boys. Peter's friends' injuries were treated with ice. Peter says that

Gender Roles, Immigrant Victimisation and the Ambiguous Boundaries
of Violence among Small Town Teenagers: Järvikaupunki, Finland

35

he has learned that if the immigrant teenagers fight and win the fight, the attackers flee quickly. But if the immigrants try to ignore the racist insults, the attackers keep at it until a fight breaks out.

Many native Finnish interviewees also considered certain local teenagers to be racist, and some said they had themselves *witnessed* attacks targeting immigrants.

Four of the interviewed boys with 'full' immigrant background (neither of the parents were ethnically Finnish and the interviewee had been born abroad) reported being involved in or victims of conflicts which were exacerbated by ethnic confrontation and/or included significant racist slander. The fifth immigrant boy reported not having been involved in physical conflicts himself, but described many cases of peer youth violence involving his fellow immigrant friends and relatives.

The experiences of the only interviewee with *Russian* immigrant background were somewhat different from the other interviewed immigrant teenagers. Immigrants of Sudanese or Afghan origin reported no physical conflicts between immigrants, whether of similar or different ethnic background. Meanwhile, most of the violent physical conflicts discussed by the one interviewee of Russian origin took place between him and other immigrants, mostly of African origin. This respondent did not report ethnic conflicts initiated by Finnish young people. While this result might be an artefact of sampling or over-reporting of ethnic conflicts by the young people most troubled by them, it could also represent an *intermediate* position of Russian immigrants on the scale of *foreign* identity: because of long-standing geographical and historical connections between Russia and Finland, Russian immigrants might escape some of the most *blatant* racism that targets teenagers with backgrounds beyond Europe.

The sample also included three teenagers with a *multicultural* background. They all had one ethnically Finnish and one ethnically foreign parent. Two of the three were born in Finland, the other had moved to Järvikaupunki from a country in Western Europe. The only minority ethnic girl interviewed was one of these three. She reported being involved in many non-physical conflicts involving racism, but had not experienced physical violence. The interviewees with a less conspicuous foreign background had completely different experiences. These two teenagers were boys who spoke fluent Finnish, were Caucasian in appearance and did not report any experiences of violence of an ethnic nature.

Confronting Animosity: Active Physical Violence by Immigrants and Victims of Bullying

The interviews with immigrant teenagers brought up a specific model of violence used in fighting the hostility of peer youth culture. In these violent conflicts the immigrants, who feel or anticipate threats from other teenagers, have an *active* role in the escalation of violence. The processes of escalation, as well as the sites, times and participants of these incidents differ in many respects from the other models violence presented here. Although the number of cases reported in the interviews is quite limited, the distinctive qualitative characteristics of this model of peer violence merit a detailed examination.

Violent hostile confrontation was used as a reaction to both physical and non-physical aggression by the opposition. Physical harassment leads sometimes to a more serious physical fight initiated by the victims of that harassment. More typically, though, the triggers of the reported violent confrontations were non-physical acts or signals and gestures of contempt. The contexts and settings where these confrontations take place are such that the confronters, usually immigrants who felt victimised by racist *disrespect,* are not inherently at a disadvantage in the situation. They were accompanied by friends or faced their opposition one on one.

Some interviewees who reported these incidents also described their feelings and motivations regarding these conflicts in some detail. The violence used was seen as self-defensive, with the intention of preventing or stopping further ostracism, abuse or ridicule. The stances of reported self-defence ranged from actively seeking pre-emptive (but not vengeful) confrontation to reactively objecting to offensive behaviour by abusive peers. None of the involved interviewees reported avoiding or backing down from imminent conflicts, as this was seen as allowing the racist abuse to persist.

Ameer (16 yrs, immigrant, single sex group interview) talks about a fight he doesn't remember well and doesn't want to tell any lies about it. He also says that he never starts a fight because he doesn't bother to fight. He emphasises that he's not a fighting type at all. However, he saw this fight as a necessity. Ameer considers himself streetwise enough to recognise quickly the characters of persons he meets. This time he had to fight because he thought that if he'd left the other person alone, the fight would have been much worse on the following day. Getting the fight over and done with settles the case. Afterwards there were no more fights. When Ameer was on 6th grade in Puotikko suburb, there was someone who wanted to fight him at school. Ameer had said that it would be better to fight after school. After school he says he asked if the other boy really wanted to fight - Ameer did this to give his opponent a chance to avoid fighting. The opponent had answered provocatively, and Ameer started immediately to fight. He got punched in the eye. He remembers causing his opponent a bleeding nose, but doesn't know if the nose was broken. Ameer gives some respect to his opponent because he had kept his mouth shut at school.

Gender Roles, Immigrant Victimisation and the Ambiguous Boundaries
of Violence among Small Town Teenagers: Järvikaupunki, Finland

37

Although the most typical cases involved immigrant young people, there are some incidents where ethnicity played no part. In these cases victims of bullying and/or their friends stood up against those who were harassing them. The narratives of these actions against *victimisation* were not as detailed as the immigrants' narratives. It is therefore unclear whether cases such as these should be located within this model or in other categories.

Catfights: Girls' Physical Conflicts

The reported physical conflicts between girls rarely resembled the models of physical conflicts between boys. Girls' reported involvement in physical conflicts was also less common than that of boys. All physical conflicts between girls were reported to have happened between individual girls. Acts of physical violence by groups of girls may certainly take place in Järvikaupunki, but in this study there was little indication of them being common.

Physical conflicts between girls were mostly described to be less serious than the conflicts between boys. This 'dismissive' view was generally shared by both boys and girls. Fights between *girls* were often called 'catfights', which referred to the specific nature of violent behaviour involved. Physical violence between girls does not seem to be connected to alcohol use or specific times of day as it is between boys.

There were only a few detailed descriptions of physical fights between girls, as both girls and boys interviewed were more interested to speak about violence committed by boys. However, some girls did have interesting stories to tell of clashes with peer girls.

> Lotta (14 yrs, in a single sex group interview) says that she has once been involved in a fight in town. She wound up fighting over a boy with another girl. Lotta isn't sure which one them actually started the fight. She and the other girl were interested in the boy (who wasn't there) and started arguing 'You're not going to touch him, he's mine'. One of them started yelling insults and they ended up fighting, pulling each other's hair. "It was a real catfight," Lotta says. After a while they both agreed that it was enough and they stopped. The girls then went separate ways. No marks were left by the clash. Lotta says that in retrospect it was quite ridiculous, nothing bad or serious.

Slap on the Face: Girls' Physical Violence towards Boys

Cross-gender physical peer violence was considered a special case by the interviewees, and it was reported to occur almost exclusively by girls' aggression on boys. Boys' physical violence on girls was seen as unfair, forbidden or cowardly. By far the most common forms of cross-gender physical behaviour were playful or *gesture-like* acts, which mostly were not seen as violence at all by the interviewees.

The most commonly reported acts of violence by girls towards boys were slaps on the face and kicks in the groin. These sorts of violent acts only went one way: according to the interviews, the targeted boys never responded with violent physical acts. In addition to slapping and kicking, biting and scratching were also used in a similar manner.

None of these acts were interpreted as violence by any interviewee. They were considered by the interviewed girls and boys to be gesture-like, not serious or harmful. However, several interviewed boys reported being annoyed or even threatened by this behaviour. They said that the kicks "really hurt" and that sometimes the girls were "over the top" with their actions, using unnecessary force. So even though this behaviour was often viewed as pranks, humour or just statements, in some cases they really did cause hurt and had real physical consequences.

The trigger for these violent gestures was usually the 'improper' behaviour of the targeted boys, as interpreted and judged by the perpetrating girls. The boys were reported to having been annoying, insulting or rude, and the violent gesture was used as a reprimand for or to counter the boys' actions. The behaviour was typically short and limited – a single slap or kick.

> Siiri and Lotta (both 14 yrs, in a single sex group interview) talk about girls' aggression towards boys. Siiri says that when provoked girls can punch or slap boys, but according to her observation boys don't hit girls. With a little titter Lotta remembers slapping a boy, and Siiri assumes that she has done the same. Lotta had slapped a boy after a quarrel. After slapping she'd started to yell at the boy, and the situation had settled. Lotta and Siiri also remember another case, when a group of younger boys had thrown sand at them at a beach, after which the girls had "given them some". The boys' reactions had been more or less passive. When asked, Lotta considers slapping a functional way of communicating in certain conflicts. She also remarks that one can recognise the severity of her aggression, when she finds herself punching hard instead of yelling or slapping. Lotta believes that attacking boys physically is an option for many girls of her age.

Sometimes, however, girls attacked boys just for fun. The boys were not always receptive to these sorts of pranks, and sometimes the girls' actions can be interpreted as bullying.

It was generally considered inappropriate for boys to hit back at the girls hitting them. This was due to the traditional gender roles and culture, including a gentlemanly code of

Gender Roles, Immigrant Victimisation and the Ambiguous Boundaries
of Violence among Small Town Teenagers: Järvikaupunki, Finland

39

behaviour and the presumed physical superiority of boys over girls. So the girls generally thought that boys were humiliated by the attacks, and boys felt that there was no way for them to respond.

Just Wrestling: Boy-Boy and Girl-Boy Playful Physical Clashes

Younger boys in particular reported participating in harmless wrestling matches or playful fights with their friends. For some of the young people interviewed, these were the only kind of physical struggles they had been part of. Older teenage boys rarely reported these kinds of incidents. Probably the physical and social growth of adolescent boys affects this, as the conflicts between bigger boys tend to be more serious in both intentions and consequences.

These playful matches between friends usually took place *after* (or in) school, *outside* youth centres, playgrounds or in the town centre. Sometimes the fights were reported having started because of an argument or dispute, but more often they were "just for fun". There were minimal consequences from these clashes. However, some interviewees reported intervention by adult outsiders, who did not understand or interpret the situation accurately.

According to Pekka (15 yrs, in an individual interview), playful fighting happens among friends only. It tends to attract some attention from parents, youth workers or other adults. Usually juveniles stop such brawling when told to and the adults also leave it at that. Sometimes juveniles get thrown out of youth centres for starting again, though playful brawling isn't very common in there.

Most of the playful clashes occurred between boys, but girls also recounted being involved in harmless physical clashes with boys of their age. Reported experiences were affected by the age of the interviewee: among the younger interviewees there were some reports of physical matches (pushing, wrestling) between young boys and girls around the same age. Older teenage girls were only involved as targets, as they were sometimes reportedly pushed around or knocked into the snow by same aged boys for joking or teasing. When such reaction was viewed as over-reaction, teenage girls reported being somewhat annoyed by this. However, most girls accepted it as part of play within their peer groups.

When girls actively participated in the *playful* fighting, they were usually older or bigger than their male opposition. The cases where girls were overpowering and hurting the boys may be classified as girls' physical violence on boys. The consequences of boy-girl playful fights are mostly non-physical in this model.

Bullying and Slander: Serious and Playful Non-physical Violence

The range of verbal and other non-physical forms of violence revealed by the interviewees was extensive. Non-physical forms of violence were mostly called bullying by the interviewees. Often the interviewees identified certain bullies, who targeted the interviewees or their friends. In some cases respondents identified mutually antagonistic teenagers, who tended to get into conflicts with each other. Many interviewees distanced themselves from bullying, but some reported being bullies themselves sometimes.

> Katja (15 yrs, in an individual interview), described intervening in bullying. She has been neither a bully nor bullied, but thinks that intervening helps in cases of bullying. She says she usually intervenes, because she doesn't want to stand watching when others get bullied. Katja's way of intervening is to tell troublemakers to go and rant somewhere else. These bullies are usually of her age, and she isn't really scared of them. Intervening tends to stop the bullying at least for a while. Katja believes that bullying usually ends in the course of time even without anyone intervening, for example if the bullied person starts avoiding the bullies.

Many of those who were interviewed portrayed *humorous* insults as part of normal talk in their group of friends and school classmates. Generally, these were not considered harmful. According to the interviews, the teenagers were capable of distinguishing between serious and harmless comments. The slander between friends was different from the serious non-physical conflicts that usually occurred between acquaintances. Both types of behaviour were depicted as rather routine and ordinary for the interviewed teenagers and regularly took place in schools and in public space after school.

There were no striking differences in reported behaviour between girls and boys. Some interviewed girls argued that boys seek direct non-physical confrontation more often, whereas girls use more indirect means such as gossip. These characterisations were not, however, very consistent across different interviews, though it was generally considered more common for girls to use exclusively non-physical forms of violence.

Bullying and conflicts taking place on various *Internet* platforms were also discussed in some interviews. These were sometimes related to *spiteful* relations and non-physical conflicts in public space, but Internet conflicts were not generally regarded to have much relevance. The interviewees maintained that 'real life' encounters were more important. Girls presented more detailed information on Internet conflicts than boys.

Gender Roles, Immigrant Victimisation and the Ambiguous Boundaries
of Violence among Small Town Teenagers: Järvikaupunki, Finland

41

Concluding Remarks

The models presented here show that both gender roles and positions related to ethnicity (or other factors connected to *discrimination*) affect the formation of violent experiences profoundly. Peer violence ensues from antagonistic reactions to apparent *ethnic* difference, and from defending one's own status against interpreted hostilities. Gender influences how peer violence plays out, and peer violence plays a role in young people's negotiation of their own gender roles. The models also show that peer violence among young people has diverse forms and can be examined from many viewpoints.

5 The Character of Violent Encounters

In this section, the relations and *interactions* of different dimensions of violent incidents are analysed.

Forms of Violent Behaviour

The basic distinction within violent behaviour made by the interviewees was the division of physical and non-physical behaviour. Violence tended to be seen as physical behaviour. The concept of non-physical violence was much more vague.

The usual forms of physical violence included punching, kicking, and grappling, wrestling and throwing or pushing around. Specific forms used by girls were pulling hair, scratching and biting. The forms of non-physical behaviour described were quite diverse. Taunting and insulting were the most widespread and commonplace forms. They occurred in all kinds of encounters and in nearly all of the models, and were reported being used both in seriously offensive and friendly manner. Other forms were sizing up, verbal or gestured threats, gossiping, teasing, ignoring, stealing items (such as hats) and making false accusations.

Relations between Combatants

Respondents typically classified their peer contacts as friends, pals, acquaintances and unfamiliar teenagers. The most clear-cut division was made between the familiar (friends and acquaintances) and unfamiliar people (strangers). In many cases people were strange, but their faces familiar. It was said that everybody knows everybody, more or less, in the small town environment.

Playful forms of physical violence only occurred between familiar teenagers, most commonly between friends interacting in groups. Similarly, only between friends were

42

Gender Roles, Immigrant Victimisation and the Ambiguous Boundaries
of Violence among Small Town Teenagers: Järvikaupunki, Finland

non-physical taunts considered harmless. The use of physical violence by girls on boys also took place only between familiar teenagers. There were no reports of this behaviour being used to reject or drive off male strangers. Possibly this is because the perpetrators need to 'know' that the target will not resort to physical retaliation.

> Extract from the interview with Tanja (14 yrs, in a single sex group interview).
>
> *Int: Are they boys of your age, younger, older?* T: Yes, about our age. *Int: Are they pals or strangers?* T: Pals. (laughs) *Int: You wouldn't dare [to slap] strangers?* T: No, I wouldn't. *Int: What about among girls, do you ever need to get physical?* T: No. Just as a joke.

In cases of serious physical violence between individuals, the combatants mostly were not very familiar to each other. There were some cases in which fights had ensued between friends or between young people who were closely related in other ways (e.g. family relationships). These incidents were often considered more serious than conflicts between strangers, and in some cases the level of violence was also severe. But it was more typical for the conflicts of this model to occur between less familiar combatants. And all cases of collective serious violence also took place between more unfamiliar teenagers.

Intentions of Violence

In order to understand violent youth behaviour and its motivations, the underlying intentions of peer violence need to be explored. Many interviewees analysed the intentions behind actions quite thoroughly themselves without any encouragement, but others seemed satisfied with more simplistic explanations.

There were very few references and no personal experiences of property crimes as reasons for peer violence. Some interviewees acknowledged that *robberies* (acquisitive crime) sometimes were a cause of violence between young people, but such incidents were not seen to happen in Järvikaupunki. Sex crimes were also not reported. The reasons behind violence were related to conflict resolution in peer relations between young people.

Most cases of serious physical violence between young people were triggered by insults or other forms of non-physical confrontation. Typically the intention was to seek retaliation for offences committed either previously or then and there, to defend personal status and to *'keep face'*. Often these incidents escalated rapidly because of heated tempers, and the interviewees often considered them quite irrational, to have happened *"without good reason"*, in retrospect.

Gender Roles, Immigrant Victimisation and the Ambiguous Boundaries
of Violence among Small Town Teenagers: Järvikaupunki, Finland

43

Interviewees often described 'losing patience' with the abusers, like Sanni (14 yrs) in a mixed sex group interview.

S: Then on the 6th grade I beat a guy in a bus. *Int: Why?* S: I don't know. He had thrown stuff on me, mud and such, and then he pushed a button to stop the bus too early and I had to get out there. Then I lost my nerves and I beat him up ... I pushed him on to the floor and started kicking and beating him. *Int: Oh, then?* I got a phone call at home for that the same evening ... Well this person had bullied me when I was younger, at the lower elementary school, at the 3rd or 4th grade, even though he was a year younger than me, and I just thought that I won't take any more.

Another commonly reported trigger was badmouthing or spreading false rumours behind other people's backs. In these cases the escalation of conflict was of more premeditated nature, but the intentions were basically the same as above.

There were some reports of seeking vengeance as the intention of peer violence. These incidents had a wide range of severity, from alleged death threats with knives to paying back in non-verbal bullying. Some cases involved 'an eye for an eye' morality (e.g. for beating up or bullying a friend), other incidents were more vicious. One interviewee reported receiving death threats for allegedly causing the institutionalisation of another teenager. Less vengeful cases of payback were also reported. These were close to the rather common intention of involvement in violent interactions: defending yourself or your friends. In non-physical conflicts outside intervention with the intention of de-escalating the conflict was also reported.

In quite a number of cases the interviewees, who were witnesses or targets of violence, were unsure of the intentions or triggers for the conflicts they experienced. Often the interviewees saw a mismatch between the apparent intentions and resulting behaviour, which was viewed as disproportionate and the outcome of a loss of temper by the combatants in question.

Time, Place and Conditions of Violence

Weekend nights in the town centre were seen by young people as the most notable hot spots for serious physical violence. The habitual use of alcohol on weekend evenings reportedly had a major influence on the development of violent conflicts. Many interviewees reported witnessing severe physical violence only among these older teenagers and adults on weekend nights. This violence can have both direct and indirect influences on the development of peer violence incidents among adolescents. Younger teenagers may themselves be involved in violence with elders, or they may emulate the behaviour they witness.

44

Gender Roles, Immigrant Victimisation and the Ambiguous Boundaries
of Violence among Small Town Teenagers: Järvikaupunki, Finland

Most respondents either didn't hang out in town late at all or had only witnessed teenage violence, not participated in it.

One of the witnesses was Katja (15 yrs) who described her experiences in an individual interview.

Int: Have you seen one or more of these cases? K: Well, it was the New Year's Eve when I saw like two or three fights. *Int: Was it the last New Year, or earlier?* K; Yes. *Int: Then it was just a short while ago. Do you remember any earlier experiences or witnessing?* K: No. *Int: How did you feel about those fights? Were the participants young?* K: They were a bit older than us. *Int: But they were in their teens?* K: Yes. *Int: How did you feel when you saw it?* K: Maybe little disgust, since I really dislike violence. *Int: Were you afraid?* K: Yes, a little, because they were so close, I was afraid that they would fall onto me. *Int: What did you do, did you for example give way?* K: Yes, we went away from the spot. *Int: But you remained in the area – where did this take place, in the town centre?* K: Yes, in the town centre.

The violent experiences of the interviewees who had participated in the weekend violence in town were not limited to this specific time and location. Similar violent incidents were reported happening elsewhere in town in connection, for instance, with house parties. In these cases the actual conditions (alcohol, gathering of teenagers, involvement of older people) were often quite similar.

Severe physical violence also took place in totally different conditions. The experiences of immigrant teenagers were mostly from sports fields and streets outside the town centre and had happened during daytime. Hours after school and locations near schools, youth centres or playgrounds were common contexts for conflicts among younger respondents. One notable case of physical violence by a boy on a girl had taken place in the countryside, in the vicinity of a summer cottage – clearly a more private space, but somewhat different from the privacy of town homes.

The contexts of non-physical violence were varied. Many interviewees described it happening everywhere, but the serious hostilities were focused on spaces where young people were huddled up and it was more difficult for the individuals to pick their company. These conditions were fulfilled best in the town centre on afternoons and evenings, after school. Playful matches and conflicts took place both in these huddled spaces and in the more secluded public space of playgrounds and local neighbourhoods.

Even though the interviews were focused on what took place in leisure and public space, interviewees often brought up disputes at school. Many interviewees considered peer violence to be more common in school than in public space. This was the majority view when it came to non-physical, bullying type of violence. However, several interviewees reported that it was also the case with physical peer violence.

Consequences of Violent Experiences

The consequences of peer violence can be divided in *three* major categories: physical injuries, processing by adult society and psychological consequences. It is worth noting that the worst physical injuries the interviewees reported suffering themselves were wounds, cuts, bruises and possibly smaller fractures. Most interviewees with personal experiences of injuries caused by peer violence had not required any professional medical care. Some of the younger interviewees especially could not name any bodily harm resulting from their experiences of physical conflict. Only one of the girls reported any kind of injuries. Physical harm constituted often only the experiencing of pain. However, there were many reports of much worse and even life-threatening injuries that had happened to friends or acquaintances.

Extract from the interview with Sami (15 yrs, in an individual interview).

Int: Have you ever got any physical damage that would've needed...? S: I've once gone to doctor. *Int: Was it bad? Was it from a punch, or was there kicking...?* S: Yes, just a punch, nothing like that. My face got bruised, nose slanted. *Int: Right. Have you witnessed more serious fights here [in Järvikaupunki]?* S: I've seen some in Helsinki. There's no use intervening in them, the police are there quite quickly. *Int: Has there been weapons?* S: Once I've seen this guy getting stabbed with a knife and... *Int: Oh! But not much now... Was that in Helsinki?* S: Yes. And then stuff like someone lying on the ground with eight others kicking them.

The actual violence behind these incidents was rather rarely witnessed; the knowledge about these cases tended to be second-hand and passed through word of mouth.

Most of the interviewees who reported involvement in *physical* violence had not faced legal action or police attention. The most usual form of interaction between interviewees and law enforcement agencies was acting as a witnessing bystander or victim. One interviewee had been accused of assault: in that case the matter had been resolved by mediation (a mandatory option in the Finnish justice system). Some interviewees talked of friends who had been facing charges or arrested by the police. The immigrant teenagers reported several cases where the young people attacking them had been arrested. No girls mentioned having been accused of anything by officials. Experiences of attention and consequences received from school staff and parents of the involved teenagers were much more common for both sexes. These consequences typically involved phone calls between families, meeting of parents and the young people involved in the school office, receiving lectures and occasionally personal penalties.

Most of the interviewees reported that peer violence did not concern or bother them much or at all. Only a few young people spoke of fear, caution or similar emotional responses resulting from experiences of violence. Possible *psychological* consequences of peer violence can be inferred from the ways many interviewees reported avoiding certain places (or, more uncommonly, types of people) at certain times of day or week. Avoiding specific parts of public space was often mentioned, but in many cases this was attributed to the fear of suspicious types of adults, or drunken adults in general. Some neighbourhoods were identified as places to be avoided because of aggressive local teenagers.

> Avoidance is discussed by Tapani (male, 16 yrs) and Meri (female, 16 yrs) in the following extract from a mixed sex group interview.
>
> *Int: Can you tell me what are such remote places that you think should be avoided?* M: (sighs) Well, I wouldn't go on my own to Bomber's [a shop] direction. I don't go there alone. T: And another place is, if you ask me, where one shouldn't go alone, not that I'm really speaking of myself but if I were female... (sighs) Let's say that I'm going to defame Tukkula area a little here. When I've been there at nights I've thought it's not very safe. If you are small and don't have anything to defend yourself with, it may end up badly. *Int: Oh? Okay.* T: Been there, done that. *Int: Really?* T: Other insecure localities are around Lampela, surroundings of the jogging track, been there, done that last winter. *Int: So you've ended up in fights there?* T: Yes.

Weekend nights in the town centre, where physical violence was considered most common, was rarely reported as requiring avoidance.

The personal psychological effects of serious non-physical violence were also usually reported to be minimal. *Bullying* was mostly considered frustrating, annoying, unfair or stupid, but almost none of the interviewees reported suffering severely from it. More concern was occasionally expressed about friends targeted by bullying, which indicates that bullying is felt and seen to be harmful, although this might not be admitted personally. Avoiding certain people was a strategy associated with coping with bullying.

The reported severity of *consequences* also seemed to depend on *age*. Younger boys interviewed were only in the first stages of adolescence, and their views of physical violence and its consequences differed somewhat strikingly from the narratives of older teenage boys. 13-14 year old boys talked about using quite similar forms of physical violent behaviour as the older boys, but reported less severe injuries. All in all, physical

Gender Roles, Immigrant Victimisation and the Ambiguous Boundaries
of Violence among Small Town Teenagers: Järvikaupunki, Finland

47

violence seemed to concern younger boys relatively little. In contrast to most 15-16 year old boys, the younger ones considered physical violence to be annoying or frustrating, but not really harmful.

Interpretations of Violence by the Interviewees

Based on the interviews it is clear that most teenagers see or want to present their approach to violence as reactive or active: according to them, their involvement in violence has a more or less valid reason, they do not behave violently unprovoked. By these statements, they lay down certain norms or codes for violent conduct. Many interviewees stated that they do not want to fight and fight only if it is absolutely necessary: if they are attacked, or anticipated being attacked, physically. Violent self-defence is the prime example of a reactive approach to violence.

> Extract from a single sex group interview with Ameer (16 yrs, immigrant).
>
> A: I asked, 'What have foreigners done to you?' He answered, 'They take our money and food' or something like that. Then I said, 'Right' and went away, because I didn't dare to fight him, he was, you know, quite tall, being seventeen. Then I said, 'Okay, I'm going away to my own country'. When I started leaving, he grabbed my neck. As he had a grip on the back of my neck, I had no options but fight.

Cases where the individual initiates violent conflict with the intention to punish for or repay some earlier direct or indirect offence targeting them can be seen to display an active stance towards violence. Similarly, using physical violence to stop non-physical bullying (often this was considered the only way to resist bullying) is an active approach. Active users of violence see it as a valid method of interaction or problem-solving in certain situations, considering violence to be a somewhat integral part of youth culture and a means for managing peer relations.

> Tapani (16 yrs, male, in a mixed sex group interview) gives an impression on his active approach to violence.
>
> *Int: Well, why did it [starting a row] happen?* T: Umm, started and started... It depends on who thinks that... I mean he had been talking bullshit behind my back. And he continued even after I had warned him, after that I was the first one to have a go at him. *Int: Was that a right thing to do?* M: That should shut him up. (laughs) T: I do nothing wrong. M: (laughs) T: Everything

> I do is justified. Until proven otherwise. Right. *Int: Do you really think it was
> nothing serious or nothing to regret afterwards?* T: If some things don't get
> settled talking, I'll settle them some way. I've had to tolerate so much during
> my life that I'm tired to take any more of that.

Many respondents, especially girls, had a *deactive* approach towards physical peer violence. They wanted to avoid conflict and did not emphasise the need for self-defence. Often these interviewees showed distaste for physical violent behaviour, considering it stupid and/or revolting.

> A deactive approach was described by Pekka (15 yrs, in an individual
> interview).
>
> *Int: Would you fight or run away?* P: I'd stand there and let the other guy
> hit me, and if there was a bruise, I'd sue him. It's that clear? I'd get good
> money.

The other extreme approach to violence is the *proactive* stance: the explicit intention to be involved in and/or initiate violent conflict. There were only a very few examples of this approach in the interviews. Mostly proactive violent behaviour was associated with other young people who were looking for and causing trouble and escalating violence. Interviewees often deemed these proactively violent young people to be responsible for drawing other teenagers into violent encounters.

In addition to displaying a certain approach toward violence, the interviewees had different definitions of violence. The most relevant factors in defining violence were the observed severity of violent behaviour and the interpreted seriousness or hostility of intentions. The severity of violent behaviour was typically judged by the actual or potential physical injuries and the overall grievousness, unfairness and excessiveness of violent behaviour. According to these criteria, non-physical violence was rarely deemed to be 'real' or 'proper' violence. Often the term 'mental violence' was used, but this was clearly seen as separate from 'proper' physical violence. Some specific forms of behaviour, for example threats and coercion, were seen to cross this boundary by some interviewees. The interviews suggest that in the eyes of young teenagers, forms of behaviour associated with bullying include most – if not all – forms of non-physical peer violence and some forms of physical peer violence. However, many forms of physical violence transcend bullying. This is not to say that young teenagers consider (physical) violence worse than (physical and non-physical) bullying, but according to this study, they do consider it quintessentially more violent. While this may seem to be axiomatic, it conveys that violence and bullying are two related but separate peer processes in the eyes of young teenagers.

Gender Roles, Immigrant Victimisation and the Ambiguous Boundaries
of Violence among Small Town Teenagers: Järvikaupunki, Finland

49

When the interviewees declared some clashes to be non-violent because the participants
were "*just playing*", the factor of seriousness was involved in defining violence. In friendly
fights there were no hostile intentions, these matches were not seen as serious but
playful and almost sport-like. A special case is the physical and non-physical horseplay
committed by boys, targeting peer girls. The interpretation of this behaviour can range
from acceptable flirtation or bonding to sexual harassment. There were very few reports
of the latter in this study. Obviously, trust between interacting teenagers is the key in
playful conflicts.

> Päivi (14 yrs, female) talks about playful pushing among her pals in an
> individual interview.
>
> *Int: Where is the borderline between playful pushing and something more
> serious? Can it lead to a quarrel?* P: I don't know. I reckon it happens daily,
> I've been pushed into snow several times, but it's not that dangerous. *Int:
> You don't take it as bullying?* P: No. *Int: Do you take it negatively at all?*
> P: (laughs) I don't know. It's more like fun.

Some cases where a playful match developed into *serious* conflict were reported by the
interviewees. Holding back appropriately and knowing when to quit were important in
keeping the clash friendly and fun.

> In the following extract about horseplay with friends, Kimmo and Tapani
> (both 16 yrs and male) were joined by Panu (19 yrs) in a mixed sex group
> interview.
>
> K: Nah, it's like healthy violence. P: It's okay as long as you don't get bruises
> ['colour'] on your face. T: Even that can happen sometimes. K: Yes, those
> things happen. T: Between friends it's okay, but if the other guy isn't your
> pal, then it's violence if there are bruises.

Girls' physical violence on boys was often considered serious, but in this case violence
was rarely seen to be severe.

> Gender roles played their part in the common notion that this type of violent
> behaviour really was not violence, as demonstrated by Otto and Laura (both
> 13 yrs, in a mixed sex group interview).

50

Gender Roles, Immigrant Victimisation and the Ambiguous Boundaries
of Violence among Small Town Teenagers: Järvikaupunki, Finland

O: You want to know what violence is? *Int: Yes.* O: For example hitting with fists. Slapping can't be called violence. Things that really hurt. *Int: But if kicking on the balls really hurts, is it violence then?* L: Well, no. O: You can't really classify that.

6 Feedback and Consultation

To get feedback on the results presented above, workshops for discussion were organised with young people and experts.

Workshop with Young People

The workshop with young people in Järvikaupunki took place at the beginning of September 2008 in a youth centre located in the Lampela study area. Local youth workers were asked to promote the workshop beforehand to the 13-16 year old young people visiting the centre. Young people were told that participants were wanted for a group discussion about a research project concerning violence. The promise of refreshments was used as a promotional hook.

Six teenagers between 13 and 15 years of age participated in the workshop for young people. The group consisted of four boys and two girls, including one foreign-born but ethnically Finnish boy. No other immigrant teenagers were present. Two of the participants had also been involved in the study interviews. Both members of the Finnish research team participated and were involved in the conversation. The workshop started with a general introduction about the research project and the aims of the study. Then the main results of the study were presented to the participants, including the different models of violence and the most important observations about the character of violent encounters. This verbal presentation was supported with printed summaries. The participants were encouraged to comment and discussion was carried on throughout the presentation. At the end of the workshop some questions were presented to the participating young people, to draw out their views on policies and practice regarding peer violence. The researchers made notes during the workshop and discussion was also recorded to ensure that nothing was missed.

The participating teenagers were generally quite interested in the discussion and engaged in conversation willingly. Yet, towards the end of the session some of the participants became disinterested and started to lose focus.

Gender Roles, Immigrant Victimisation and the Ambiguous Boundaries
of Violence among Small Town Teenagers: Järvikaupunki, Finland

51

The first issue for discussion was the study results in order to assess the validity of the study data and results. The participating teenagers thought that the models sounded *familiar* and *real* to them. They agreed vocally with many observations and voiced no objections. As different teenagers naturally have different experiences, not all models were equally familiar to the participants. The young people at the workshop commented and focused especially on the topic of ethnic and racist conflicts, wanting to point out that many times they are *accused* of racism erroneously. The intervening adults, especially at school, often hold the native combatants responsible whenever a violent conflict breaks out between native and immigrant teenagers. This was seen to be unfair.

Secondly, the understanding and interpretation of youth conflicts by adults was discussed more broadly. The participants thought that there are often misinterpretations of intention or behaviour by adults. Sometimes young people are blamed for something they did not do, and sometimes playful fights between friends are taken too seriously by adults. *Misunderstandings* and unfair dealings were reportedly more common in *school* and with teachers than in leisure time in public space or with youth workers and police. The participants said that youth workers at the youth centres in particular are more aware of young people's intentions and the nature of different conflicts.

Finally, the young people were asked to express recommendations for action on peer violence. The need for action was also assessed. The participants did not see peer violence as a big problem. They thought it is often associated with certain 'special cases' and *troublemakers*, whose behaviour is difficult to alter. They argued that the problems are bigger in school than in public space. *School* conflicts are both more common and often go unnoticed or are not dealt with properly by the school personnel. When the participants were asked whether the issues of conflict resolution and violence should be discussed more by the school at the level of elementary classes (before they turn 13 years old), they gave some support to this idea.

Workshop with Experts

The workshop with experts also took place in September 2008 at a local conference venue. Experts on youth violence and youth workers in Järvikaupunki were invited to the workshop by contacting them by email and phone calls two week prior to the event. The workshop was held with four experts on youth violence: a social worker with the local police, two youth workers from Non Fighting Generation (a Finnish organisation dealing with youth violence), and a worker from a local organisation offering outpatient services for people encountering violence in their close relationships. Due to timetable mismatches, no *municipal* youth workers were able to participate. They were met separately on the 25th September in a shorter meeting where a similar presentation of the study results was given. Some comments from this meeting are also included in this report.

First the background of the study and the purpose of the workshop were elaborated for the participating experts. Then the study design, the models of the peer violence and notable observations based on the analysis of the character of violent encounters were presented. After going through the main study results, the experts were presented with questions regarding the reliability and relevance of the results and conclusions. They were also asked to formulate recommendations based on the information presented and their own experiences. The experts asked questions throughout the presentation and made a lot of helpful comments.

The experts had no objections or reservations regarding the study results. The workshop agreed that the experiences recorded might have been quite *different* if the sample had included young people coming from more severely disadvantaged backgrounds or with more serious criminal histories. The research in general and the study results at hand were welcomed as relevant and useful in developing policy and practice.

The results and discussion led to the development of recommendation from several different perspectives. Regarding young people's leisure time, the experts saw that more organised – and controlled in some way – activities should be provided for the young people, including on the *weekends*. This should not be seen as a need for rigid surveillance by parents or elders, but as a need to enhance, support and expand the already present structures of professional youth work in centres, in the field and at different venues, and by organising events and activities.

The experts agreed that the majority of concrete cases of assaults and observed violence between young people involves older teenagers, those of 15-16 years age and older. The violence, bullying and wrestling, that is most common among younger teenagers goes by largely unnoticed. Work needs to be done in helping the *younger* teenagers to recognise and deal with harmful violent behaviour properly, to encourage effective *prevention* and *intervention*. These subjects should be included in health education and basic codes of behaviour in schools and leisure activities. Proper intervention by all parents and professionals encountering peer violence among young people is needed to establish the boundaries of acceptable behaviour.

Regarding young people's experiences of peer violence in general, the situation in *schools* and the work done in schools was seen as most important. The regulations in practice in schools and the society 'outside' are different, and this ambiguity should be addressed. Cases are sometimes dealt with inadequately in schools, but legal processing can also be counter-productive or disproportionate in their response. Arbitration procedures used in youth justice in Finland and other work done by the police, social workers and anti-violence organisations in Järvikaupunki may contain good practice, which should perhaps be adapted to other environments (e.g. schools) and disseminated more widely. Young people's good experiences of dealing with *youth workers* and *police*, reported by the interviewees and the participants of the workshop for young people, support this conclusion.

Gender Roles, Immigrant Victimisation and the Ambiguous Boundaries
of Violence among Small Town Teenagers: Järvikaupunki, Finland

53

There were some differences between the views presented in young people's and expert's workshops. The young people's focus was on their everyday experiences of conflict and its inadequate processing, false accusations and misunderstandings. The experts' workshop discussed the general structures and problems of young people's leisure and peer violence and looked for ways to enhance current practices. Both groups noted the important role of schools in processing peer violence. Ethnic confrontations received more attention from young people and less in the expert workshop, where general anti-violence work among teenagers was emphasised.

7 Some Final Reflections

This analysis of peer violence produced *two* models of youth violence, where *ethnic* confrontation was a key factor. According to this study, having noticeable and 'uncommon' ethnic appearance in small towns like Järvikaupunki largely determines the nature of violent experiences for a teenager with a foreign background. Experiences of violent conflicts related (according to the perspectives of interviewed young people) to ethnicity were very common among them. In contrast, incidents of playful violence or of violence between girls and boys were not reported at all by these interviewees. For the immigrant teenagers interviewed, violence was unequivocally a serious issue.

Ethnic confrontation and the lack of mutual understanding and goodwill between native and new inhabitants increase the intensity of peer violence among young people and produce specific forms of violent encounters. Interestingly, ethnic or 'racist' conflicts were not connected to interviewees' foreign background as such, but to apparent foreign characteristics. If the *looks* and *language* abilities of the interviewee were no different from the majority population, there was no difference in the experiences of peer violence either. Many peer violence incidents related to ethnicity seem to result from pro-active, predatory rejection of difference. But in some cases, the young people who feel discriminated against participate actively in the escalation of peer violence themselves.

In all models of peer violence presented here, *gender* affects young people's participation and role in violent incidents. The vast majority of physical violence occurs between combatants of the same gender and the qualities of violence reportedly differ substantially between all-male and all-female physical conflicts. Almost all cases of serious physical violence involved only boys, with girls mostly acting only as witnesses. As a whole, the physical violence encountered was less severe for girls than boys.

Cross-gender peer violence by girls on boys has well-established cultural forms and functions in Järvikaupunki. The boundaries of acceptability and harm perceived by young people are exceptionally vague in this area of violent behaviour. Generally, girls' violence was also interpreted differently than boys', its characteristic comical nature was emphasised and overall significance downplayed. *Traditional* gender roles where men protect women are present in the expressed disapproval of boys' violent behaviour targeting girls, and girls' experiences of more intimate (sexual or relationship-related) peer violence are probably underreported and 'hidden' in this study.

Many violent incidents analysed in this study were interpreted by young people as harmless, *playful* and/or non-violent. The most important condition for perceptions that violence was harmless was a level of familiarity between participants. This seems quite obvious, considering that trust and the right interpretations are obviously needed to keep an incident from escalating. A certain amount of trust, predictability or superiority also seems to be needed for girls to make physical contact on boys. Furthermore, the age of the combatants has a significant bearing on the actual and interpreted harm of physical violence, especially when only boys are considered. Probably the difference in sheer size, weight and strength between 13 and 16 year old boys explains some their different experiences and interpretations of peer violence. In the world view of the younger boys, physical violence seems to be less harmful, at least in a bodily sense.

In addition to harmless violence, *fair fights* were also often considered non-problematic. By refraining from excessive behaviour and showing reactive or active approaches to violence, young people express the fairness of their involvement. The perceived severity of violent interactions greatly influenced the way young people described their importance and meaning. Fairness could also suggest that most physical violence takes place between roughly same aged individuals, and based on the interviews this really seems to be the case. Conflicts between older and younger teenagers were mostly non-physical, and usually initiated by the older combatant both in physical and non-physical incidents. However, when judging fairness, the interviewees usually considered the physical size of combatants rather that their age. Naturally, these two are quite heavily correlated at least between boys of 13 and 16 years of age. Probably the effect of adolescence on size and strength also explains why physical matches between boys and girls were more commonly reported among younger teenagers.

As reported by most of the experts, the most severe cases of peer violence take place on weekend nights and in the town centre. Yet much of the lower-key peer violence among 13-16 year olds goes by unnoticed in other parts of public space, for example in parks and on sport fields. The results also give some support to the expressed concern that the most significant *arena* of everyday peer violence is in *school*. This study affirms that young people commonly have experiences of serious physical and non-physical violence in school. Peer violence in both schools and in public space needs to be more explicitly acknowledged and addressed properly by adults and young people alike.

Gender Roles, Immigrant Victimisation and the Ambiguous Boundaries
of Violence among Small Town Teenagers: Järvikaupunki, Finland

55

References

Aaltonen, S., (2006). *Tytöt, pojat ja sukupuolinen häirintä [Girls, boys and sex-based harassment]*. Helsinki: Yliopistopaino.

Etelä-Savon TE-keskus, (2006). *Etelä-Savon maahanmuuttostrategia [Immigration strategy of Southern Savonia]*. Available from: http://www.tyojakoulutus.fi/Pdf/mamustrategia.pdf [Accessed 1 October 2008].

European Commission, (2007). *Objective 1 programme for Eastern Finland*. European Commission, Regional Policy. Available from: http://ec.europa.eu/regional_policy/country/prordn/details. cfm?gv_PAY=FI&gv_reg=ALL&gv_PGM=1999FI161DO002&LAN=5#cont [Accessed 11 June 2008].

Eurostat, (2007). *Regional GDP per inhabitant in the EU27*. Eurostat Press Office. Available from: http://epp. eurostat.ec.europa.eu/pls/portal/docs/PAGE/PGP_PRD_CAT_PREREL/PGE_CAT_PREREL_YEAR_2007/ PGE_CAT_PREREL_YEAR_2007_MONTH_02/1-19022007-EN-AP.PDF [Accessed 11 June 2008].

Harinen, P., (2005). Nuoret monikansallistuvassa ja –kulttuuristuvassa yhteiskunnassa [Young people in an international and multi-cultural world]. *In:* Wilska, T-A., ed. *Erilaiset ja samanlaiset: Nuorisobarometri 2005 [Similar and different: Youth barometer 2005]*. Helsinki: Yliopistopaino, 98-110.

Harju, J., (2003). Heinojen murhien tuomioille KKO:sta viimeinen niitti [Sentences of the Heino murders finalised in the Supreme Court]. *Helsingin Sanomat*, 5th June.

Helsinki Times, (2008). Auvinen sought to inflict maximum damage in Jokela shootings. *Helsinki Times*, 18th April. Available from: http://www.hs.fi/english/article/Auvinen+sought+to+inflict+maximum+d amage+in+Jokela+shootings/1135235675118 [Accessed 11 June 2008].

Hilden-Paajanen, T., (2005). *Pahojen poikien piiri: Joensuun skinien epäilty rikollisuus 1995-1998 [Circle of bad boys: the suspected crimes of Joensuu Skinheads during 1995-1998]*. Thesis (PhD) University of Tampere.

Honkatukia, P., Nyqvist, L. and Pösö, T., (2006). Violence from within the reform school. *Youth Violence and Juvenile Justice*, 4, 328.

Honkatukia, P., (2001). *"Ilmoitti tulleensa raiskatuksi": Tutkimus poliisin tietoon vuonna 1998 tulleista raiskausrikoksista ["Reported rape": Study on rape crimes reported to police in 1998]*. Helsinki: Tilastokeskus, Oikeuspoliittinen tutkimuslaitos.

Honkatukia, P., (2000). "Lähentelijöitä riittää...": Tyttöjen kokemuksia sukupuolisesta ahdistelusta ["There are lots of those men...": Girls' experiences of sexual harassment]. *In:* Honkatukia, P., ed. *Lähentelystä raiskauksiin: Tyttöjen kokemuksia häirinnästä ja seksuaalisesta väkivallasta [From advances to rapes: Girls' experiences of harassment and sexual violence]*. Helsinki: Nuorisotutkimusverkosto, 13-76.

Iivari, J., (2006). *Tuomittu maahanmuuttaja [Convicted immigrant]*. Helsinki: Stakes.

Kivivuori, J., (2006). Trends in Juvenile Delinquency in Finland. *In:* Honkatukia, P. and Kivivuori, J., eds., *Juvenile crime in Finland: Trends, Causes and Control*. Helsinki: National Research Institute of Legal Policy, 15-56.

Kuure, T., (2001). *Muistio nuorisoväkivallasta. Nuorisotyö ja polarisaatio-oletus [Memo regarding youth violence. Youth work and the polarization hypothesis]*. Ministry of Education. Available from: http:// www.minedu.fi/export/sites/default/OPM/Nuoriso/nuorisoasiain_neuvottelukunta/julkaisut/ muut_tutkimukset/vakivalta/liitteet/nuorisovxkivaltamuistio.pdf [Accessed 11 June 2008].

Näre, S., (2000). Nuorten tyttöjen kohtaama seksuaalinen väkivalta ja loukattu luottamus tunnetaloudessa [Sexual violence against adolescent girls – hurt confidence in the economy of emotions]. *In:* Honkatukia, P., ed. *Lähentelystä raiskauksiin: Tyttöjen kokemuksia häirinnästä ju seksuaalisesta* väkivallasta [From advances to rapes: Girls' experiences of harassment and sexual violence]. Helsinki: Nuorisotutkimusverkosto, 77-135.

Perho, S., (2005). The construction of girls' and boys' positions in a racist youth milieu. In: Suurpää, L. and Hoikkala, T., eds., Masculinities and Violence in Youth Cultures. Helsinki: Finnish Youth Research Society, 48-74.

Purjo, T., (2006). Pahoinpitely ja kiusaaminen eri asioita [Assaults and bullying are different matters]. Helsingin Sanomat, 26th August.

Reinboth, S., (2004). Eveliina Lappalaisen surmaajan tuomio aleni KKO:ssa [Killer's sentence lowered by the Supreme Court in the Eveliina Lappalainen case]. Helsingin Sanomat, 23rd June.

Salmivalli, C., (1998). Koulukiusaaminen ryhmäilmiönä [Bullying in school as a group phenomenon]. Helsinki: Gaudeamus.

Suurpää, L., (2002). Erilaisuuden hierarkiat: Suomalaisia käsityksiä maahanmuuttajista, suvaitsevaisuudesta ja rasismista [Hierarchies of difference: Finnish conceptions of immigrants, tolerance and racism]. Helsinki: Nuorisotutkimusverkosto.

Tilastokeskus, (2007a). Väestörakenne [Population structure]. StatFin-tilastotietokanta. Available from: http://pxweb2.stat.fi/database/StatFin/vrm/vaerak/vaerak_fi.asp [Accessed 13 October 2008].

Tilastokeskus, (2007b). Väestöennuste [Population forecast]. StatFin-tilastotietokanta. Available from: http://pxweb2.stat.fi/database/StatFin/vrm/vaenn/vaenn_fi.asp [Accessed 13 October 2008].

Tilastokeskus, (2007c). Elinkeinorakenne ja työssäkäynti [Industry structure and employment]. Väestötilastopalvelu. Available from: http://www.stat.fi/tup/vaestotilastopalvelu/index.html [Accessed 13 October 2008].

Tilastokeskus, (2007d). Kaupunki- ja seutuindikaattorit [Town and region indicators]. Kaupunki- ja seutuindikaattorit. Available from: http://www.stat.fi/tup/kasit/index.html [Accessed 13 October 2008].

Width, T., (2008). Koulusurmat nousivat ykkösuutiseksi maailmalla [The school killings became number one news in the world]. Helsingin Sanomat, 29th September.

Young People Hanging Around without Leisure Time Facilities in a New Democracy Suburb: Perkova, Estonia

Kadi Ilves and Judit Strömpl

1 Introduction: Setting the Scene

Peer violence is a topic of brisk discussion in Estonian society. Hardly a week ticks by without some bad news of hard violent acts inside and outside schools' walls. Traditional fighting between two boys, however, does not evoke the attention of media any more. The stories in daily newspapers focus on so called extraordinary violence, for example the growing physical violence amongst teenage girls. There have been several cases when groups of girls 'trashed' some classmate. Another series of articles reported the beating of a schoolboy by a group that included adult men. Later it became known that the victim himself was a perpetrator of school bullying and the beating was a revenge organised by the father of the victim. The school year 2008 began with news about a boy's knifing after the first school-day. In addition to these events the news of school shootings coming from around the world, and especially from neighbouring Finland, evoke anxious discussions about the prospective use of violence among Estonian young people. Different institutions and agencies dealing with young people express in these articles their vision and explanation of possible peer violence in Estonia. There is lot of blaming the bad school system and reckless parents. It is interesting that in these discussions the Child Protection Association (an NGO) is prominent as a blamer, but the representatives of child protection office and also youth work are not visible at all.

The biggest street conflict where Russian school students participated actively happened on 26 April 2007 in Tallinn. It concerned the removal of the bronze statue of a soldier – a memorial to dead Soviet soldiers in the 2nd World War. The bronze soldier carried different meanings for Estonian and Russian members of the Estonian population. The bronze soldier symbolised the Soviet occupation of Estonia for most Estonian people, while for the Russian part of population it symbolised the victory over Nazism. This dual meaning of the memorial became even more important and symbolic over time in relation to the so-called integration policy of ethnic minorities in Estonia, which was not very successful. The biggest minorities are Russian, Ukrainian and Belarusian. Almost one third of population are Slavs who use mostly the Russian language in their everyday communication. The biggest aim of integration was to make these people speak Estonian. At the same time the Estonian own independent national identity was in the process of development. On many occasions, the forging of this identity made use of the historical memory of Soviet occupation as a huge trauma for Estonian national and state development, which undoubtedly is true. Unfortunately the topic of trauma is linked to blaming the Russian people who were identified openly or in a more hidden way with Soviet occupants. At the same time the Russian people living in Estonia also went through their identity work, including seeking to explain how they were 'here'. For those who have found their place in Estonian society their ethnic origin was not a question, but for those who experienced loss of status since Estonia's independence in 1991, the Soviet soldier as a symbol of liberation was essential to their pride. It justified their being in Estonia. It gave them the role of positive heroes. When the Estonian government decided to remove the bronze soldier, they felt in some respects that this symbolised their own casting out. Some believe these sensitivities were largely ignored by the Estonian government, but were slyly exploited by Russia. The perceived provocation succeeded in producing a violent response: Tallinn's centre was occupied by rival factions for three hours without any intervention by the police. The Estonian capital had never seen such a violent event in public space in peace time before.

The topic of youth violence is also the topic of scientific research and youth work practice. There are numerous articles and conference papers where practitioners in education and youth work discuss about peer violence and other troubles with young people. Youth violence in Estonia has been studied concerning three main areas of research: juvenile delinquency, school bullying and sexual abuse of children and minors. The first area has been developed since late 1960s when sociological empirical studies were first allowed to be carried out in the Soviet Union. The topic of peer violence was observed first of all at that time in relation to violent offences such as homicide, robbery, personal tort, and rape (Saar et al. 2003; Saar 1988; Raska 1980). Quantitative studies on latent youth crime and violence were carried out over recent years using self-report questionnaires where some questions on peer violence and disadvantaged neighbourhoods were included (Staketee et al. 2008; Markina and Šahverdov-Žarkovski 2006).

The studies connected with school bullying are mostly quantitative and looking for an explanation of causes of violence (Kõiv 2006; Peets and Kikas 2006; Ainsaar 2004). Ainsaar (2004) analysed the more frequent places where young people meet violence. Among others (school, home), the street as public place was included in the analysis. The results show that most of secondary school pupils encounter violence at school or connected to school relationships. A mixed method study on young people's interpretations of violence was carried out by a research group at the University of Tartu (Strömpl et al. 2007). The topic of violence in public space was touched on only briefly, because young people who participated in the study focused primarily on school violence.

In the studies on sexual abuse questionnaires were used (Soo 2005; Soo and Kutsar 2004). Furthermore, some local research on young people's lifestyle, leisure time and alcohol and drug abuse were carried out in some cities of Estonia (Murakas et al. 2007; Rootsmann et al. 2007; Kruusvall 2004; Aimre et al. 2003; Heinla 2000).

On the basis of media presentation of peer violence and previous research it seems that there is insufficient attention paid to young people in Estonia. This situation affirms also the character of youth research in Estonia in general, where there are only some studies that focus on the youth perspective. In fact there is a lack of knowledge about young people's experiences and interpretations of violence. We do not know where they are and what they do when they are out of home, school and youth centres.

The study described in this chapter is important both for understanding young people's perspective on their experiences with violence and for their better integration into society. The results of the research provide a good basis for the development of disadvantaged neighbourhoods by local authorities and the better organisation of youth work.

2 Locality in Focus

Some Background Information about Tartu

Tartu is the second largest city of Estonia, and also the centre of Southern Estonia. The city is best known for being the home of the University of Tartu, founded by King Gustavus Adolphus of Sweden in 1632. The first written records of Tartu date from 1030 in an ancient Russian chronicle. The city lies 185 kilometres far from Tallinn, capital city of Estonia. The population of Tartu is c.100,000 (98,696 individuals on 01.01.2008 according to the Estonian Statistical Office 2008), its geographical area is 38.8 square kilometres and it is divided into 17 districts. The river Emajõgi (in English 'mother's river') flows through Tartu for the length of 10 kilometres within the city limits.

The majority (about 80%) of Tartu's residents are Estonians, 16% Russians and 4% representatives of other ethnic groups. The number of young people 10-14 year of age is 5,136, and 15-19 year of age 6,937. There are 26 schools (25 for Estonian and one for Russian children) that provide general education to 13,850 students and five vocational educational institutions with 3,661 students. There are 12 higher education institutions with 22,008 students. Beyond formal education, there are also nine hobby schools with 1,661 students, 41 hobby clubs that offer activity for 3,009 young people, 15 youth organisations with 1,202 members, nine open youth centres and two municipal youth agencies (Tartu in Numbers 2008). Tartu is the so-called intellectual centre of Estonia; the slogan of Tartu is 'City of good thoughts'.

It is important to note that Tartu has been a rapidly developing city during the last ten years. All districts of Tartu have changed their image as a result. The formerly poor districts have quickly developed while some other ones, which previously were prosperous, have become more neglected. People who were becoming more affluent moved into more fashionable and expensive city area near to the city centre or rural area around the city. By contrast, those people who lost jobs and became poor moved outside of the city to find cheaper accommodation in the countryside.

The changes in the city structure were connected closely to the general stratification process in Estonia after the emancipation from the Soviet regime. This process was mostly regulated by private capital transfer, and not by local government and public administration. After joining the EU in 2004 and in a context of economic growth, many people could receive favourable bank loans for purchasing better accommodation. However, only people with stable incomes could apply successfully for bank loans. Those who had little money on their bank account had no opportunity to use this possibility (for more about stratification in Estonia, see Kutsar 2002). Since 2007, however, Estonia has experienced a serious economic recession, and the number of unemployed and impoverished people has begun to increase (Estonian Statistical Office 2008).

It is important to remark that in Estonia there is no significant number of *immigrants* in the classical sense – the incomers from foreign states. In Tartu, there are only few 'coloured' people who, in neighbouring states such as Finland and Sweden, are known as the target group for discrimination and hate-crimes. The local ethnic minorities in Estonia are mostly people who have lived there since Soviet times. It was a general practice of the Soviet regime to mix people of different ethnic origins. People were sent into different places to work. It was a practice of obligatory working for some years in places to which people were directed. For this reason, we cannot speak about the voluntary immigration of people: they were not incomers from abroad but often compulsory settlers inside the same state (the Soviet Union).

Notwithstanding their long residence period, however, these ethnic minority people are only slightly integrated in the native Estonian culture and society. Therefore native Estonians and those from other ethnic groups, such as so-called *Russian*-speakers, constitute different communities and virtually do not communicate with each other. The ethnicity of the *'alien'* people is mostly not relevant for indigenous Estonians. They divide all people living in Estonia to two groups – *native* Estonians and 'others', and the latter are quite often disdained by them. This is not expressed publicly but rather in the form of disregard and ostracism.

Description of the Chosen Area

Perkova is placed between the town centre on the one side and an old industrial region on the other. Historically Perkova was an old working class area, which arose between the industry area near the river and the railway. Typical buildings are about 100 years old one-two storey wooden buildings. During the Soviet time some four-storey blocks of flats were built for people with higher status, but there are not many of these houses. A considerable number of buildings in Perkova are in poor repair and only a few of them have been renovated. Yards and/or gardens around the houses are mostly untidy, as are the streets. There are some parks which in the evenings and night-time are without any supervision and street lighting. In addition, there are numerous problems in respect to *illegal* alcohol sales, and also high level on alcohol misuse among residents.

The majority of factories in Perkova and also in the neighbouring district, which were developed during the Soviet period, are now bankrupt, closed or reorganised. Large and empty factory buildings are deserted and not subject to any maintenance. During 2008 the biggest of them was destroyed.

Perkova's surface is about 230 hectares. In 2007 the population of Perkova was c. 9,000 residents; it is the second largest district of Tartu by number of residents. The number of young people 7-18 year of age living in this area is 1,288 (688 boys and 600 girls). There are two schools providing general education and three youth centres.

There are no leisure institutions for young people in Perkova, and young people do not have any possibilities to practice any kinds of sports and/or other activities which are interesting for them. Only a bowling-club operates, but its entrance fee is overly expensive for teenagers. The operating youth centres have diverse target groups and they offer quite diversified alternatives of leisure time activities for young people. One of them provides mainly for 'good' young people who participate willingly in diverse leisure activities and do not have any behavioural problems. The troublesome young people of Perkova are not engaged in that centre and some who do use that centre come from outside of Perkova. The second youth centre is also not open for all young people because it is linked to an orphanage. However, there is a section called 'open youth centre' which ought to be open for all young people. This open youth centre now offers some leisure activities for young people aged 7-10 but not for those 13-16 years old. The third youth centre lies in the heart of Perkova; however, the employees of that centre have not been successful in involving young people in its activities. Also here, there are hobby groups mainly for 7-12 years old children. In addition, the youth workers of all three centres have interchanged often and some of them do not have an appropriate professional qualification.

The criteria which were used for choosing Perkova were:

- Residents have a relatively low social-economic status, income and level of education.

- There is a relatively high level of unemployment among the residents.

- According to some experts (the probation officer, the chair of Tartu juvenile commission), quite a large number of young offenders live in this area.

- Almost all of our experts pointed out the considerable number of marginalised families with alcohol problems, and relatively bad living conditions of people in Perkova.

- One of the two schools in the area has an especially bad reputation among interviewed specialists. The experts also mentioned the insufficient infrastructure and limited access for young people to leisure activities. Beyond this inadequate infrastructure there is a large number of empty buildings both in Perkova and in a neighbouring district, including factories, restaurants and shops.

- The district is not in the focus of local authority, police and/or other decision makers, because it has not known as a particularly bad area. Instead, the district has for some time lacked attention from public authorities.

- Ethnic minority groups are well represented in the area.

3 The Approach Adopted

Choice of the Disadvantaged District

Perkova as a disadvantaged area was chosen on the basis of expert interviews. Altogether six individual semi-structured interviews with experts were carried out. The experts were asked to participate according to the principle that various spheres in respect to troublesome young people and young people's troubles were represented. Those interviewed were: the head of child protection department of local government of Tartu, the chairmen of local Juvenile Commission (which deals with youth in trouble including young offenders), a probation officer working with juvenile probationers, *two* youth workers from two very different youth centres in Perkova and a youth police officer. Not one of those invited to contribute declined to be interviewed. Experts were asked to characterise the most problematic districts in Tartu for young people and to describe problems that have taken place there. Already the first two interviewed experts named Perkova as one of the most disadvantaged areas of Tartu and all of the subsequent interviewees concurred.

In addition to this information from the expert interviews, we also used the available data from a recent research study carried out in Tartu about youth subcultures (Rootsmann *et al.* 2007). At the beginning of the study we could not use any statistical data concerning Perkova because Tartu's city government did not collect such kind of data regarding single districts. However, since September 2008 there are now available data about the area which describes figuratively the very rapidly developing and changing situation of Tartu and also the whole of Estonia (Tartu in Numbers 2008; Murakas *et al.* 2007).

Interviews with Young People

Interviews took place from October 2007 to January 2008. To find participants we focused on young people on the street and therefore many afternoons were spent in

Perkova walking around the places where young people usually prefer to pass their leisure time. It was quite difficult to find young people for the individual interviews. They hang around together as a group and mostly would not agree to give an individual interview. The reason was they probably did not trust a stranger making them a slightly odd offer to participate in research about young people's encounters with other young people in public space. Therefore some young people declined to give an interview. Eventually we succeeded on the streets and at a café in contacting six boys and one girl who agreed to give an individual interview and additionally three groups of young people who agreed to participate in group interviews. Accordingly seven interviews were carried out on the streets. 17 additional interviews took place in three different youth centres and most of them were individual interviews. Seven interviews were initiated with help of youth workers.

Altogether 24 interviews were conducted but two of these were later excluded, so data from 22 interviews have been analysed and form the basis for the findings. The first excluded interview was a test-interview with a 15 year old girl to identify the questions in Estonian language: how young people understand the questions. The interviewee gave a good advice how to use language and how to find young people. The second interview which was completely excluded was done with a group of too young (11-12) girls. Their age became clear only at the end of the interview. We decided to invite them to participate judging by their looks. Each of them had bleached hair and artificial nails and therefore they looked like 13-14 year olds. After the interview the age of interviewees was checked to ascertain young people's eligibility. A third problematic interview was done with a group of young punks. One of them was in the wrong age group: a 23 year old young man, and his remarks were ruled out. Other members of this group were 14-16 years old and therefore eligible for this research. Finally it should be mentioned that one 15 year old girl participated both in a group and an individual interview. She was the only girl in a boys' group and because of that did not get enough possibilities to express her opinions during the group interview. As a result, a separate individual interview was conducted with her.

The interviews took 38 minutes on average; the longest lasted one hour and 15 minutes and the shortest 16 minutes. The group interviews predictably lasted longer than individual interviews; those who were interviewed singly, especially boys, displayed a limited capacity for concentration and appeared to get bored quickly. All Russian young people spoke Estonian pretty well and there was no need to translate the questions or interviews. All interviews were transcribed and a quite detailed observation diary was kept containing descriptions of the interview situations.

Among the 22 interviews were 17 individual interviews, three in-pair interviews and two interviews with larger groups. Altogether 32 young people participated, 19 boys and 13 girls. Ten boys and seven girls in individual interviews, four boys and two girls in the three same-sex pair interviews, and five girls and four boys in the two mixed-sex group interviews. Two interviews were carried out with Russian young people, which add up to six interviewed young Russians. Regarding age, there was the following distribution: six 13 year olds, seven 14 year olds, fourteen 15 year olds and five 16 year olds.

Obstacles to Implementing the Individual Interviews

The overarching research plan was to conduct individual semi-structured qualitative interviews with young people aged between 13 and 16 living in Perkova. At the same time we wanted our qualitative methodology to be as flexible and natural as possible. For us was very important that the young people who participate in the research to feel safe and comfortable (Eder and Fingerson 2002). Furthermore, from our former research experiences with young people we learned that it gives an additional value to the understanding of teenagers' language use and ways of representing their experiences when they are in small groups. Being together they naturally use the language of their own culture and the researcher can ask additional questions for clarifying the meanings of used words and notions. In an individual face-to-face interview there is a greater risk that a young respondent will try to meet the expectations of the adult researcher and give answers that from his or her point of view are thought to be the 'right' ones. This is especially important in the context of Estonia where the educational experience still bears many signs of the former authoritarian system. This can mean that in an individual interview the young person will speak not about his or her 'real' experiences and understandings, but will use the common widespread interpretative repertoires (see also Bahktin 1999; Potter and Wetherell 1987).

We therefore started with group interviews. Later, when we already had quite good data and were more certain that we could understand the young people's language use and earn their trust, individual interviews were then carried out. For most of the young people who participated in our research violence was a sensitive and unpleasant topic. One girl in a group interview asked for example to change the topic, because she felt herself uncomfortable to discuss this. It however depended on what exactly the interviewees called *violence*. For most of them not all aggressive demeanours were considered to be violent.

Analysis and Interpretation

During coding and analysing the data the qualitative software package Atlas.ti 4.1 version was used. In the beginning we decided to use an inductive open coding method to clarify the richness of qualitative data. This means we did not code the data according to the research questions. As a result of this inductive approach we produced a number of codes that were not directly connected with preliminary research questions but nevertheless characterise peer violence amongst young people in Estonia. On the next stage of coding we settled on only those codes which were connected with purpose and questions of our inquiry and assembled these to the following code families: Physical violence, non-physical violence, place, time, intention, combatants, consequences, own youth group, conditions and dynamic of encounters, and young people's interpretations of violence, ethnicity and gender. On the basis of families and codes there were subsequently found to be five models of violence which characterise interviewed Estonian young people's behaviour in encounters.

4 Models of Peer Violence

During the analysis *five* models of youth violence were established. The names of models are derived from young people's stories – how and what they talked about in relation to their own or others' behaviour during the encounters. These stories included both descriptions of activities, characteristics and perspectives in terms of participants and situations, and interpretations of meanings from the respondent's point of view. The models of youth violence, which were assembled on the basis of interpretations, proposed by Estonia's young interviewees, are the following:

- "Just for fun": different violent encounters, mainly non-physical for making somebody ridiculous;

- "Chastisement of rules violators": in-group and out-group physical and non-physical violence regulating relationships;

- "One for all and all for one": collective violent encounters for defending a group member against other groups or individuals;

- "Collision of ideologies": group rivalries focused on territorial and ethnic conflicts, local or sub-cultural identities. The 'neo-Nazi Skinheads';

- "Girl's stuff": gender related violent encounters, individual, collective and contemporary.

'Just for Fun': Different Violent Encounters, mainly Non-physical for Making Somebody Ridiculous

Spitefulness and Pushing of Weaker Group Members

The first type of just-for-fun violence takes mostly place *inside* the young people's own group. Incidents can happen between individual group members as well between a single person and some other group members or whole group. However, the most prevalent are conflicts between individuals. Sometimes a victim's family members can also be involved. Then assailants can also identify the family's property and vandalise it. The other group members participate in conflict as bystanders or witnesses. The purpose of these kinds of encounters seems to be the wish to laugh at one or both protagonists, in other words to have fun. The victim of fooling and mockery mostly is a weaker or younger group member(s) whose function in the group sometimes is being a simpleton. He or she may have also a specific nickname. The leader(s) of group accept that kind of fooling and mockery inside the group. This kind of having fun is not intended to teach a lesson or cause severe harm. Because of that these encounters are neither long-lasting nor sweeping, but usually are limited by non-physical violence or by facetious pushing. After encounters participants' friendship usually continues, despite the fact that during the conflict the victim can get offended and even burst into tears, which indicates that some hurt and harm has been caused. The interviewees did not speak about repetitious assaults toward the same victim. So we suppose that such just-for-fun attacks usually are single and unpremeditated cases; however some of these can be intentional.

Extract from an individual interview with Peeter (15 yrs).

P: It happened last weekend, for example. An older boy spited 'Brainy'[nickname of victim] till he was in tears /.../ Spiting was as the spiting always is, with pushing and shoving. /.../ He started to cry and whatsoever. We all were friends again when he stopped. There was no conciliation.

Spiting Younger Children on the Street

The next just-for-fun incidents take place *outside* the young people's own group but are aimed also to make fun and/or to achieve somebody's attention. In the opinion of the interviewees these acts are again not really violence but joking. Such acts can happen on the streets during the day, when young people meet each other after school or while hanging around in leisure time. Usually the participants are not drunk. The encounters occur between a group and a single individual. However, sometimes incidents between groups can take place. Victims can again be younger or somehow weaker than teasers and mockers. Incidents can also take the form of spiting, mocking, fooling and laughing at victims as well as shoving and pushing them or taking their things away playfully. Mostly the encounters do not last for a long time and are restricted to a certain location, for example at shopping mall, where young people congregate for a while just to hang around. In the interviews only assailants described these cases and therefore it is not possible to assess the potential hurt for victims. The opinion of the respondents (who had perpetrated such behaviour) was that this did not cause any harm and therefore that such incidents are not really violent.

Extract from an individual interview with Katrin (15 yrs).

K: When we sometimes have a good state of mind ... Once we came from bookstore and a little boy walked on the street and then we said like for a laugh ... but he understood that we joked and he didn't say anything bad because we just asked "Ciao! You don't want to know us, do you?"

More Violent Spiting and Mocking

The third mode of just-for-fun violence was perceived and described as real violence. The reason for that kind of distinction from cases described previously might arguably be the role of the interviewee in the conflict described – the two previous modes of just-for-fun violence were recounted by a witness and an assailant, but the next one derives from an interview with a victim of 'just-for-fun' violence. This kind of spiting (or some other kind of behaviour) usually occurs outside of young people's own group and seems to be more serious compared to more 'friendly' forms of the same kind of behaviour because the purpose is more explicitly to damage or hurt the other in order to express their own power and also superiority. Mostly it takes place spontaneously without any certain purpose. Nevertheless such acts may have and sometimes do have very serious consequences to the victim(s) and perhaps to both parties, because the conflict may continue for quite a long time and occur in public space where other people can see and hear it. However, witnesses and/or bystanders to such acts appear to rarely have the motivation of courage to intervene, especially if they are young people themselves, for they fear they may become the next victims of the same assailants. Adults, on the other hand, may not even perceive such behaviour as violence, because it may look like a (word)play between young people.

Extract from an individual interview with Jane (14 yrs).

J: My classmate and I walked down the street and met a group of 4-5 young people. They walked toward us. Then they started to shove my classmate and told her that she must watch where to walk. Then they pursued us, talked to my classmate mockingly, called her names and pushed her again. I knew that when I confronted them the situation would become even worse, because there were more of them. We just walked forward and kept walking until they left us alone, remained behind and walked away. That was the worst case that happened to me.

Chastisement of Rules Violators: In-group and Out-group Physical and Non-physical Violence Regulating Relationships

Chastisement inside the Own Group

Punitive encounters are quite frequent *inside* youth peer groups. The main goal of such encounters is to correct the behaviour of a group member who has transgressed some explicit or unspoken rules and to call him or her to order. The punisher's goal is not to cause severe physical and/or psychological hurt, but causing hurt to a certain degree is essential. So victims can get quite severely hurt and harmed; mostly the interviewees spoke about psychological hurt. Sometimes assailants may change the mode of punishing during the different phases of conflict. For example, they may first try to explain things with words; if this does not work they use physical force or the threat of physical violence. The Estonian teenagers did not describe cases where chastisement meant casting out a group member from the peer group or ending the friendship. Sometimes group members who were punished in this way did leave the group soon afterwards but it was rarely clear that it was specifically the violent experience that had triggered their departure but the actual reason of his/her leaving remained unclear.

A group member can be punished because of his presumed homosexuality. Supposedly other male members of that group sensed their own sexual orientation to be threatened by this 'gay' group member. As a result, they "just had" to beat him. Chastisement such as this can be serious and can lead to exclusion from the group. Excessively large differences between group members' orientations, attitudes, and values can be reasons for ending the friendship.

> Extract from an individual interview with Toomas (14 yrs) who told a story about a previous group member who was punished for 'wrong' sexual orientation.
>
> T: For example a boy last summer ... that boy was totally out of control. He was such a weird guy. He was beaten in such a way that his face was really roundish afterwards. He was beaten one by one ... by turns. All members of our group were against him because he became a gay, totally homosexual and then we... finally he couldn't live in Tartu anymore. Now he lives somewhere near to Tallinn. /.../ He went through with a guy who gave him money for kind of strange things. He got money from the guy with whom he did those suspicious things.

Punishing individuals for informing could be found inside youth peer groups which were described as real gangs, engaged with drug dealing. Mostly these groups consist of adults, but teenagers aged 13 and over can be used as runners and sometimes petty (local) dealers. A 16 year old interviewee told us a story about an act of punishing an informer in connection with him giving information against a drug dealer. The punishment of the informer takes place between an individual group member and a whole group, which believes it has the right to chastise him. The informer will be beaten seriously because informing against the group leader is a very grave contravention of the rules of the gang. So he is likely to experience severe physical and psychological hurt and may also need medical help.

Extract from an individual interview with Jaan (16 yrs) who described a case of punishing an informer.

J: Some shit happened. That case was in connection with narcotics. A guy was sent to jail and he suspected somebody of informing against him but nobody knew anything. Inside our group and in town people started to fight and a friend of mine also was informing against that guy. And my friend was beaten seriously by the other group because of that.

Chastisement of Outsiders

The chastisement of outsiders means mostly acts of punishing people outside of young people's own group. Chastisement of outsiders can rather happen in the form of fighting between youth groups and not as much as between individuals. More serious methods can be used including severe physical violence such as beating and vandalising and sometimes also using different kinds of weapons, such as sticks, knives, and bottles. However, punishment can be perpetrated also more softly – with words, which seems to be more typical towards and between girls. These encounters are also often tied in with self-defence and/or revenge.

The punishment of outsiders may take place in various ways and for different reasons. Respondents reported conflicts where they were assaulted by a group or by a member of another group. A successful self-defence was presented as the giving a lesson to an assailant. Mostly the descriptions portrayed physically violent encounters which ended in the defeat of the opponent. The interviewee proved his superiority by teaching his protagonist a lesson. The heroism was even more emphasised because of unequal position of opponent: in these stories the enemy is invariably older and stronger (for example, an adult against a minor), or there is a group against an individual. Some stories of this kind took on the form of fairy tales and it was not always clear where truth stopped and fiction began. By checking out the formal information, some large group-to-group fighting that was described by interviewees had not actually taken place in Tartu. Stories such as those were therefore not used in our descriptions of violent encounters.

Extract from an individual interview with Jaan (16 yrs) who told a story about teaching a lesson to an aggressor.

J: In principle it happened like that: someone wanted to beat me up from what he was threatening. He waved his knife at me on the railway near the packinghouse. He came there with his group and wanted to beat me. So I defended myself and he got beaten and then he went away. This guy was 19 in my opinion, but I was 16 or something. I don't know, he came to beat me, but he got beaten himself.

Conflicts with drunken people were also described in the interviews as a certain kind of punishment. The interviewee presented drunken people as troublemakers who need punishment for being a nuisance. According to interviews these conflicts took place late in the evenings at places where the teenagers were hanging around. Encounters would usually take place between a single drunk adult and a group of 2-5 juveniles although sometimes it was drunken young people who were the target, especially if they engaged in provocative behaviour (words or actions) towards the assailants. Moreover, the assailants were sometimes also drunk. Such assaults are mostly physically violent. Non-physical modes of assault, such as abusive language, are usually just precursors to more direct physical aggression.

Mark told a story about punishing a drunken adult aggressor. Extract from a single sex group interview with Mark (15 yrs) and Henri (13 yrs).

M: We were on the street three of us together and walked toward E-store [a large furniture store] from Linda Street. My friend was walking in front of me. I walked behind him and had two bottles of beer in my hands. I had already drunk a half of one beer and both of my friends also had bottles of beer in their hands. A man came towards us, one of my friends of mine said him "Jou!" Then that man started to say something like "what do you want?" and "why do you look at me, monkey?" or something. I got to them and asked "what's going on?" That man came to me and just fisted my chin. Then I asked "what are you doing?" and hit him on his head with my bottle. Then we left and he brawled there for a while. We went to Y-park and then I said to my friend that let's go back to the shop and look where that man is. The man came again towards us and started to shout out that all of us will be beaten by him. Then I took a stick, my friend also took a stick and that man also took a stick. I asked: "why did you hit me?" and then he bawled: "but why did you hit me?" I answered: "to defend myself because you wanted to beat me". Then that man started to beat me with his stick but my friend saw

what was going on and went for him with his stick. It struck that man to face
and he got a black eye. Then we wanted to get away but police were already
there and seized us. My friend is in jail now because he had done another
assault a couple of years ago. That man has also threatened us earlier like
that and once before he had had a fight with my friend. But we did not do
anything. He's always been the same.

'One for All and All for One': Collective Violent Encounters for Defending a Group Member against other Groups or Individuals

Respondents told us of different cases concerned with defending members of their own
youth peer group against some other group or individual. Most prevalent seemed to
be cases in connection to the defence of friends against hostile individuals or small
groups. Stories about mass fighting between whole groups were quite uncommon
(though collective encounters have taken place between Perkova's young people and
young people from other districts). The preparation of conflicts is sometimes thought
over carefully because the purpose is to gain superiority over the other group and
protect the honour of your own group. However, besides this kind of well arranged
fighting unarranged encounters may also take place. In that case the unsolved conflict
may emerge again and again between same or different combatants or even between
larger groups. Conflicts between an individual and a group are mostly physical. Youth
groups tend primarily to address disagreements initially by non-physical methods, first
of all by words. They use physical violence only if non-physical solutions do not work.
Sometimes there is ongoing verbal violence between members of two groups wherever
they meet each other. The conflict may subside, fester or escalate; it will end only with
the engagement and agreement of the leaders of the warring groups.

Extract from a single sex group interview with Martin and Karl (both 15 yrs).

M: The last fighting I remember took place between us and Pargikad [a
youth group from another district]. K: About 50 people took part in this
conflict. M: We were in the minority, there were more of them but yet they
were beaten by us. Our guys were greater and stronger. K: A girl from the
other group started that. She spread rumours about things. We met near
the school. M: The girl who spread the rumours was from Pargikad and so
that group came. We promised that we will beat them. Then the groups got
together and a guy from our group said to them to come here if you want to
fight. K: They came and then it happened. They broke down totally. M: They
got beaten and it was the end of conflict. K: The police were everywhere but

they could not do anything because there were so many young people. M: A guy from Linnuküla [district of Tartu] said that they have weapons with. But he is an idiot and you cannot believe him. K: Some guys had beetles [beetles are used for playing baseball] with them and other such things but nobody had guns or anything like that. M: Beetles are the usual weapons in conflicts like that. K: People had knives and such things on them. Someone got hurt by a knife. M: With a knife? I know that people got hurt with beetles but I don't know anything about stabs.

'Collision of Ideologies': Group Rivalries Focused on Territorial and Ethnic Conflicts, Local or Subculture Identities

The term 'ideology' indicates here different kind of principles or sets of principles around which the young people get together as a group. These principles or rather differences between principles of diverse youth groups are the reason for conflicts between these groups. The conflicts under discussion are characterised by the collision of diverse *world views* and *behavioural principles*, for example dress style, holding and securing a territory, interests or attitude toward other people, including various minorities. These conflicts mostly took place between whole groups and less between individuals. However, sometimes a group harasses an individual member of any other youth group. People meeting during these conflicts as rivals may in fact be acquainted with each other. Unfortunately there were not any complete stories in the interviews and because of that we could not present any extract of two first models of ideology violence. Young people represented these cases only as remarks or comments in connection to some other cases and the model became completely 'visible' by the time analysis of the interviews had been concluded.

Defence of Perkova against Strangers and Undesirable People as Expression of Local Identity

Young people living in Perkova proclaim that the district 'belongs' to them. Because of that a conflict can happen with youth groups coming from other districts and hanging around in Perkova. The fighting starts especially quickly when the strange group behaves badly; for example, if they are impudent toward domestic youth or vandalise something. Mostly conflicts between groups take the form of physical fights which can start spontaneously or be premeditated.

Quarrels between Different Subcultures

Another type of encounter is organised by Perkova's young people against members of some special subcultures. Representatives of the Emo subculture or the so-called 'Mainstream Guys' are both undesirable in Perkova and especially vulnerable to attack by the 'Boys of Perkova', especially because of their lack of connection with this area's look, style and attitudes. The assailants prefer to harass them as a group and not as individuals. Mostly such encounters are non-physical spiting, mocking and name-calling. All stories about that kind of conflicts were told by young people who were not members of the subcultures mentioned above. We only conducted one group interview and one individual interview with individuals from Punk subculture. These interviewees told about fear of being attacked on the streets of Perkova. Therefore they prefer to spend time on the streets as a group and avoid being alone.

Estonian Skinhead Violence against Russian Minority

These conflicts happen between an individual Russian young person and groups of Estonian Skinheads. Conflicts between Skinheads and other Estonian youth are to some extent distinct, because these are not as much *hate-crimes* as against Russian minority. Skinheads are often drunk at the time of assault and they are usually physically violent towards victims. Typically the intention is to cause serious hurt and injuries. Skinheads tend to perpetrate their violence in the evenings, when it gets dark and they usually use some kind of weapons, for example knives, some other special edge-tools or even tear-gas. However, no Skinheads individuals or groups were interviewed for the present study. Therefore all descriptions of conflicts originate from non-Skinhead interviewees so the accounts are, at minimum, second-hand.

Ethnic Identities and Violent Conflicts between Estonians and Russians

The third type of conflict on the basis of different 'ideologies' is encounters between youth of Estonian and Russian ethnicity. Russian interviewees reported that they prefer to spend leisure time outside Perkova because they are afraid of Estonian young people's spiting or other kind of harassment. The Estonian interviewees confirmed that from time to time in Perkova there are violent encounters between young people from the two ethnic groups. Russian interviewees blamed Estonians for verbal violence, and Estonian interviewees described encounters which were allegedly started by Russian young people. Both Estonian and Russian interviewees stated that conflicts between the two ethnic groups are generally restricted to non-physical exchanges. Only rarely do such conflicts become physically violent. Like other 'ideological' conflicts these confrontations are usually between groups or an individual and a group, rather than between single individuals. Mostly the youth group of one ethnicity starts to spite, laugh at, and ridicule passer(s)-by from the other ethnic background.

Extract from an individual interview with Georg (15 yrs) who described a fight between Estonian and Russian youth.

G: This summer there was a Russian gang... They started to abuse us at once. Usually they start with obscenity and then things are going on. Mostly it happens between the Russians and us. I don't know why they like to abuse us. Scuffles are uncommon, mostly it's words.

'Girls' Stuff': Gender Related Violent Encounters - Individual, Collective and Contemporary

Girls' Violence in the Internet

Non-physical conflicts between two girls or a girl and a group of girls begin in the 'real world', for example, at school, on the street, or somewhere else. Then the assailant(s) open for the victim an account on a social networking and discussion Internet site (for example: www.rate.ee or www.orkut.com). On that page the assailants post photos and texts about the victim, which usually are ironic and mocking toward her. As a rule that account is made public, which means that all interested people can look at the account and sometimes also add to the material or comment on it. The objective of the assailants is to humiliate and disgrace the victim publicly. Assailants sometimes also spread information about the web page among their friends and acquaintances. Besides individual relations in the Internet are also possible interactions and encounters between groups in physical space. Encounters which have begun on the Internet may end on the streets in the form of real physical fighting. Some interviewees also told us about using Internet for attracting friends to the street fights.

Extract from an individual interview with Kristi (16 yrs, a Punk girl) who described how her classmates used a public Internet site to spite her.

K: Rather some kind of virtual psychological violence. For example someone does an anti-club against someone else or something like that. I know that my classmates made that kind of club against me. They opened an account at Rate. They had a lot of fun. In my opinion it is very foolish. How do they have a mind to do something like that? Why do they care that somebody does not like Rate and is different compared to them? They took some photos with mobile phones and ... Possibly they opened even two accounts for me. I have never logged in and even haven't looked at these photos. One of them was with a pink toy. It was a reference to my dressing style. I wear mostly dark clothes. It is very silly that they have worked hard to make such an account and I don't care about that. It doesn't hurt me. They had plenty of fun, they giggled all the time. The reason was the material which they published was totally false. /.../ some of my friends, whose opinions

> I care about, looked at the photos and comments at Rate and also teased
> me about it. But actually I don't care about that. My friends know it doesn't
> hurt me.

Conflicts in Connection to One's Body Weight

A special girls' issue in conflicts relates to body weight. Skinny girls spite the others who
are not as thin as they are for being overly fat. Usually the assaulted girls have a normal
body weight and a constitution appropriate to their age. Mostly such conflicts are non-
physical; they take place between an individual and a group of girls or between small
groups. The conflict can be ongoing and be expressed in a public place where peers
(especially boys) of same age can witness what is going on. The assailant's purpose is to
shame the victim and to draw peers' (boys') attention to themselves.

> Extract from a single sex group interview with Maria and Isabel (both 15 yrs).
>
> M: Yes, due to weight. Other girls are not as big built as I am. Really! Actually
> I don't think I am fat but if other all are thin like whip sticks, then... that
> affects the way they see me. I don't like the fact that they spite me, and
> because of that I have to change myself. Till now I didn't diet yet, because I
> don't want to spoil my health. I: Why are you lying? You said that you diet
> and don't eat evenings as much as earlier and blah-blah-blah!

5 The Character of Violent Encounters

Verbal, Psychological and Physical Violence

Violent encounters among young people from Estonia are very complex. The interviewees
made clear distinctions between verbal, psychological and physical violence. However,
when describing their own experiences, there were in fact very few stories about 'pure'
physical, non-physical and/or psychological violence.

The teenagers mostly did not mention isolated activities like hitting, name calling or
slapping but spoke about more comprehensive behaviours like spiting, mocking, and
beating. The research was not designed to produce an exhaustive list of all possible
types of peer violence in public space but to build on descriptions of encounters which
young people had experienced and/or witnessed. If they named the conflicts somehow

(for example 'mocking'), then the interviewer asked them to be more specific about the meaning of term, if such elaborated was needed. Estonian young people described a considerable range of conflicts which could be classified both in terms of physical violence and non-physical violence. However, some clearly different modes of violent behaviour could be identified:

(a) Physical acts: Hair pulling, spitting, shoving and pushing, dragging, hitting and beating, taking away things, kicking, use of different kind of weapons.

(b) Non-physical acts: Rumours and gossip, name calling, shouting, laughing/ridicule, stalking, insult and innuendo, verbal threats, ignoring/ostracising, using Internet networking sites and chat rooms for hurting others.

Often the assailants' behaviour may become more severe during the course of a conflict. During an encounter the assailant(s) often practice more than one way of causing hurt and they may also combine mutually different acts according to their imagination. Mostly victims are primarily targeted initially with different forms of verbal violence, for example, shouting, laughing/ridicule, insult and innuendo, and verbal threats. The intimidation of victims continues with threatening them with physical violence, before being really physically violent. This is a customary incremental process in violent encounters between young people.

Assailants use physical violence only when the non-physical modes of 'having fun', 'teaching a lesson' and other rationales are not successful. However, sometimes they combine both non-physical and physical types during the same incident. For example verbal modes like shouting, ridicule, name calling, and shouting can be accompanied, almost simultaneously, with spitting, shoving and pushing, hitting and beating, taking away things or even using different kind of weapons. So-called 'purely' physically violent encounters are quite uncommon according to the interviews. The choice of methods depends incidentally on resistance and/or capitulation of victim, too. For example if the victim will resist, then the conflict may end, or in direct contrast, become even more serious.

The interview data point to a framework of rules which are (at least theoretically) present in young people's violent encounters. First, it seems that inside young people's own group there are preferred verbal and less serious physical modes of 'treatment' for prospective victims. However, the settlement of encounters with unfamiliar or hostile people elicits the use of more serious methods and sometimes also weapons. Second, in general boys are not physically violent towards girls. Some interviewees also told us that they do not hit or beat younger individuals. However, the latter rule seems to be more important for boys and not as much for girls.

'Have Fun' and 'Strengthen the Norms'

The intention of youth violence is mostly explained by interviewees as to have fun and not as much to cause hurt. Sometimes, however, 'fun' for the perpetrator can mean severe humiliation or even physical injuries for the victim. To have 'fun' may mean in this case that the perpetrator uses the humiliation of the victim as a possibility to relax and to deal with their own tensions. During the analysis became obvious that sometimes young people who use such kind of behaviours do not understand that they cause physical and/or psychological hurt. If 'joking' toward a young person and their family is perpetrated by group peers, the victim usually knows their assailants. Often also in-group encounters more than one assailant is involved which may increase their insolence. In cases where group leader(s) allow 'joking' toward group members this can also be seen as the way in which the leader(s) establish their position: through jokes and ridicule, they can indicate to the wider group who is in control.

The other type of youth violence is perpetrated with intention to teach a lesson. On the contrary to just-for-fun violence the purpose of 'teaching a lesson' violence is to cause some hurt to the victim. It means the punishment of somebody who has transgressed the rules of youth world or culture. These rules can be in connection with dressing style, belonging to one or another youth subculture, having the 'wrong' sexual orientation, social conventions or personal tastes. Similar violence could also take place as a form of revenge, whose purpose can also be to make an example of somebody. The victim must be injured as a result of the 'teaching' because they have then been given a chance to 'learn' their lesson. It seems that by punishing a drunk adult the victim 'needs' a lesson about interfering in young people's activities: they are punished simply for being bothersome and uncomfortable in the eyes of the assailants. Drunkenness and the loud-mouthed behaviour of victims is really only an excuse for young assailants to go on the offensive.

Similar intentions arise in conflicts where the purpose is to defend the honour of their own youth group or even the whole district. These encounters belong to the model named "one for all and all for one". Also the encounters on the basis of world views or so-called 'ideologies' have often the same intentions. Besides protection of honour the purpose of that kind conflict is to cement a distinction between 'Us' and 'Them'. The latter could be individuals as well as other youth groups or subcultures. 'They' are mostly seen as hostile and dangerous people who jeopardise the stability or principles of the youth group. For those reasons it is 'necessary', at times, to punish, teach or warn 'Them'. Arguably the overarching rationale advanced by young people for their peer violence is to strengthen their own in-group norms at the expense of those of outsiders, strangers and others who are perceived as different.

Consequences Depend on the Position: Victim or Perpetrator

According to interviewees it seems that young people differentiate between the consequences of physical and non-physical violence. The first has, in their view, some 'real' consequences, for example severe physical injuries, which may require medical help. In contrast, non-physical forms of violence, including verbal ones, are considered to be less hurtful, hardly violence at all, and indeed are frequently used amongst friends 'just for fun'. Nevertheless, the severity of any violent act depends on intention and duration as well as on outcomes for the both parties to the conflict. The meaning of consequences is in fact contingent on the position of the *story teller*. A perpetrator sees rather different *consequences* than a victim because the meaning of conflict is clearly very different for each of them.

Respondents who described their experiences as victims thought that every kind of violence is hurtful. They spoke about the severe psychological hurt they experienced through non-physical violence directed towards them. Beyond this psychological hurt some interviewees who described their experiences as victims of physical violence also reported physical injuries like bruises and black eyes. *None* of the interviewees was a victim of conflicts involving *weapons*. However, some of them described cases they had heard about or witnessed in which weapons had been used. They described mostly injuries which were inflicted by edge tools like knives or by beetles and sticks. Even then, none of the interviewees mentioned the need for medical aid for victims of conflicts that had involved weapons.

Respondents describing encounters in which they were assailants or witnesses told rather different stories. Behaviour which is judged as violence by victims may be named as a joke by assailants and sometimes also by witnesses. Some bystanders, however, can be on the victim's side and also understand the harm caused. In case of encounters between young people of different ages the age gap probably plays an important role. To children approaching the teenage years, older teenagers can appear like adults; they evidently have different power positions in comparison to nine or ten year old children. Therefore also the consequences of 'joking' (as teenagers may see it) can be viewed as violence on the part of younger children because of *unequal* power relations.

With regard to the consequences of physical violence, both parties can have several injuries. For example the assailants may use different kind of physical violence as 'aids in teaching' which can cause severe physical hurt to victim. Likewise the assailants themselves can be hurt physically. Both combatants also can get quite serious psychological harm during an encounter. The results probably depend on drunkenness of the parties involved. Where both combatants are drunk, some of the implicit constraints to peer violence are ignored, and the likelihood of greater injury is therefore increased.

For girls the issues in connection with the body and figure are very important. Victims of so-called *weight* violence may sometimes undertake quite drastic methods to diet and become more like their classmates, some models or other idols. Therefore violence related to body weight or other similar sensitive issues can cause severe psychological hurt and even lead some victims to engage in self-harm and suicide attempts.

According to interviewees, the interference (that happens to appear, or is called, or is asked for help) of adults in violent encounters amongst young people does not change the progression of conflict nor end it. It simply displaces or delays it. Moreover, some interviewees suggested that adult passers-by or witnesses who dared to intervene could be beaten up by the young people involved. The other possible result of interference could be the continuation of conflict in some other place; young people are adamant that such conflicts should be ended 'properly'. This is hindered if somebody incompetently gets involved in the conflict. Nevertheless, in opposition to the observations made above, some young people reported that conflicts end mostly as a result of adult interventions. The appearance of the police or some member of the security industry usually puts an end to youth conflicts in public space. The police are especially feared by young people because of the possibility of legal proceedings, prosecution and punishment. Some interviewees reported such procedures in connection with themselves or their friends. They had acquaintances who had been sent to prison or a special school for troublesome youth. On that basis, it was clear that at least some young people are well aware of the potentially serious outcomes of engaging in peer violence and, as a result, they try to avoid being involved in those encounters that may produce the more risky consequences.

Russian and Estonian Young People have Similar Attitudes Toward Violence

The Estonian and Russian participants in the research showed no differences in their attitudes toward peer violence. We cannot bring out separately typical encounters in connection with Estonian or Russian young people on the basis of our data. These conflicts mostly take place between an individual and a group which both represent different nationalities. Also conflicts between groups of Russian and Estonian young people are possible both in Perkova and Tartu. According to interviews fighting and other physically violent encounters are quite rare. The last conflicts of this kind took place about two or three years ago.

During the interviews, a discussion was encouraged concerning the event regarding the bronze soldier in Tallinn, which was that time still relatively recent and still in the news. Questions were asked whether some conflicts concerning to these events had taken place in Tartu. But the interviewees broadly ignored the challenge. They answered that it was too far from their everyday interests. Maybe the time that had elapsed since April 2007 meant that the bronze soldier events were already in their more distant memory.

Group Conflicts are Rarely Physically Violent

On the basis of interviews we can conclude that generally most types of peer conflicts take place between single individuals or between an individual and a group. Conflicts where an individual risks starting a fight against the group are very unusual. Encounters between whole youth groups on both sides also occur rather infrequently. As respondents told us, the last large group conflict happened in Tartu about two or three years ago. According to the police, those involved in this group conflict included Estonian and Russian young people, as well as representatives of various youth subcultures, such as Skinheads, Emos and Punks. So, this conflict cannot be classified as a conflict with a distinctive rationale, purpose or clear opponents.

Some interviewees could not remember any group conflicts in Perkova. However, others did describe fighting between small youth groups, but mostly the same stories recurred in different interviews. Nor did the police and media report any big youth group conflict in Tartu during the last couple of years. So we can conclude that any kind of group encounters are rare both in Tartu and in Perkova, but information about those that have taken place is widespread and well known among youth. The stories about such encounters are passed down like traditional tales and it is reasonable to suppose that some of these stories were recounted once more during this research.

Perkova's young people do sometimes engage violently with some other groups outside Perkova. This is when they feel the need to protect territory against incomers. The rule "one for all and all for one" seems to be an essential one in youth groups from Perkova. Friendship and brotherhood are main factors which keep youth groups together. All young people from Perkova are members of one and the same overall youth group (the so-called 'Boys of Perkova') despite the fact that most of them are also members of smaller groups within the 'Boys of Perkova' group. Because of this they are ready to defend the honour of their own district. Youth groups from many districts sometimes meet each other in the centre of Tartu rather than anywhere else. However, from the distant past it is known that there used to be some group fighting inside different districts, including Perkova.

Sometimes group-conflicts (especially "one for all and all for one" and 'ideological' conflicts) begin at one place between two combatants (for example, at school) but they cannot solve that and it continues, and grows, at some other place (for example, on the street) and time between larger groups. When individual members of two groups are at odds then actually the whole groups are at odds with each other. In this case the individual is taken as a representative of the other group and not just as a single person. The variance of this kind of encounter in relation to 'ideological' conflicts results from the dispute resting less on individuals and more on principles. The young people who sometimes fight because of different *world views* can get along with each other outside the youth groups. Disagreements come to the surface if they meet as members of youth groups in a conflict; otherwise their relationships as individuals can be reasonably harmonious.

On the one hand conflicts between groups can take place spontaneously as an immediate response to the encroachment of strange people. On the other hand these can be also premeditated and a calculated means of striking back. The latter is mostly a result of prolonged opposition of groups. Mostly conflicts between groups are not physically violent. The reason for this lies in the danger that physical fighting between groups can develop to very serious levels and produce severe and unwanted consequences: for example, beyond physical injuries, the intervention of the police and subsequent sentencing by a criminal court. Sometimes it is enough when all group members just get together around the harassed or victimised group member and show their power as a group. Nevertheless, real fighting is sometimes needed or at least one should be violent verbally and threaten physical force in order to represent the dominant position in comparison to the opponent.

According to the interviews the roles of *assailants* are not fixed during the conflicts. The assaults are mostly spontaneous and because of that roles develop during the event's dynamic. Usually in case of group encounters some group members remain bystanders and observers and only some active members are the actual fighters. Similarly in cases of encounters between an individual and a group some of the group members are not active and remain as passive bystanders. Their role could be also gate-keeping or guarding the assailants against unwanted witnesses.

According to interviews we can deduce that encounters within distinctive youth groups are quite usual in Perkova and normally tied to struggles over power relations inside the group. The interviewees did not call these *conflicts* 'violence' because these are connected more with friendly interactions between group members who rarely seek to cause real hurt to each other. However, the interviewees who had been victims of that kind violence have different opinions. In-group encounters may be non-physical as a rule but there are some exceptions.

'Good' Girls Hurt the Soul

As earlier studies on violence reported, boys are more violent because they use the more visible physical violence that produce signs of hurt on the body of the victims. Girls, in contrast, use more psychologically violent acts that hurt the soul of the victim, even though they tend to be described and defined as more peaceful in their interpersonal relationships. Yet, this is true only as long as the invisible psychological harm is not taken into account.

Compared with conflicts between boys and even between boys and girls the conflicts between girls are special. If boys told us more about physical fighting, then girls' violence seems to be mostly non-physical. Some interviewees claimed that girls do not fight physically with each other. They rather use more refined ways to achieve power and domination over their opponents.

However, during the interviews *two types* of girls emerged who differs essentially from each other. There are so-called 'good girls' who conduct themselves in manners 'appropriate' to girls and 'bad girls' who deviate from the norms of proper feminine behaviour. It seemed that most female interviewees wished to leave an impression of a 'good girl' who does not fight with anyone and always behaves well. This attitude was particularly typical for those girls who participated in individual or same sex group interviews. In mixed sex group interviews the boys' voices dominated and the girls' voices were hardly heard. Maybe this could help to explain that girls are involved in peer groups in public space mainly as the male members' girlfriends. In the opinion of 'good girls' they do not use any kinds of violence but sometimes they just have to use some power to 'teach a lesson' to somebody. Violence is a 'dirty' thing for 'good girls', but verbally or psychologically influencing a violent encounter is, in contrast, a 'clean' way to defend and explain any involvement in violence. In this way, even 'bad girls' can engage in a more widespread repertoire of violent behaviours, including physical violence.

One more difference between the two groups of girls is important to point out. Usually a 'good girl' does not fight with a boy which is in her opinion contemptible. A 'bad girl', however, does not recoil even from fighting with boys because that shows her equality in the boys' community. Among the interviewees there were only a few female participants who identified themselves as 'bad girls' and therefore we can give only a general and not a comprehensive overview in respect to their experiences and interpretations. However, if the results of other studies are brought into the picture then we can also find another explanation for their physically violent activity. Children under 10-12 years use physical power in conflicts of mixed sexes and the gender separation starts from around 13 years (Strömpl *et al.* 2007). It seems that deviation from feminine character is not acceptable among Estonian youth culture. This and other studies (see for example Markina and Šhahverdov 2007) show that among Russian teenagers girls' fighting in general is more tolerated than among Estonian teenagers. However, two experts described some conflicts among female teenagers which had taken place in Perkova just before our research. In these conflicts the assailants were young female perpetrators or in other words *really* 'bad girls'.

On the basis of interviews it is possible to draw a conclusion that girls fight for 'softer' reasons. For example they have disagreements concerning, amongst other things, dress style, body weight and looks, backbite, jealousy, and power relations inside a youth group. The more common intentions of conflicts of girls were revenge, fun and a wish to teach a lesson. Girls spite, mock, ridicule, gossip, ostracise and/or call protagonists with different quizzical and scornful names. Another special characteristic of 'good girls'' violence is invisibility. That means it is quite difficult to prove the occurrence of a 'violent' assault because there are no visible signs.

The girls' encounters take place usually between individuals but the interviewees also described some fighting which took place between an individual girl and a group of girls.

As a rule these conflicts do not last a long time. The encounters happen often on the basis of current emotions and are not at length premeditated. However, some kind of encounters, for example, those in connection to Internet pages, may continue for quite a long time.

Variability of Conflicts in Function of Time

Violent activity among young people takes place in general during evenings or afternoons after the classes at schools. The exact time depends on seasons, too. In autumn and winter-time when it becomes dark earlier the teenagers spend less time on the streets and parks and go home earlier (around 2000-2100 hours). In spring and summer-time days are longer in Estonia; it is light until 2300 hours and the young people spend much time outside. The weather is warmer and drier and the social life also starts later. For solving conflicts with violence, *darkness* is needed. After the school day when the pupils go home mostly verbal violence could take place. The young people reported about insulting, calling names or ridiculing each others.

Some more serious conflicts have their own pathway of development. They start as a rule on the weekends or free days when the adolescents meet each other in the afternoon. First they talk and make plans for evening. According of these plans the first aim is to provide themselves with some *alcohol* (beer and cider are the most popular drinks among Estonian youth). When they have got some bottles of beer, the conversation continues. The conversation has an important role in dynamics of conflicts. Somebody tells something that another group member does not like, or somebody reminds something from the past that could provoke a conflict. If these misunderstandings happen in a place dark enough and there are no police or other adults around, the young people often start fighting quite spontaneously. Conflicts and fighting inside youth groups or between friends begin this way. Conflicts between different groups are, in contrast, rarely spontaneous and unplanned. Mostly young people arrange the time and place of fighting in advance; for example, some of them who are falling foul of some other group or member of the group meet somewhere and call or e-mail to other group members to invite them to fight. In these cases the darkness is important factor because it seems to protect combatants from attention of adults, including the police. It also gives a certain kind of protection against identification.

Smaller conflicts and their resolution through fighting happen more often while serious quarrels between different groups are quite seldom, maybe once in the year. True, in case of more substantial confrontations mostly we can speak about a *series* of violent events. However, our interviewees reported that they are likely to avoid any such big sequences of fighting, or try to find more peaceful ways of solving conflicts.

Duration of Conflicts

According to the interviewees the simple short-time fighting between individuals are much more common than repeated long-time complex conflicts. However, the violent behaviour of combatants could be complex during the conflicts. The conflicts inside youth groups are more simple and short-time than conflicts between youth groups. In the latter case, further conflict sometimes takes place at the same time as some solutions are being explored; this can re-ignite the conflict. Some conflicts between youth groups holding different world views or 'ideologies' can persist for a long time without any resolution. Fighting can ensue every time they meet each other. Nevertheless, for the most part, violent encounters between young people are solved or sorted out on the same day as they begin.

Far from Adult Eyes: Places of Peer Violence

The place where the fighting occurs depends on who are the participants and how impulsive the fighting is. A need for fighting among friends, as described before, can happen wherever the group has come together. Different groups usually congregate in their particular established place. During the interviews the teenagers mentioned different places in Perkova. These are sections of parks or places where not many adults are likely to be.

In the case of planned fighting between different groups young people tend to choose places *outside* Perkova. These places are chosen well to avoid the attention of adults and especially the police.

The long-time conflicts which could take place repeatedly between the same combatants or the same youth groups could also change location. According to the interviewees' opinions some of these conflicts begin at school but are then continued on the streets.

A special place for young people's encounters is the Internet. Specifically, social networking and communication pages are phenomenally popular among young people in Estonia. This kind of violence is special because it does not occur in public space in the classical sense (streets, parks or other outdoor physical places) but these Internet pages are still in the public domain. For teenagers the open Internet sites, which are made to promote social interactions between people, are of the same value as streets and other outdoor public spaces when it comes to 'proving' domination or humiliation. Young people meet each other there and become acquainted as well as form their own opinions about other people. They can cause hurt through the dissemination of these opinions. Just like dark parks and empty streets, open Internet pages are far from adult eyes – parents usually do not have the knowledge to navigate this terrain either and therefore cannot supervise young people or prevent conflicts on the Internet.

Interpretation of Violence by Young People

On the basis of interviews with Estonian and Russian young people one can conclude that the notion of violence is a formidable and sensitive topic for 13-16 year old young people in Estonia. On the one hand violence means for them serious crimes such as homicide or rape. On the other hand the interviewees associated the term 'violence' with school and relations in school which is their everyday reality.

Describing their everyday communication and events young people spoke about diverse *aggressive* behavioural acts, but they did not refer to all of them as violence. For example, fighting between equal numbers of peers or peer groups is not considered by teenagers to be violence but more a friendly relation between peers or a way to solve conflicts. In contrast, from an adult perspective there is in teenagers' (especially boys') relations a great deal of aggression which can be viewed as violence.

The positions of the protagonists in violent encounters play an essential role in peer relations. One aim in such aggressive acts is to clarify the hierarchy in these relations. Young people explained that sometimes they bully a new member of a group just to test him or her. If he or she rises to such a test 'worthily' then he or she will become a full and equal group member and a good friend. According to the interviewees violent acts inside young people's own youth group could be attempts to strengthen one's position among peers. However, they distinguished different aggressive acts. The teenagers compared fighting between equal sides with martial arts or sports like judo. A boy who gets a black eye during the judo training, is happy; this shows to him and other peers that he is a 'real man' (compare this point with the results of a study made by Sunnari *et al.* 2002; Messerschmidt 2000).

Violence according to teenagers always includes psychological aspects, which is often not presented or acknowledged in all (so-called non-violent) types of fighting. The aim of violence is to cause psychological, emotional (in Estonian teenagers' terminology 'mental') pain, to humiliate the victim. Violence for young people means *unequal* positions of the sides involved in the encounter. It is an intentional hurting of the opponent who is in a weaker position and has no choice but to give in and leave. Young people consider mental violence to be more dreadful than physical violence. Mental violence indicates unequal relations between perpetrator and victim. The inequality can be both vertical (for example between teacher and student) and horizontal (between peer group and a lonely student). Similar results were established by Strömpl *et al.* 2007.

Interpretation of Gangs by Young People

Even though some male interviewees named their own group as a gang, their stories about the group did not accord with notions of real criminal gangs. According to their stories their group seemed more like a *fellowship* or brotherhood. During the interviews it became obvious that these boys wanted to comply with interviewer's expectations and told such stories because of that. We conducted four interviews with members of a boys' group of Perkova. The first of these interviews was a pair interview and two others were individual interviews. In the pair interview one participant was the leader of the youth group and he named the group as a gang. The other group members who were interviewed some days later also named their group as a gang. It is therefore possible that group members shared the interview experiences mutually and agreed with each other about meanings and issues. However, Estonian youth have good possibilities to obtain information from the Internet and also share news about gangs and themes related herewith. Young people aged 13-16 may be very skilful in using the Internet which offers many options to learn about youth subcultures in other countries. It then becomes possible to adopt preferred language, style and image.

Emergent Challenges

During the research some phenomena concerning peer violence emerged that appeared to be unusual and arguably not known before:

- Girls physically fighting: Both in our interviews with young people and with experts became obvious that girls use more and more physical violence in their relations. This fighting as a rule happens in public places such as parks, yards, and empty buildings.

- Body, looks and clothing style: Violence concerning body weight and looks is also more characteristic for girls' relations.

- Alcohol: Alcohol drinking as such is not a new phenomenon, but the amount of alcohol consumed by teenagers has grown and the age of young drinkers has gone down. There are many new alcohol products (light beer, cider, vodka and gin long drinks and cocktails) that are clearly aimed to young people though the law officially prohibits selling any alcohol to a person under 18 years.

- New technologies: Estonia was quite successful in developing new technologies and Internet is available for almost everyone. Computers are one of most mentioned attractions in youth centres. Young people have good skills in using new technologies that offer them wider opportunities for different activities including violence.

- Youth subcultures and sexual minorities: In the Soviet Union Western-type youth cultures were prohibited and men's homosexual orientation was criminalised. So we can tell that these cultures and the ideology around them are quite 'young' in Estonia. Therefore, the conflicts are sharp where old traditions and new possibilities clash.

- Powerlessness of adult people: Young people are frustrated by a situation in which they cannot get enough support from adults, but have to care about their well-being themselves. This is maybe a result of notion of freedom and equality in a new liberal democracy as it is constructed in Estonia.

6 Feedback and Consultation

Workshops with Young People

In September and October 2008 we carried out two workshops with Perkova's young people to present to them the results of our research and ask their opinion in relation to transforming Perkova, and Tartu as a whole, into a better place for young people. Though in the study design it was only planned to hold one workshop with young people, a second workshop was necessary as the first one did not turn out to be successful (as described below). In both workshops we used the same advertisement and agenda. As organising the workshop in Renju youth centre was complicated due to limited interest of both young people and staff, we offered two cinema cards as a present for participants who were involved in the entire workshop. In contrast, young people in Kilja youth centre were very interested in the workshop and therefore we did not use cinema cards there as incentives. However, some refreshments and sweets were supplied in both young people's workshops.

In the workshops, it was planned to discuss with the young people what disturbs them in Perkova, what could be undertaken to reduce troubles, what the young people's own contribution to improvement could be as well as what adults, youth work and the city government should do.

The first workshop took place in Renju youth centre in Perkova in September 2008. This centre consists of two different sections. The first one, an orphanage, provides residential care for homeless young people. The second, called an open youth centre, is a meeting place of Perkova's adolescents who do not need residential care.

All seven participants of the first workshop - one girl and six boys - were residents of this orphanage. Five of them were 13-14 years old and two over 18 years old. As young people over 16 years old were not a target group for our workshop (and indeed for the research as a whole) we did not apply the opinions of the latter two young people to the report at hand. However, we could not exclude these young people from the workshop because younger participants might also then refuse to be involved. Youth workers from this centre were not present at the time of workshop and they also did not offer assistance in planning and preparing the workshop. Furthermore, we did not succeed in carrying out the workshop in the way we planned it. The seven young participants listened carefully to our short presentation of the study results and discussed the topics actively until we asked them to express their own opinions with regard to the arrangement of youth work. These questions seemed to frustrate most of participating young people and they left the room one after the other. They did not tell us the reason but some older participants wanted to smoke outdoors and younger participants just followed them. Only one 14 year old boy remained there and continued active conversation with us. We suppose young people from the Renju orphanage are not involved as equal participants in the arrangement of the centre's youth work but are treated by staff as customers of the residential care service. Therefore they were probably not interested in – and certainly not accustomed to - taking part in debates like our workshop. On the other hand, it may have been more interesting for them if we asked for the kind of care these young people would need, but this was neither our topic nor our responsibility.

After the first workshop we tried to conduct the second workshop at the other section of the same youth centre. However, the youth workers of the open youth centre were not interested in helping us to organise the workshop and therefore we had to cancel it.

Negotiations in connection with the second workshop with youth workers of the youth centre Kilja were more productive. The second workshop took place at the beginning of October 2008. The youth workers assisted in the planning and preparation of the workshop. Seven girls aged 13 to 16 participated and three of the youth workers. All participants engaged fully in the discussions. All in all, this workshop was much more successful than the one in Renju youth centre. The main difference between the two workshops was that, in Kilja, the three youth workers were actively involved both in the preparation and execution of the workshop. This workshop turned out as a event where both young people and adult youth workers participated. Although this was not our plan, we let the circumstances guide us and we found that it was successful, because we all could experience a pleasant opportunity to discuss sensitive and important topics together. After the workshop all participants were of the opinion that they will start a new tradition in Kilja – regular informal round tables where young people can have a conversation with adults, express their own opinion and ask questions that are important to them.

The young participants were willing to add their own experiences concerning our results. The stories told to us were largely tied in with school life. It seemed that the topic has the greatest reality in the context of school for young people who did not participate in our research as interviewees. The most difficult questions were connected with the responsibility of young people as active changers the situation in Perkova. Post factum we thought that it was really a difficult and unexpected question for teenagers who are not used to be involved in different decision making processes. They reacted to this question with surprise. The teenagers also could not tell us about their expectations of adults in making their lives more safe, they just expressed their wish to live in a safe city. Young people also could not suggest anything to the responsible people in Tartu city government. All their wishes to the city centres were connected with things they already knew. For example they spoke about wish to have more hobby groups; however this seemed to be just a formal 'right' answer. If young people have no positive experiences with something they cannot wish it. For example one positive and new experience was offered by the workshop itself; the young people in Kilja liked it very much.

Workshop with Experts

As with the young people's workshop, we also encountered various problems in conducting a workshop for decision-makers and youth work experts from Perkova and Tartu. Primarily we introduced the study results to experts from the Youth Policy Service (YPS) of Tartu City Government. We hoped to invite these experts to our workshop and discuss which youth workers should also be invited. Instead we were asked to participate in a seminar of youth work topics which was for both youth workers and young people. This seminar took place in early September 2008. After our presentation of the research results, we tried to start a discussion with the participating experts and youth workers. Though they all seemed interested in the results, they did not appear interested in engaging in a discussion on peer violence in public space. Only the presentation of the results seemed to be interesting for the experts.

An expert from the YPS suggested talking to Tartu's Social Welfare Service or Child Protection Service experts about the problem in question. According to him, YPS deals with youth leisure time issues, but peer violence or other young people's problems are rather a matter for social care. Most other experts we tried to invite to a workshop did not answer e-mails or could not find time for participating in the workshop. In the end it turned out that only the youth workers from Kilja who participated in the workshop with young people (as described in the previous section) were interested in discussing strategies toward peer violence in Perkova. During these discussions the idea of street youth work in Tartu was brought up by the youth workers.

Conclusions

The absence of youth workers from the open youth centre, youth workers' passivity in involving young people in activities, experts' disinterest in discussing youth problems and an unwillingness to deal with these conveys a quite good picture of the problems relating to youth work in Tartu. These matters demonstrate figuratively how and why Perkova's young people, who are less active and therefore left outside any hobby groups, are left alone without adult supervision and care. According to the results of research conducted in Tartu, two of the three youth centres in Perkova are very unattractive and unpopular among young people (Murakas *et al.* 2007). Only the Kilja youth centre is valued as an interesting place. So, on the basis of workshops we can suggest that it is the attitude of youth workers and their involvement in joint activities with young people that may be the key issue for successful youth work in Perkova and Tartu.

7 Some Final Reflections

The most positive experience of our study is that young people were willing to participate in our research. When we asked them to explain their experiences and opinion on peer violence, young people were interested in these topics and in making known their view. They liked to get attention from adults and were interested to communicate with us, as researchers. What was important was to communicate with the young people at an equal level and to accept their concepts and opinions and positions. In their narratives it became obvious that young people in Perkova do not often experience that they are taken seriously by adults which leads to a general distrust between young people and adults.

Another important point is that this research also indicates to the *gap* between rhetoric and practice of youth work in Tartu. Formally everything seems to be very nice – several laws and regulations enact children's and youth rights and principles of youth work (for example: Child Protection Act, Youth Work Act). There are eleven youth centres in Tartu and since 2004 the city joins the UNICEF's directed movement of Children's and Youth Friendly Cities. However, this situation is an imaginary one because a large *majority* of young people do not participate in youth centres or other activities addressed to them, as indicated in recent research (Murakas *et al* 2007*).* The lack of efficiency is hidden under *wordy rhetoric*; in reality, plans are not realised and regulations mentioned above are not applied. For example the rhetoric of *participation* of young people in youth work is very popular in Tartu, but actually it looks like this: youth workers just sit in their offices and expect (wait for) young people to take the responsibility for active participation. Even children and young people who need urgent help and protection are also expected to seek this help and protection themselves. *"Estonia has a liberal policy and everyone is responsible for his/her welfare"*, as a child protection worker said in one of the expert interviews. Research findings pointed out that the 13-16 years children need sometimes more efficient help for their lives and future and that in reality young people suffer from the too much liberalism existing in policies and institutional functioning.

Additionally, there is also a division between so called *good* and *troublesome* young people. Troublesome young people are apparently neglected by youth work specialists, because the 'mainstream' youth work's vision is connected with good youth only. Troublesome youth have access to the *special* youth work, after breaking some laws (for example, dropping-out the school). This special youth work is performed by the police, the Juvenile Commission, special schools and/or probation officers and means in fact a form of tertiary prevention. Young people in trouble, who do not break any laws are left *alone* and are expected to manage themselves. According to interviews with experts and young people, we can conclude that there is a *retrograde* understanding of youth work in Tartu – young people have to commit a misdemeanour to have the possibility to participate in youth work.

There is *no street youth work* at all in Perkova and in Tartu as a whole. The street youth work is not needed up there, accordingly to the decision makers of the Youth Policy

Service of the City Government. So young people in trouble are *not* involved in the youth work, their 'voice' is not heard and there are no resources for secondary prevention. Troublesome young people and young people's troubles in Perokva and probably beyond tend to remain 'out of sight and out of mind'. Their propensity to violence, in different forms and at different levels, is one issue that merits closer attention and intervention. Therefore, a public debate and changes inside concerned institutions are needed urgently to improve young people's conditions and status in society.

References

Aimre, I., Raska, E. and Uueda, M., (2003). *Noorte vägivald, narkomaania ja kuritegevus Tallinnas. Eakaaslaste vaade probleemile [Violence, drug abuse and crime of young people in Tallinn. The young people's view on the problem]*. Research Report.

Ainsaar, M., (2004). Väärkohtlemise ohvriks sattumise kogemused noorukieas [Experiences of victimization in young age]. *In:* Soo, K. and Kutsar, D., eds., *Seksuaalse väärkohtlemise kogemused ja hoiakud Eesti noorte hulgas* [Experiences and attitudes of Estonian young people concerning sexual abuse]. Tartu: Tartu University Press, 50-54.

Bakhtin, M., (1999). The problem of speech genres. *In:* Jaworski, A. and Coupland, N., eds., *The Discourse Reader.* London: Routledge, 121-132.

Eder, D. and Fingerson, L., (2002). Interviewing Children and Adolescents. *In:* Gubrium, J. and Holstein, J., eds., *Handbook of Interview Research. Context & Method.* Thousand Oaks: Sage Publications, 181-202.

Estonian Statistical Office, (2008). *Statistical database.* Available from: http://pub.stat.ee/px-web.2001/l_Databas/Population/databasetrce.asp [Accessed: 15 October 2008].

Heinla, E., (2000). *Sotsiaalsete riskiteguritega lapsed Tallinnas: võimalus ja/või parutamatus kasvada seaduserikkujaks [Children with social risk factors in Tallinn: opportunity and/or necessity (inevitability) to grow up as offenders]*. Tallinn: TPÜ Rahvusvaheliste ja Sotsiaaluuringute Instituut.

Kruusvall, J., (2004). *Tallinna kuue linnaosa koolide 8. klassi õpilaste turvalisuse ja riskikäitumise uuring (2002-2004) [Research on safety and risk behaviour of 8 grade pupils at schools of six district in Tallinn]*. Tallinn: TPÜ sotsioloogia osakond, Tallinna Sotsiaal- ja Tervishoiuamet.

Kutsar, D. ed., (2002). *Living Conditions in Estonia. Five Years Later.* Norbalt II, Tartu: Tartu University Press.

Kõiv, K., (2006). *Kiusamiskäitumise mitu tahku [Different faces of bully]*. Tartu: VALI trükikoda.

Markina, A., Šahverdov-Žarkovski, B., (2006). *Alaealiste hälbiv käitumine Eestis self-report meetodil läbiviidava rahvusvahelise uuringu andmetel [Delinquency of adolescents in Estonia on the basic of data of Second international self-report delinquency inquiry]*. A research project co-financed by EU Daphne I and Ministry of Law of Estonian Republic.

Markina, A., Šahverdov-Žarkovski, B., (2007). *Eesti alaealiste hälbiv käitumine. [Estonian juvenile delinquency]*. Tallinn: Justiitsministeerium/Ministry of Justice.

Messerschmidt, J. W., (2000). Becoming "Real Man". *Men and Masculinities,* 2 (3), 286-307.

Murakas, R., Veski, L., Rämmer, A., Alvela, A., Lepik, A. and Maasalu, A., (2007). *Noorte vaba aeg ja noortekeskuste tegevus. [Leisure time of young people and operation of youth centres in Tartu].*

Research Report. Institute of Sociology and Social Policy of Tartu University. Available from: http://www.tartu.ee/data/Uuringute_kokkuvote_Noorte_vaba_aeg_ja_noortekeskused.pdf [Accessed: 15 October 2008].

Peets, K. and Kikas, E., (2006). Aggressive Strategies and Victimization During Adolescence: Grade and Gender Differences, and Cross-Informant Agreement. *Aggressive Behavior.* 32, 68-79.

Potter, J. and Wetherell, M., (1987). *Discourse and Social Psychology.* London: Sage Publications.

Raska, E., (1980). *Seadusega pahuksis: portreevisand noorest kurjategijast [At enmity with law: a portrait of a young offender].* Tallinn: Eesti Raamat.

Rootsmann, M., Mänd, M., Mänd, M., Kikerpill, K. and Palm, J., (2007). *Tartu mitteformaalsed grupid noorte endi tõlgendusel [The informal groups of Tartu in young people' interpretations].* Tartu: Linnavalitsuse Noorsooteenistus.

Saar, J., (1988). *Kiivakiskunud elu [Deviated Life].* Tallinn: Eesti Raamat.

Saar, J., Markina, A., Ahven, A., Annist, A. and Ginter, J., (2003). *Crime in Estonia 1991-2001.* Tallinn: Tallinn Technical University Press.

Soo K., ed., (2005). *Erikoolides ja laste hoolekandeasutustes elavate noorte hoiakud ja kogemused seoses seksuaalse, vaimse ja füüsilise vägivallaga [Sexual experiences and attitutdes of young people living in special schools and welfare institutions].* Tartu: Tartu University Press.

Soo, K. and Kutsar, D., eds., (2004). *Seksuaalse väärkohtlemise kogemused ja hoiakud Eesti noorte hulgas [Experiences and attitudes of sexual abuse of young people in Estonia].* Tartu: Tartu University Press.

Staketee, M., Moll, M. and Kapardis, A., eds., (2008). *Juvenile Delinquency in six new EU member states.* Daphne II, Utrecht: Verwey-Jonker Institut.

Strömpl, J., Selg, M., Soo, K. and Šahverdov-Žarkovski, B., (2007). *Interpretations of violence among Estonian teenagers.* Tallinn: Ministry of Social Affairs.

Sunnari, V., Kangasvuo, J. and Heikkinen, M., eds., (2002). *Gendered and Sexualised Violence in Educational Environments. Femina Borealis 6.* Oulu: Oulu University Press.

Tartu in Numbers 2008. Available from: http://www.tartu.ee/data/TARTUarvudes2008_est_2.pdf [Accessed: 10 May 2008].

Street-based Youth Groups and Sub-cultural Clashes in a Post-industrial Working Class Area: Trewaun, Wales

Jennifer Maher and Howard Williamson

1 Introduction: Setting the Scene

Political and *public* concern over youth violence in the United Kingdom has increased steadily over recent years. The British mass media have reported new and urgent social problems of Antisocial Behaviour Order (ASBO) youth (Mulholland 2007), Yobs (Doward 2007), 'Hoodie' youth and youth gangs (Akwagyiram 2008). Images of deviant young people congregating in public space have combined with a growing fear of youth violence and weapon use to create a disturbing picture of modern UK youth. For example, headlines from UK newspapers in 2008 report 'Marginalised British youngsters leave adults living in fear, says US magazine' (Dodd 2008) and a '40% rise in violent crime by under-18s' (Taylor 2008a). Weekly reports of high profile gun and knife incidents involving young people have firmly established peer violence among young people as a public plague. These high profile *incidents* emerge from the general low-level violent encounters of young people, yet attention rarely falls on the everyday 'mundane' experiences of peer violence in public space.

Youth involvement in binge drinking (Ward 2008), weapon usage (BBC News 2008a), violence for 'buzz' (Bennett *et al.* 2006), youth sub-cultural rivalries (BBC News 2008b), 'happy slapping' (Balakrishnan 2008), gangs (Akwagyiram 2008) and increasing female violence (Casciani 2008) have increased the panoptical gaze of the public, government and media on young people. Concern and fear over young people's behaviour surpasses our understanding of it; there is relatively little concerted research in the UK into the nature and dynamics of contemporary peer violence in public space. Much of the knowledge about young people and violence involves older age groups (e.g. British Crime Survey) or is largely based on school bullying and domestic violence.

Although peer violence in public space is increasingly an issue of concern for the media, politicians and communities, UK knowledge is largely based upon anecdotal information and popular media imagery. More generally, research by UK organisations has identified youth peer violence as an important area of research. For example, the Welsh TV social affairs programme 'Week In Week Out' (BBC News 2005) reported that almost 2,500 children in Wales have attacked other young people in the past 12 months, according to police figures. Six in 10 boys and four in 10 girls said they believed they could beat up someone else if they were provoked (BBC News 2005). Burman (2004) identified that 98% of females (aged 13-16) witnessed interpersonal physical violence, 58% worried about being sexually attacked, 41% were victims of deliberate hitting/punching/kicking, 91% reported being subjected to verbal violence, while 10% described themselves as violent, and 10% reported committing seven or more different types of violent acts. Outside of the family, boyfriends are the most common perpetrators of sexual violence on young people (70%), followed by someone recently met (17%) and then fellow pupils (10%) (NSPCC 2007).

At present, *academic* research on peer violence among young people is focused around youth *gangs* and *school* bullying. The UK media (Leapman 2008; Taylor 2008b) and more recently academics (Maher 2007; Sharp *et al.* 2006; Bennett and Holloway 2004; Bullock and Tilley 2002) have identified the presence of youth gangs across the UK, documenting a variety of violent behaviours and, more recently, fatal injuries resulting from conflict among their peers. Schools have been identified as the locus of much peer violence involving young people (Wilson *et al.* 2006; Wood 2005; Kidscape 2002; Cawson *et al.* 2000). Furthermore, the link between school bullying and peer violence in public space (Kidscape 2002) has been verified by Pitts *et al.* (2002) who reported that levels of 'in-school' violence are found to be closely related to levels of violence in the neighbourhood. NCH and Tesco Mobile (2005) highlighted the movement of peer violence between public and cyberspace - identifying a contemporary form of bullying.

Efforts to combat high profile peer violence largely fail to discuss more widespread forms of peer violence experienced by young people – as a result they remain under-researched and largely unnoticed. *Everyday peer violence* is likely to be young people's first experiences of violence (outside the home) and essentially the time in which young people develop strategies to cope with peer violence. It is therefore a useful first step in combating both low-level and high profile peer violence in public space.

This locality study, based in Trewaun, Wales, provides a first step in understanding young people's experiences and interpretations of this phenomenon, through the analysis of in-depth qualitative interviews with young people aged 13 to 16. As the UK scene has been set - in terms of the current public debate, academic research and media coverage of peer violence in public space - the next step involves a focused look at the study locality and the study design. The attitudes and experiences of the young people interviewed are then presented in eight models of violent encounters and seven key dimensions identified during analysis of the data. Interview extracts - from the young people's interviews - are used to enhance the models and dimensions. The report concludes with reflections and recommendations from dissemination workshops. The research analysis and workshop feedback is combined to expand the limited knowledge available on peer violence in public space in the UK.

2 Locality in Focus

Trewaun is a large town in one of the valleys within the Rhondda Cynon Taff (RCT) Local Authority, in South Wales. The Brecon Beacons National Park borders the valley to the north of the area; to the south, new industry and business continues to develop in localities close to the capital city of Wales, Cardiff (approximately 20 miles from Trewaun). Between 1905 and 1924 Trewaun – originally a small pastureland village - was transformed into a vibrant town at the height of the coal mining industry in South Wales. The locality's key role in coal and steel exports worldwide supported the development of large communities dotted along the valleys. In 1916 the population of Trewaun was 54,000, compared to 15,839 today (National Statistics 2001).

De-industrialisation across the valleys in the 1980s and 1990s resulted in all but one colliery closing, dramatically reducing employment opportunities for working class families. The fragmentation of communities that took place throughout the UK during de-industrialisation was particularly evident within the valleys themselves. Following national trends (Barclay 1995; Hills 1995), increases in poverty and social exclusion were predominantly concentrated in the more marginalised local authority estates (Jones and Adamson 2001) – many currently identified as part of the Welsh Assembly Government's (2006) Communities First Initiatives (tackling social exclusion in deprived communities in Wales).

The 2001 Census identifies 46,040 people in the Trewaun and surrounding research area, of which less than 1% are from minority ethnic groups. The area is characterised by its similarity to other areas identified in the 2001 Census, with the exception of a higher older population (65+) and slightly lower youth population (5-19 yrs); a higher number of owner occupied houses and therefore less social housing; a high population (33%) of non-educated 16-74 year olds; a lower number of self-employed; and an above average number of long-term sick and unemployed (National Statistics 2008).

Trewaun is characterised by run-down housing estates, depopulation, family breakdown, underperforming schools and decaying amenities, large-scale unemployment and general community decline (including the loss of many services). The growth of a service industry has produced the types of jobs in which working class young people, significantly young men, are largely disinterested and for which they generally lack suitable skills. Young people living in Trewaun have low aspirations, face limited employment opportunities, and are experiencing dramatic social change and little certainty about their futures.

The Welsh Index of Multiple Deprivation (WIMD) is the official measure of deprivation (referring to problems caused by a lack of resources and opportunities) for small areas in Wales. Overall, the WIMD 2005 (Welsh Assembly Government 2005) identifies both the South Wales coalfields and major cities as the most deprived areas found in Wales, with instances of third generation *unemployment* and high rates of chronic illness. Trewaun includes areas that represent both higher and lowest levels of deprivation.

From the Child Poverty Index it becomes evident that the UK, being the fourth largest economy in the world, conversely has one of the highest levels of child poverty of all industrialised countries. Although Government measures have reduced the number of children living in poverty in Wales from 33% to 27%, poverty still affects 170,000 children in Wales (Children in Wales 2007a). There has also been an increase in the proportion of working households in poverty; due to low wages. Recent figures show that Wales continues to have the highest rate of child poverty in the UK and has comparatively above average rates across the EU15 and EU25 countries (Children in Wales 2007b).

Crime rates in the RCT are low in comparison to other areas covered by the South Wales Police (for example, 80 crimes per 1,000 population compared to 111 crimes per 1,000 population in Merthyr). Levels of community engagement are low, while reports of youth annoyance have increased from 8,089 in 2003/04 to 8,796 in 2004/05 (Audit Commission 2006). There are no official local statistics available on violence among 13-16 year olds.

3 The Approach Adopted

Study Design

Prior to commencing the field research in Trewaun, contact was made with local Welsh youth service providers. *Five* expert interviews with local youth services and other relevant service providers (e.g. Head of the detached youth team, personnel at a local independently-run youth centre, Police Community Support Officers) were conducted. From this preliminary contact, the town of Trewaun was identified as a hub, where young people from across the valley were inclined to congregate. The proposed site was confirmed as an appropriate *'disadvantaged area'* through an examination of the indices and data mentioned in the section above.

At the start of the research, accompanied by local detached youth workers, the researcher made direct contact with young people on the street or in unsupervised recreational areas (e.g. skate park). As the research progressed, the follow-up meetings with young people were conducted in the evenings. Posters were also handed out and displayed in areas frequented by the relevant age group, in order to increase awareness of the research amongst young people in the area.

This strategy resulted in 66 young people agreeing to take part in the research, of which 27 young people were interviewed. Although individual interviews had originally been identified as the desired research strategy, some young people wished to be interviewed in groups. This resulted in 19 recorded interviews conducted with 14 individual and 5 groups. These interviews took place in a number of locations on and off the street: on street corners, under shelters, in cafes, in youth clubs and in sports centres. Where possible the young people were asked to meet or follow the researcher to a suitable indoor facility (the majority took place in a town centre youth facility) due to the wet, windy and cold weather and dark evenings that characterised the fieldwork period (September 2007 to January 2008). The young people were all initially encountered on the streets, and thereby satisfied the eligibility criteria. Young people encountered in public space in Trewaun, but who lived elsewhere, were occasionally interviewed outside the area and closer to where they lived. An interview schedule according to the common guideline was utilised to ensure key topics were covered; however, the interview was largely unstructured. Ethical considerations regarding consent and confidentiality reflected the broader guidelines of the British Society of Criminology and the University of Glamorgan.

Interviews were transcribed verbatim in a style compatible with NVIVO 7 (Qualitative Software Package). NVIVO 7 was used to *analyse* data from a grounded theory perspective (Strauss and Corbin 1998). To allow young people's transcripts to 'speak for themselves', analysis began with open coding allowing simplified categories and concepts to emerge from the data. These categories eventually gave way to the establishment of a provisional set of focal concepts (dynamic explanations) and main themes (models). With the research questions in mind, progressive focusing and the logical categorisation of data enabled the linking of concepts and development of eight models of violence. The circular process of analysis concluded with data saturation.

Research Constraints and Considerations

As with much qualitative research, especially that involving young people who congregate in public space, there were a number of deviations from the original research design. First, identifying the correct *age* of young people proved difficult. In particular, it was problematic identifying the exact age group on the street, finding young people of the lower age range, contacting minority ethnic young people and working with young people who remained within their groups while being interviewed. Second, securing a time and place in which to conduct the interviews was problematic on account of: the difficult weather conditions, the fluid movement of young people and their groups around the area, the impact of time on young people's presence in an area, and concern for researcher and interviewee safety throughout. Third, the impact of *situational* factors influenced the quality and quantity of information received from interviewees. For example, the use of *alcohol* and *drugs* by young people, the presence of the police and their focus on youth street presence and the presence of other - rival or friendly - young people in the locality affected the interviews conducted.

As a result of these factors, group interviews supplemented individual interviews; the majority of interviews took place off the street itself and the length and quality of the interviews varied considerably. Despite these challenges and changes the research unearthed a rich vein of data regarding peer violence in public space, helping to illuminate its complexity and contributing both to comparative international analysis and national understanding.

Sample Information

The majority of male and female interviewees were older teenagers (15 and 16 years). The mean age of the sample is 15 years of age. 15 interviewees were male, 12 were female. The sample is exclusively *White British* – consistent with the largely *uni-cultural* population of Wales. The sample was not asked questions about 'class', as this tends to be an abstract concept for young people (it is dependant on a number of dimensions: location of home, school, parental occupation, for example).

Respondents were asked to identify the size of their core group. Girls reported having an average of ten friends, while boys reported an average of 14 friends. In line with the history of youth sub-cultural affiliation in the UK (Pearson 1983), young people were also asked if they identified themselves with a particular group type. The majority of young people identified some group affiliation, with Chav/Townie (12 young people) being the most common; 9 interviewees did not report any particular youth group affiliation.

Identifying the number of the sample who reported being a victim or offender of physical or verbal violence (as defined by the young person, not the interviewer), boys were more likely than girls to report being a victim and offender.

Overall, in the sample there are slightly more young men than young women and more in the older age group in the range, with over half being affiliated with a *youth style*. The majority of males identified themselves as victims and offenders of both verbal and physical violence, while nearly half of females identified themselves as offenders or victims (with the exception of verbal violence).

4 Models of Peer Violence

In line with a central research objective, particular attention was paid to gender[1] as a key factor for understanding peer violence in public space. Additionally, six other factors emerged as important dimensions for classifying specific types of violent interactions (see Figure 1 below). Young people clearly made a distinction between physical and non-physical violence when describing the importance and meaning of the violent encounter. Their description of and explanation for violence differed significantly according to whether it was internal (in-group) or external (out-group), or individual (one-on-one) or collective (groups). The use of a weapon during a violent incident was identified as 'extreme' violence, different from 'normal' violent encounters. Modern technology, such as mobile phones, email and chat rooms were used by young people to engage in a contemporary form of bullying (e.g. 'happy slapping' and cyber-bullying).

Finally, interviewees reported distinct violent encounters dependant on the premeditated or spontaneous nature of the conflict (e.g. a planned fight with rivals compared to a verbal exchange that escalates into violence between two acquaintances). From this framework multiple models are evident. The following *eight* models represent those factors which most commonly emerged from the data. Each model is illustrated by a story or experience taken from the interviews with young people and includes descriptions of violence perpetrated, experienced and witnessed.

Figure 1: Framework for models of peer violence

Male	Female
Physical	Non-Physical
Internal	External
Individual	Collective
Weapon	Non-weapon
Traditional	Contemporary
Spontaneous	Premeditated

Eight 'static' models of peer violence among young people in public space are presented below – based on the framework identified during data analysis:

- 'The Scuffle': Individual, traditional, spontaneous, physical violence among boys.

- 'Bars, Bats and Bricks': Individual, physical violence with a weapon among boys.

- 'Fight Club'[2]: Collective, premeditated, physical violence with a weapon among boys.

- 'Cat-fight': Individual, spontaneous, physical violence amongst girls.

- 'On the Prowl': Collective, spontaneous or premeditated physical violence amongst girls.

- 'Cyber-violence': Girl's premeditated, contemporary, non-physical violence.

- 'Play-fighting': In-group, physical and non-physical violence.

- 'Out of Order': Boy's physical violence towards girls.

The Scuffle

The scuffle - a traditional method of resolving conflict - is the most common form of out-group violence between boys. Technically, the scuffle involves one or more persons quickly engaging with another young person or group in a violent manner. This type of violent encounter is often the consequence of a non-physical (usually verbal) dispute (which is seldom viewed by boys as 'actual' violence). The encounter is usually spontaneous and brief, aimed at establishing dominance or status. Boys identified a regular pattern of individual violence – feelings of anger or aggression (often exacerbated by the influence of alcohol) in reaction to a perceived 'dis'' (disrespect) or challenge to status resulted in a physical scuffle to balance emotions. Punching, kicking and shoving are commonly part of a scuffle, with bruising and facial cuts the most common injury outcome.

> Extract from a mixed sex group interview with John (15 yrs).
>
> *Int: So what would make you fight someone?* J: Well, I get wound up easily, and I lose my rag easily ... *Int: So mostly verbal things?* J: Yeah, something verbal. I've had too much hassle off people when I'm drunk. Wolf whistling like, some boys were passing Wolf-whistling [at my girlfriend] and that makes me so angry. Especially if I've had a good couple of cans of lager. *Int: So normally, would you be okay with it if you had no alcohol?* J: No, I won't, I hate it. It's just with a can of [a premium brand of strong lager] I'll be ready for it, I don't care after it... *Int: So what happens, you walked out of here, you haven't had anything to drink and someone wolf whistles at you, what do you do?* J: Stop them... well I would tell them, 'No, I'm not happy' and if they wanted to fight, I would fight.

Bars, Bats and Bricks

Boys, most commonly reported witnessing and using weapons during violent encounters. Of those reporting use of a *weapon*, most often this was acquired during the fight rather than brought for a premeditated conflict. As weapon use usually falls outside the rules of conflict, it is uncommon in individual fights. As a result, the presence of a weapon is interpreted by interviewees as a noteworthy and distinct model of violence. Blunt objects (e.g. bats, bricks or rings) were most commonly identified as weapons during these encounters, although knives and guns (airguns) were also *witnessed*. This type of encounter reportedly starts as a scuffle, but escalates when a weapon is introduced. The following extract describes the use of a weapon, acquired during a violent encounter considered by the respondent to be in self-defence.

Extract from a single sex group interview with Pauli (16 yrs).

P: Well I hit some guy with a brick. Int: *Why, what happened?* P: I don't know, I just hit em with a brick. He came at me, like and I just smacked him once and again and then I stood on his head. *Int: What did he do?* P: I don't know. *Int: Did he start it?* P: Yeah. *Int: You mention standing on his head, does that happen much?* ... P: Well I've done it, cause I was drunk. *Int: So what happened beforehand, why?* P: I don't know what happened, I don't know, there was a fight, he started coming at me and I just smack... he got my back up.

Fight Club

Collective violence reportedly took place between older groups from different areas or groups with a different cultural affiliation. Boys were commonly acquainted, but such conflicts could also involve strangers (who come to the locality). Long-standing *'historical'* rivalries between villages were adopted by male groups, resulting in a high number of reported collective physical encounters. This type of violence involved high numbers of young men (and occasionally young women) – with encounters of over a hundred young people reported. The conflict is largely pre-planned, with rules on numbers and types of weapons (if any) to be used. Additionally, violent combat was repeatedly reported by boys and girls between the two main rival sub cultural groups – the Goths and Townies (who also include Chavs and Spice Boys). Whereas in model 2 the weapon was acquired during the fight, in the following extract weapons were purposefully carried for the fight.

Extract from a single sex group interview with Pancho and Joche (both 15 yrs).

P: We've never been beaten, we're too good, we are (laughs). J: We were going to fight the boys from Nant at the weekend but they didn't turn up. *Int: You were going to fight with who?* P: They were going to come down with metal bars and that. J: And fight the boys at the weekend, the Nantymel Boys. *Int: So how did you know that they were meant to come down?* J: Because we have people from the same school as them come down here and tell us. *Int: It's not girls by any chance?* P: Yes. Other youths – Yeah (laugh). *Int: How did I guess?* P: Well we had our own people as well, you know. *Int: So were you ready for it?* P: Yeah, well! J: Well, not really, we hadn't got enough people (laugh). P: Well, not really, we were supposed to be in Tedstown when they came down. *Int: So did you guys get some bars and weapons, or were you just going to face them?* J: Face them. P: We just waited at the train station, just waited to see what happened. *Int: Okay, so you just waited to see what happened. So how many people were involved, like waited for them to come down?* J: There were about 20 of us. But they didn't turn up? ... *Int: What about you guys going to other areas, are there any people who are protective of their area?* P: Nantymel, really and all that. J: it's like that with Newton really. T [new boy shouts from another table]: Oh Newton, that's one that don't like us, going down there.

Cat Fight

Girls were less likely to report physical violence. Their encounters differed from those involving boys in terms of prevalence, severity and interpretation by young people. Overwhelmingly, boys identified girls' violence as insignificant and childish, while girls identified it as significant and distressing, but often less serious than boys' violence. Although girls' violence was also influenced by alcohol use, this was not as significant as in boys' encounters. Additionally, the types of violence used, its causes and motivations differed from that discussed by boys. Girls were more likely to report a long period of verbal conflict and a shorter episode of physical violence than boys. The desire to stop future physical violence, to seek revenge for defamation or slander of character (e.g. rumours, gossip) or to build a reputation (e.g. attract the boys' − or indeed a boy's - attention or incite fear in other girls) were common reasons given for physical encounters.

Extract from an individual interview with Sofia (15 yrs).

S: I was walking through town with Rhea and this girl came up and grabbed me. *Int: What happened?* S: We were walking through town when I was attacked by this girl. *Int: Who was she, did you know her, or have a problem with her before?* S: No, she came up behind me and grabbed me to the ground, em gripped my hair and pulled my head back and got me to the ground. And she starts hitting and kicking me. *Int: Really, was she hitting and kicking hard?* S: Yeah, all on my head and body. *Int: Why did she do this?* S: I don't know. ... *Int: What age was this girl?* S: She was the same age. *Int: What did Rhea do?* S: She ran to her house and got her father. Then that girl went and I just went up to her house. *Int: Has anything else happened since then?* S: No. ... *Int: What about yourself, were you hurt?* S: Yeah, my neck.

Extract from a single sex group interview with Nicola (15 yrs).

N: Oh, I felt very guilty on the train once when I was fighting with Kelly. She wouldn't get out, but she was mouthing me for days. But she wouldn't fight me. So I just kind-of like... we were on the same train, cause I missed two trains. I said to her 'look get up come over here and we'll sort it out'. She wouldn't so I just dived on her and started hitting her. *Int: So what did you end up doing?* N: And then some women grabbed me and slammed me against the window to get me off her. So I gripped that women and she gripped me and I said 'go on then.' (laughs). And then when I got off the train her mother was screaming at me and her mother went like that 'don't be scared of her, hit her'. And Kelly went like that no she just hit me and her mother started on me. And then that girl started mouthing again, so I turned around and said 'Kelly keep that up and I'll hit you again' and she went and run off then. But then afterwards I felt guilty afterwards cause she was younger than me. It started off in Starmans [youth centre] really cause she was mouthing me and that. And I went to hit her in Starmans and I got banned for two weeks from there.

On the Prowl

Girls were less likely to describe involvement in collective physical violence. As with collective violence among boys, girls reporting this model of violence often referred to prior hostility towards the combatants, in addition to the use of alcohol prior to the violent incident. The encounter is often premeditated, but does not involve the organisation reported in boys' violence. In the first extract below a (Chav) girl reports planning to track down a particularly disliked sub-cultural group (Goths) in order to attack them. The second extract describes an act of collective premeditated physical violence carried out by girls alongside their fellow boy group members, to avenge another group member. The level of violence and injuries received are reportedly more serious than those emanating from individual encounters, in fact they are more akin to violence seen in individual male encounters (punching, kicking, pushing, and tripping).

Extract from a single sex group interview with Nicola (15 yrs, Chav/Townie).

Int: Okay, so you had a fight with three Goths in one night, what was that over? N: Well me and my cousin Stacey were drinking and then I don't know really, she went and said, 'should we go fight them?'. So we fought with them and... *Int: So you planned to fight with them?* N: Well, yeah (laughs). I don't know what happened after that, we followed them down to the bus stop up by the Kebab shop and hit them in there and the one, she went up to the kebab shop having a panic attack, so me and Stacey followed the lot of them in there and we fought them in there. We're on bail and everything for that.

Extract from an individual interview with Pink (15 yrs).

Int: Has there ever been a situation where someone was attacked or in conflict like that and the rest of the group have gone to get revenge? P: Yeah, it happens more with the boys I think. Even if one of the girls have got hit, the boys will go out for revenge, like. Say one of the boys got hit, when one of the boys Craig got jumped and we all went up to Tybach and went looking for the boys who jumped him. We were all, there was like 20- 25 of us all gonna jump em, cause it was one of ours and he was on his own and there were like 10 or 11 of them. So we were all going up to take them out one by one to see how they would like it. Okay, an assassination. *Int: Did they find them? P:* Yeah (laughs) but there were about 40 of them so they decided to just turn back around and (laughs). *Int: So did it result in any kind of violence? P:* Some of the boys did fight in school, they picked em off in school, the boys did, cause they were in the same school. Cause they picked them off in school instead of outside.

Cyber-violence

Most of the girls reported engaging in and/or being victims of non-physical violence, which ranged from spreading gossip and name calling to verbal threats of physical violence and stalking. With the increased ownership of mobile phones and access to Internet chat rooms among young people, new and more intrusive forms of bullying or non-physical violence was reported. This type of encounter was reportedly more worrying and upsetting than bullying in person as the perpetrator had access to the victim any time of the day or night (once the technology was on). Cyber-bullying often involved disturbing threats of violence, passing on personal information and personal insults. It was also reportedly a precursor to physical conflict. As there was often a period of repetitive contact in which victim could not cool off, physical conflict could escalate more quickly. 'Happy slapping' would also come under this heading – as the key feature is the use of mobile phones to record the violent encounter. This type of cyber-violence was commonly reported by young people in terms of viewing or owning the footage, rather than as the victim or main offender. The extract below documents the effects of this contemporary bullying on a girl who reports usually avoiding conflict.

Extract from a mixed sex group interview with Becks (15 yrs).

Int: Have you ever had any bad experiences with other groups or people? B:
I've never got into a real fight, so, I've had shouting matches with some, but,
it never went any further than just screaming at each other. *Int: Have you
ever felt it could go further?* B: Yeah, it depends whether, well when I felt
it could go further I was drunk. But it was more the excitement. Because it
was like this girl was really annoying me, she was texting me and everything
saying that she was going to batter me and then she didn't come down, so I
was like okay then. *Int: Okay, so she was actually texting you on your phone,
does that happen often?* B: Yeah, well not too often, but yeah.

Play-fighting

Physical and non-physical encounters between one's own peer groups was the most
commonplace violence reported by boys. This type of violence was less common among
girls, and usually involved the opposite sex. In contrast, violence by boys towards girls
was seldom discussed or identified as a problem in play-fighting. Girls reportedly avoided
physical conflict of any type with their girlfriends, as physical violence was viewed as an
unforgivable breach of friendship. Verbal conflict between girls was almost routine; it
was seldom viewed as violence. Boys viewed both the physical and non-physical violence
within the group as standard *fun* with their 'mates'. Interestingly, physical violence was
more often easily forgiven by boys than non-physical violence (if a personal comment
was made about family or a girlfriend). Violence among friends and peer groups is
qualitatively different from the other models of violence due to the notional sense of
balance and boundaries (not going too far), *self-regulation* and *fair play* to which young
people reportedly subscribe. What becomes increasingly evident is the fragility of this
'balance', especially when protagonists are under the influence of alcohol. That said, as
the extract below details, in-group violence is largely viewed as 'different' from other
types of violence.

Extract from a single sex group interview with Michael, Raul, Pauli and Scott
(all 16 yrs).

Int: What about fights between each other, within the group? M: Once or
twice (laughs). *Int: So what is that usually over?* S: Girls. R: Money. P: Too
many cans of lager. *Int: Too many cans?* S: Well, girls or money. Girls or
money – someone lending someone something? M: Well someone not
paying something back like, once you've had too much to drink, it means

they fight over money... *Int: So what about verbal conflict?* M: I (yes), loads
of that happens between us lot, like the banter between us all, like, and then
it's over. *Int: So it is okay?* S: Just ripping each other, like. R: Yeah havin' a
laugh. P: But then we've had too much to drink then it can get a bit violent
then. *Int: Yeah?* S: But the next morning then it is tidy enough. *Int: So it moves
from the verbal to the physical?* M: I (yes) well a bit of boxing and slapping,
like... *Int: Okay, then what about when you are fighting in your group, you
know when to stop?* M: yeah, well no, some don't know when to stop. *Int: So
what happens then?* M: then we will stop it for them. *Int: Okay, what does
that usually mean, when is enough, enough?* S: The last man standing. *Int:
Okay, so if someone is on the ground then you wouldn't kick them?* S: No you
wouldn't kick them, friends and that, you wouldn't kick them. P: With drink
it can go too far. *Int: In what way does it go over the top?* M: When it turns to
punches. *Int: What's going over the top?* M: Well if someone gets personal
like. *Int: In what way?* R: Well if they are talking about family, like. P: Or if
they say something you don't want anyone else to know.

Out of Order

More private *'domestic'* violence (violence between young people in a 'relationship') was
the least reported type of violence. Physically violent encounters between girls and boys
are viewed as inappropriate. Both boys and girls identified boys' violence towards girls
as unacceptable and distinct from all other types of peer violence. Younger boys and girls
were quicker than older youths to confirm this is not a problem – thereby suggesting this
type of violence is associated with older youths in relationships rather than their younger
peers. That said, it is commonplace for older boys to be in a relationship with younger
girls (as was the case below), thus making this an important model in this study. The
girl in the extract below identifies this type of violence as a serious, but largely 'hidden'
problem among her peers. Domestic peer violence, like adult domestic violence, was
most likely to occur in private, away from other group members.

Extract from an individual interview with Taz (16 yrs).

*Int: Okay so you have never had a weapon pulled on you or you have never
used one?* T: Only my ex-boyfriend who smacked me across the head with
a baseball bat for no reason. *Int: Is that why he is an ex?* T: Yeah. *Int: Is
that usual - would guys usually hit girls?* T: I think a lot more of them do,
to be honest, well I was with him for two years and he battered me all the
way through. *Int: Really, is that okay, like is it something they hide or don't*

care if people know? T: Well basically all his mates knew what he was doing, cause when I was going to school, I had, like, bruises all down my neck and it did look genuinely like love bites, so obviously everyone thought it was love bites, but it was in fact his hand prints and stuff. You know? It's mainly the older boys like, you get all the boys 20-odd now they do batter their girlfriends. But nobody knows about it until they finished and then the truth comes out. Because when I was with my ex, there was no way I would say he was hitting me about when I was with him. But then after, like, all his mates knew it anyway cause they had seen him do it a couple of times, like I remember in the middle of a pub, during my mate's father's wedding he head-butted me and all the boys jumped on him and beat the hell out of him, like, so. *Int: Humm, nice guy.* T: Nah, but the younger boys, like the ones that come in here I don't think any of them would hit their girlfriends, like, so.

Conclusion: Continuity and Change

The models of violence advanced above highlight the various types and levels of everyday peer violence among boys and girls in South Wales. Peer violence is established, not as an occasional phenomenon but very much as part of the historical, cultural *norms* and sub-cultural practices of young people.

The models identify the issues of continuity and change as key to understanding peer violence within the local community. Boys are represented in these models by their efforts to continue the 'traditional' norms linked to masculinity and local identity (e.g. area rivalries, protection of 'resources', and hostility towards outsiders). The *spontaneous* nature of boys' peer violence, alongside the absence of a model representing non-physical violence reflects the overwhelming focus of boys on physical violence. *Traditional* female roles are also evident in the sexual violence model and support for male collective violence. The absence of a weapons model for girls similarly reflects the small number of girls who carried or used weapons. Although much of the violence presented has roots in *local* traditions, it is also important to identify the influences of change in peer violence.

As Trewaun expands and changes, its young people must accept increasing upheaval. *Cyber-bullying* and levels of physical violence by girls and *'happy slapping'* by boys are new types of peer violence, which already represent distinct challenges in terms dealing with peer violence. Change will continue as the increased presence of 'outsiders' and the influences from the global *media* influence young people's perspectives on violence.

In summary, the eight models discussed capture *snapshots* of young people's experiences and perspectives on peer violence.

5 The Character of Violent Encounters

As identified in the models above peer violence among young people is *complex*, involving a number of dimensions - who, what, where, when and why? This section uses these dimensions to present a more in-depth analysis of the interview transcripts. First, a detailed look at the types of violence reported by young people is presented using the distinction between physical and non-physical violence, followed by details of the combatants involved in violent episodes, the times and places, and finally the conditions affecting the encounter. Subsequently, the intentions, consequences and interpretations of young people of the violent event are discussed. Extracts from the interview data and cameos from observations provide illustrations of these issues.

Types of Violence

Peer violence falls into one of two categories – physical or non-physical. Within these categories there is a range of violent acts which lie on a continuum of seriousness. The severity of a violent act was often evaluated by respondents according to the possibility of injury, the number and type of combatants and presence (or not) of a weapon. Non-physical violence was most often referred to by girls – this included 'mouthing' (talking back to someone), 'bitching' (saying negative things about someone behind their back), ostracising, insulting or threatening using technology (see 'Cyber-violence' in the section on models above) and shouting verbal abuse. Persistent threatening or verbal abuse between girls can lead to physical violence. This behaviour is largely viewed as humour rather than violence by older boys, and is central to group life. That said, boys also identified non-physical violence (mouthing off and 'winding up') as a precursor to physical encounters, especially when sensitive issues are ridiculed. Boys placed a high value on non-verbal behaviour (e.g. hand gestures or 'eyeballing' - giving a look), especially where encounters with out-groups or strangers were concerned (see 'Fight Club' in the section on models above)

Physical violent encounters dominated all young people's interviews. The least severe and most commonly reported level of physical violence among girls reported involved shoving, pushing, pulling hair, slapping and scratching. Although less frequent, types of physical violence more likely to be witnessed amongst boys (including punching, head butting, kneeing and elbowing) were also identified by girls.

Violent encounters amongst boys often involved more serious types of physical violence – from shoving, punching and kicking to stamping and weapon use. Boys also identified specific types of violence such as 'happy slapping' and 'jumping someone' – these types of violence generally involve more than one young person and include mid-level violence including punching, slapping, and kicking. The force used and outcome of the act rather than the act itself often defines its severity.

Roles and Relationships of Combatants

The various 'people elements' add to the complexity of peer violence: essentially the type and relationship between combatants greatly influences the type of encounter. Initially, there is an obvious division in terms of gender - with boy on boy, followed by girl on girl being the most common encounter. The violent encounter can also involve a different number of combatants - one-on-one, group on one and group-on-group - which alters the nature and evolution of the violent incident. The relationship between combatants also influences the violent encounter — with acquaintances and own group conflicts being the most commonplace (but not the most serious violence), followed by stranger (usually more serious violence), and then friends and family being the least (and usually least serious) reported. The experience of in-group violence differs greatly to out-group violence. In-group conflict is frequently reported but is usually less serious (and motivated by different factors) than out-group encounters. Finally, the *role* (positive and negative) of other participants such as *spectators*, friends and adults were key to the escalation and outcome of violent conflict.

Gender

Overwhelmingly, violent conflict takes place between same sex combatants. Girl on boy violence and boy on girl violence were reportedly nothing more than play-fighting (see 'Play-fighting' in the section on models above) or flirting among friends. However, as Taz noted (see cameo in 'Out of Order' in the section on models above) there can be a more sinister side of violence perpetrated by older boys towards girls. Interestingly, this type of violence is often covert, in contrast to all other types which are regularly replayed through stories and gossip by young people.

> Boys largely discounted physical girl on girl encounters, like Toffel (15 yrs) in an individual interview.
>
> *Int: So what is the difference between girls fighting and boys fighting?* T: Oh, I don't know. *Int: Do you think girls fight properly; would you consider it a fight?* T: Pushing innit (laughs) and grabbing the hair and... *Int: So would you consider that a fight?* ... T: It's like mucking around and that, it's like they go at it and go mental, like and that is all. *Int: So they are not as violent as boys?* T: No not really.

Gender is an important variable for understanding the frequency, type and intensity of violent encounters.

Number

One-on-one physical encounters were reported by both boys and girls. It was identified as the most acceptable and 'fair' encounter to engage in. In contrast, a group assaulting an individual was seen to contradict the 'rules' and perceived balance of a violent encounter. That said, while this notional sense of balance was often applied to in-group and acquaintance conflicts, it was less apparent in stranger and rival group violence.

The expressed need of boys to protect and defend their group could turn individual fights into a collective encounter. This process of escalation is often found in area and group rivalries.

> Extract from an individual interview with Pink (15 yrs).
>
> *Int: Do you usually see one-on-one fights or group?* P: It tends to, well it is meant to be one-on one fights, but it starts off one-on-one, but then one of the friends would jump in and then it would be like two on one and then the other friend jumps in and its like groups start fighting, it's like it's manic, it gets escalated.

Conflicts between boys often escalate quicker than girls, as they are quicker to react to a perceived 'dis'. As the number of combatants rise, so too does the level and type of violence used (see 'Fight Club in the section on models above).

Relationships

The relationship between combatants generally refers to the proximity or attachment between the combatants. The relationship can be viewed in terms of personal relationships (e.g. family and partner) and in-group (best friend and *friendship* group) and out-group (acquaintances and strangers). The closer the relationship, the less likely young people are to engage in serious violence. Amongst 'best friends' there is reportedly much non-physical violence, but little physical.

> Extract from an individual interview with Pink (15 y).
>
> R: But if you know who you are talking to, I think if it was one of the girls and they really annoyed me I would probably lose my temper, but it would never get physical, I would never hit one of the girls.

Group friendships are more open to physical violence, particularly with boys, as it is presented as a group norm.

> Extract from an individual interview with Toffel (15 yrs).
>
> *Int: So do you guys fight within your group?* T: I (yes) we have mucking around fights, but we don't actually hit each other all the time, like. *Int: So what is the difference between mucking around fights and being in a proper fight?* T: Well mucking around is like pushing or just chucking each other to the floor and a proper fight is like kicking each other and punching, hurting each other basically.

Acquaintances and strangers - out-groups - are more likely to experience more serious types of violence as identified by the area rivalry detailed inFight Club (above). When area rivalries occur, they are often led by core group members from each area, with an entourage of the fringe members of the group and 'friendly' neighbouring groups (borrowed for the occasion). Out-group violence is reportedly more severe than in-group violence in terms of type of violence used and outcome (injury sustained or strain on the relationship). Pancho comments that out-group rivalries do not happen very often, but "but when they fight they fight!" In contrast, in-group violence which is much more prevalent, Michael suggests, is self-regulated to prevent serious violence or injury:

> Extract from a single sex group interview with Michael (16 yrs).
>
> *Int: Okay then, what about when you are fighting in your group, you know when to stop?* M: Yeah, well no, some don't know when to stop. *Int: So what happens then?* M: Then we will stop it for them.

Other Participants

The important role of 'observers' (bystanders) in peer violence became increasingly evident. In particular observers (usually peers) can inhibit, facilitate or escalate peer violence. The *roles* of participants are dynamic – that is, they can move between being active or passive participants during a single violent incident.

> Extract from a single sex group interview with Joking and Fred (both 16 yrs).
>
> *Int: When you are looking at fights, do other young people get involved in them?* J: Yeah, sometimes you'll see people like sticking in the odd punch or kick and that. *Int: Like a sly dig type of thing – is that okay?* F: Nah, it's them fighting, so just leave them alone. Either stop them or just leave them

> at it, don't get involved because otherwise it will just kick off and you'll be
> fighting them then. *Int: Have you seen that happen?* F: On the odd occasion.
> *Int: So what happens when a fight breaks out?* J: Normally you just see a group
> of people circled around people that are fighting. Sometimes people try to
> break it up and sometimes people just let them at it till they calm down.

While a small number of young people suggested they avoided witnessing violent
conflict, the majority reported stopping to watch (as passive observers). Group members
witnessing a friend in combat reported cheering and encouraging the encounter
if it was a 'fair fight' (in line with the code of the streets) or becoming involved as a
combatant or guardian (watch out for other young people or adults) if they perceived
their friend to be in trouble. Group members could also act as shields against outsider
(adult) interference during an encounter. Girls played an important role in instigating,
organising and encouraging boys' violence (prior to and during the violent incident).
Additionally, girls can assist in de-escalation, by taking the boys out of the situation or
using non-physical intervention. Obviously dependant on the role and relationship to
the combatant, escalation and de-escalation in peer violence is heavily influenced by
peers.

Movement through Time and Space

The timing of the violent encounter is looked at across three time dimensions: the
frequency of an encounter (how often between the same combatants); the *duration*
of an encounter (for how long does the encounter last) and the actual *timing* of the
violent episode (time of the day, day of the week and time of the year), and two space
dimensions: location and movement through different places. Again, the dynamic
nature of peer violence is apparent in this dimension – as few violent episodes followed
the same pattern.

Time

Peer violence can largely be divided into simple (one-off) or complex (prolonged)
encounters. In general, individual conflicts were more frequently experienced than
collective conflicts; however, collective tensions and therefore conflicts tended to exist
for a significantly longer period of time. Individual physical, unlike non-physical, conflict
among girls were less likely to be sustained over a long period of time. Prolonged non-
physical encounters between girls were commonplace as 'everyone knows everyone'
and there are limited places to hang out in order to avoid other young people. The longer
the dispute lasts the more likely non-physical violence will escalate to low-level physical
violence, such as pushing and shoving, although the close proximity of combatants also
encouraged girls to resolve issues after a one-off physical encounter.

Physical and non-physical violence between boys presented a more complex pattern of violent encounters. Essentially, boys tend to view violence as less serious and so were more likely to fight, make up and fight again with the same people. Simple violent encounters involving boys usually involved combat with a stranger or distant acquaintance. Collective violence was reportedly frequent - every time certain groups met – however, as interviewees tended to remain in their own area, these encounters were less frequent than other types of violence.

Non-physical violence in-group existed continuously (it was part of the everyday group behaviour), while non-physical violence between acquaintances and strangers tended to exist in the (short) moment (often immediately prior to the physical conflict). Due to the higher rates of violence and the normalisation of violence among boys, this pattern is to be expected. The *length* of an encounter varied considerably according to the type of violence used and combatants. For example, physical conflict among girls usually occurs within a short time-frame (see 'Cat Fight' in the section on models above) although there was often planning and a long period of escalation prior to this. In contrast, boys often reported physical encounters to be impulsive, unplanned, spontaneous – and therefore more likely to be of short duration (see 'The Scuffle' and 'Bars, Bats and Bricks' in the section on models above). The one *exception* to this is when a group fight has been organised in advance.

> Extract from an individual interview with Taz (16 yrs).
>
> T: Yeah, it is not like, our [girl] fight is literally two minutes and it is over with. *Int: Is that the same with guys, any the guys you know about?* T: Some of them drag it out, but none of the fights I've ever seen have lasted more than 5 or 10 minutes. It's never been really battering each other to the death, like, it's always like one wins just like that, so. *Int: Is it usually one-on-one or a group on a group?* T: That depends really, sometimes you'll have just two people fighting and then other times you'll have the Taibachers and Nantymelers come together – you've got 50 on each side and then there is a big riot and that could go on for like half an hour, an hour.

The capacity for violence to escalate is important in the time dimension of peer violence. Essentially, the pattern of violence escalation from non-physical to physical increases in probability over a long period of time and with increased frequency of encounters. Young people also identified peak periods of witnessing and engaging in physical violence – during the *evenings* and on the *weekends*. During the *summer* the combination of dry weather, long periods of freedom (and boredom) and the holiday atmosphere (high numbers of young people and alcohol use) results in more frequent and serious physical violent conflict amongst young people (and the opposite prevails during the winter). Due to the *lack* of specific activity events (e.g. concerts) in the area, Hallowe'en night, Guy Fawke's night and the Christmas holidays – are often an exception to this rule. In particular, the Hallowe'en is often viewed as a period of excessive criminality and violence by young people (due to the use of fireworks, bonfires and party atmosphere).

Space

Young people identified certain urban and rural areas with types of violence. For example, the bus station, library steps, train station, skate park and outside the youth facility in Trewaun, were commonly identified locations for individual or spontaneous out-group violence reported by boys and girls. Rural areas – such as sports fields and parks were more likely to be used for organised or spontaneous collective violence, especially area rivalries (during the summer months, when large numbers of different groups congregate in these areas). In general, the urban locations identified are those most often frequented by young people, with the least adult supervision (in the evening) and with the possibility of area observation (to protect resources). These locations are also key situations for area and group rivalries (territorial conflict) to occur (as rival groups will know where to find their rival peers).

> Extract from a single sex group interview with Michael and Raul (both 16 yrs).
>
> *Int: Have you ever had any trouble with other groups, or other young people in the area?* R: Newton. M: Well, there is a lot in Trewaun that don't get on, but it is just, like people from down there, from Newton, just don't get along with people up here. *Int: So Newton don't get on with Trewaun?* R: Newton boys won't even come into Trewaun like, will they? M: No. *Int: Why, will that cause trouble?* R: Well I don't know, they will just end up fighting and that sort of thing.

Territoriality is linked to the most serious types of physical violence used. This is less about owning an area, and more about protecting one's 'resources', such as girls, services, or illegal activities, and one's identity. Young people identify closely with their area, and identify rival groups through the name of their area. Perhaps due to the limited movement by most young people outside their immediate home/school area, this identity is central to who they are and as a result it is important to defend.

Young people documented the movement of non-physical and physical encounters to and from the street to indoor public areas (such as schools or youth clubs) and cyber areas (such as email and chat-rooms). The *school* played an important part in developing conflicts and in disseminating information on organised violent conflicts. Additionally, revenge for an incident in one location could be exacted in another more convenient location. For example, Pink highlights an example of this movement of violence from the street to the school - where a boy and girl friendship group avoided group conflict with a larger group, in order to engage them in smaller numbers in school where they would be more vulnerable (see extract in 'On the Prowl' in the section on models above). Furthermore, young people from various rival areas are forced to meet in school (as young people of secondary school age living outside of Trewaun must go to school in Trewaun), thereby creating an easy time and place for rival encounters. If bullying or verbal violence begins in school, it is possible for it to continue and escalate outside of school and vice versa. A good example of this includes contemporary bullying with the use of texting, emails and chat rooms to threaten, insult and spread rumours in a more consistent and premeditated way - reported among girls, though not boys.

Personal and Situational Influences

Both individual and situational conditions influence peer violence in public space. Individual conditions include the influence of young people's personal approaches to violence. Situational conditions include the presence of violence and aggression *catalysts*, for example, alcohol and weapon use are highlighted by respondents as key influences on the incidence of violence. These influences are discussed below.

Individual Conditions

During the analysis patterns in young people's reactions to peer violence became apparent. In particular, interviewees identified a number of measures taken to avoid or create a violent encounter. Four types of 'personality' (in terms of orientation to violence) emerged which linked to the approach most commonly reported by each young person, these were: the deactive approach – avoidance of violence; the reactive approach - defensive violence; the active approach – tolerance and acceptance of violence as an everyday cultural reality; and the proactive approach - actively seeking violence (see Figure 2 below). In proposing these 'personality types', it must also be emphasised that they are dynamic and not fixed. This typology reflects a preferred orientation which is 'ordinarily' adopted, but an individual's position may change according to various factors and circumstances. Depending on the dimensions previously discussed, young people identified a change in their response during specific violent encounters: a typically deactive young person may become reactive in response to a friend's victimisation, or a proactive young person may choose a deactive response when the odds are too imbalanced.

Figure 2: Personal approaches to peer violence

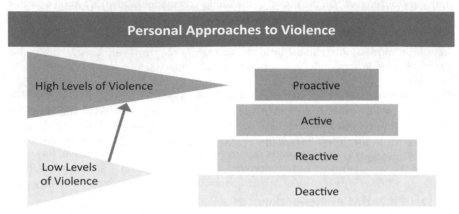

Lucy and Aggi are good examples of deactive personalities, when asked how they dealt with conflict they reported "I just walk away, go somewhere else" (Lucy) and "Just walk away." (Aggi). In contrast, Becks displayed a reactive approach to violence.

Extract from a mixed sex group interview with Becks (15 yrs).

B: Well I was on holiday and this girl just walked up to my friends and started bothering them like that. And the English girls said stupid Welsh bitch and I turned around and I said what did you say? And she went like that, came right up to my face, like that, so I went 'womp' and she went down and she got back up and she head-butted me. As she head-butted me, my top tooth came down, like half my top tooth came out and I thought, well I ain't having that now. So I went whack, head-butt, stomp and thump (laughs). It was the first time ever to fight and I was drunk.

Pancho and Joche's account of escaping a good 'roasting and kicking' from a group in a rival area is consistent with an active approach to violence. Essentially, they accept conflict as part of life in the valleys:

Extract from a single sex group interview with Pancho and Joche (both 15 yrs).

J: Well we'd do it to them and they'd do it to us, so it is just... *Int: Is that part of growing up here?* J: We are all like that though, ain't we? P: We don't go looking for it, it comes to us. J: It comes to us.

Lastly, the extract detailing Nicola's account of hunting down and beating up a group of Goth girls for fun (see 'On the Prowl' in the section on models above) is a good example of a proactive personality. Additionally, when asked how she felt about watching peer violence, Nicola replied "I just want to join in really".

Situational Factors

Although weapon use is not prevalent in the research location, young people reported carrying or using a variety of melee weapons (blunt and sharp). Overall young people negatively perceived weapon use and ownership - with most young people agreeing that weapon use is uncommon and unacceptable. Weapons such as air rifles, knives, bats, knuckledusters and bricks were reportedly used by some young people. However, many of the weapons used were reportedly 'found' at the scene – such as poles, glass bottles and stones. The display or use of weapons during an encounter is viewed as the most serious level of violence:

> Extract from an individual interview with Sean (16 yrs).
>
> *Int: Would you call a fight a fair fight or as you say a dirty fight – is there a difference between the two?* S: Well if there's a dirty fight, it normally means there's gonna be weapons involved, but normally a clean fight is just fists, like, and heads.

The use of weapons was most evident in out-group violent encounters, rather than individual or in-group conflicts.

While drug use (smoking cannabis) was argued to have something of a calming effect, alcohol consumption was asserted by young people to be a significant influence on peer violence. Alcohol was identified as *central* to instigating in-group and out-group violence among boys and out-group violence among girls. According to young peoples' estimates, alcohol use was present in half to almost all cases of boy's violence. A particular premium brand of strong lager - termed 'Rocky' by local young people due to its reputation to make boys more aggressive and violent - was repeatedly identified as the drug of choice to prepare for violent encounters.

> Extract from an individual interview with Pink (15 yrs).
>
> P: Yeah, if the boys have drunk like 'Rocky', then they think they are Rocky. [...] Yeah, they go looking for fights and scream at people across the road to come over and fight them and stuff, just for fun and that. And then there

> are some girls that think they are hard, even though they are like pansies, and it is like (laughs) oh my god what are you doing. *Int: Alcohol, does that make people worse?* P: Well with some of the boys, they are bad anyway, but when you give them 'Rocky', it's like oh, just stay away from them.

The notional sense of balance and boundaries offered by young people as part of a *code* of conduct for peer violence was often upset by alcohol consumption. In particular, boys reportedly 'crossed a line' with peers in their group and were more likely to use excessive violence on strangers while under the influence. Likewise, girls were more likely to react, or indeed initiate, violence among their peers and family members after alcohol misuse.

> Extract from an individual interview with Taz (16 yrs).
>
> T: No, if I smoke hash I just mellow out, I just sit down and have a laugh with all the boys like, but. I've tried a load of drugs, like speed just makes me happy; I just go around like an idiot. Pills, I don't like them at all, I was really bad when I had them, and I was collapsing. I tried cocaine, but that just gave me a bit of a bit of a rush. It only lasted for half and hour, so I didn't see the point in paying for it. No, to be honest drugs don't make me violent, it is just the alcohol.

Overall, the presence of personal and/or situational factors increases the level, intensity and frequency of violence among peers.

Intentions

Young people, when attempting to explain their violent encounters, did not discuss acquisitive crimes (e.g. robbery, snatching items) or sexual deviance (assault or rape). Data analysis identified two dimensions of intent - moralistic (belief) and predatory. Although the lists below are not extensive, they seek to capture the main intentions underlying peer violence.

Moralistic intentions: Avenge slights to 'honour', saving face/keeping face, defending a friend or someone else, loyalty, defending resources (turf or possessions), status enhancement, self-defence, establish boundaries, social control, avoid becoming a victim, balance the scene/situation (odds), resolve a problem, to confirm identity, consistency (what I've always done).

Predatory intentions: Revenge, teach a lesson, to release tension/frustration, gaining resources, alleviating boredom, bit of a laugh, fun/buzz, getting in first (attack form of defence), rejecting difference, makes me feel better, to drive others away, no reason/ just because.

Inconsistencies often emerged between the expressed intentions of violence given by young people and the actual behaviour and outcome of the encounter. For example, moralistic reasons (self-defence and group defence) were often given for out-group violence. Yet when described, out-group violence often appeared to involve primarily predatory intentions - such as the release of tension or frustration, to protect territory and resources and for fun or buzz

> Extract from a single sex group interview with Joking (16 yrs).
>
> J: It's like, just punching each other non-stop, going at each other even when you're tired and you've no energy left and you're still hitting them, even if they are down in the floor and they can't move. *Int: Is that a bit excessive, when someone's down and you're still hitting them?* J: Yeah, it's like you just need to get it out of your system for a bit, but once you're like that at least you should just stop.

In-group violence is often described as intending to be fun and entertaining but a strong underlying intention appears to be reinforcing social control and boundary setting (including establishing status within the group) amongst members. Boys, rather than girls, reported *regulating* in-group violence in order to prevent 'real' violence from occurring (see 'Playfighting' in the section on models above). Boys also reported the importance of protecting and defending their friends, which also ties in with balancing the odds in a fight. Loyalty, solidarity and masculinity characterised many of the boys' friendship groups, thus making them more likely than girls to report engaging in conflict to defend or gain revenge for a friend as the 'code of the streets' suggests they should.

> Extract from a single sex group interview with Pancho and Joche (both 15 yrs).
>
> P: No, say one of my mates is fighting or something and you have to join in to help them. J - You don't have to join in, like. P: Well unless it's one-on-one, proper, now. *Int: So if it is a one-on-one fight then you don't have to join in?* J: No unless it goes nasty, then you go in. P: Then you go in. *Int: So what is getting nasty?* J: If your friend gets beat up then you have to jump in.

Physical violence by girls was inferred by other girls to be for the purpose of enhancing status among boys and to protect resources (e.g. relationship interest). Girls were more likely to report engaging in non-physical rather than physical violence. However, a girl's refusal to engage in verbal conflict may quickly escalate the conflict to physical violence (Cat-fight above). Like the boys, escalation from non-physical violence to physical was reported, especially if there was some perceived score to settle or some previous history of verbal conflict.

While violent boys with the intent to establish status and restore *honour* can achieve these aims through non-physical means – specifically one boy backing down from the fight – girls tend to see this as a further challenge or insult. Essentially, the movement towards more physical violence often resulted from the non-compliance of the opponent to engage in the conflict (see 'Cat Fight' in the section on models above). Non-physical violence is often perpetrated by girls with the intention of establishing control and status, defending resources and friends, saving face, teaching a lesson, alleviating boredom and in order to drive others (outsiders or people who are different) away. The importance of sub-cultural and geographical identity was clearly evident amongst both males and females. Thus, the need to confirm one's identity and reject those who are different was highlighted in the area conflicts and group rivalries described.

Outcomes

Interview analysis identified three main consequences of peer violence: injury, legal penalties and relationship changes. Injury could involve physical and non-physical (such as emotional or psychological hurt). Legal penalties usually occurred when the police became involved in the conflict. Relationship changes (e.g. loss of friendship) among peers were most frequently discussed by young people.

Significantly given the extent and severity of physical violence discussed, interviewees rarely reported serious injury as a consequence of their violence. The majority of physical injuries required no medical attention, as Pink recalls.

> Extract from an individual interview with Pink (15 yrs).
>
> P: It's like scratches and bruises and there is hardly ever black eyes anymore, really, cause it never really goes that far anymore. Normally really, they just have a little scrap that's about it. But some of the boys do put each other on the floor and start booting them.

Boys reported more serious injuries than girls, though most serious injuries were witnessed rather than perpetrated. For example, Scott reports witnessing a boy jump off stairs onto another boy's head, thereby breaking his jaw. Boys were more likely to discount the emotional effects of violence – suggesting that conflict was humorous and entertaining. This combined with the lack of 'real' physical injury resulted in many boys (especially older) alleging that there was no impact or consequence resulting from their experiences of violence. Girls (and one younger boy) responded more emotionally to both physical and non-physical violence and reported feeling fearful or upset in the aftermath.

A clear indication that peer violence often falls underneath the community radar comes from the few reports of legal or official consequences. Although interviewees identified physical encounters which resulted in police or adult intervention, the outcome was seldom punitive. This is evident in Nicola's account of the outcome of her attack on a Goth group of girls.

Extract from a single sex group interview with Nicola (15 yrs).

N: Well they tried taking me to court for fighting, but they couldn't get enough evidence on me cause on the CCTV cameras [Close Circuit Television, used for street surveillance] everyone was crowding us and they couldn't see nothing. So they didn't have enough against me and I said it was self-defence. So they couldn't really do nothing.

Nonetheless, when adults do intervene in young people's peer violence, the consequences can be relatively serious: exclusion from school, being banned from youth clubs, curfew and arrest. Taz describes what happened after a drunken violent encounter with another girl.

Extract from an individual interview with Taz (16 yrs).

T: Then when I was in bed the police come to arrest me from where I was in bed and I hit the female police officer as well, so I spent a nice night in the cell and I woke up and I couldn't even remember getting arrested. I woke up with all with broken toes, broken knuckles and had cut my head by there where I was head-butting the cell door. I was punching the hell out of the cell doors, I was going nuts.

Young people identified the change in peer relationships as the most significant consequence of violence. The apparent differences between boys and girls are noteworthy. In-group violence between boys seldom impacted upon their relationship – essentially, by the next morning it had been forgotten. In contrast, girls were more likely to report holding a grudge and continuing the conflict for months (thereby causing friction in the whole group).

The suggested 'rules' and boundaries identified by boys, can partially explain the difference. In-group violence is monitored and controlled by peer pressure: if a member breaks the norms, they may be subject to physical violence or ostracised by the group (identified as the most serious consequence). Girls were most likely to lose friends as a result of violent encounters. Breaches in friendship resulted in an escalation of conflict, with increased verbal conflict and long-term animosity between combatants. That said, girls were not overly concerned with exacting revenge or settling a score, following a violent encounter. Boys, in contrast, identified the need for resolution in the aftermath – the outcome was usually identified as equilibrium (settled the score) or disequilibrium (still owing one or planning revenge). If the result was equilibrium, the violent conflict was seen as successful and no grudge remained. If interviewees felt disequilibrium, revenge attacks were planned and hostilities between combatants affected other group members (see 'Fight Club' in the section on models above).

Interpretation of Violence by the Young People

The definitions and interpretations of violence presented by young people clearly displayed a diverse and dynamic approach to violence by young people. Young people's understanding of what is and what is not peer violence varies considerably from the definition used at the start of this project – with the divide between physical and non-physical violence particularly problematic. Younger boys and both younger and older girls were more likely to identify all types of encounters as *'real violence'* and described the efforts taken to avoid them.

During analysis the concept of a 'ladder of violence' became useful for understanding young people's perspectives. Essentially, the further up the ladder, the more likely interviewees were to define behaviour as violence. The ladder is made up of a number of variables; the increased seriousness in the nature of the violent act (stamping being very serious), the situational factors evident – especially the use of weapons, the 'fairness' of a fight (dependant on the number, age and vulnerability of people involved), and the resulting consequences (especially serious injury) (see Figure 3).

Figure 3: Interpretations of violence

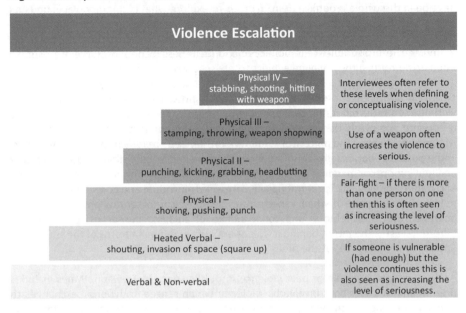

The norms held about violence and the boundaries drawn by young people are usually upheld by those combatants closest to the group. As a result, stranger violence and out-group violence is likely to be viewed as the most serious type. Furthermore, the *discrepancy* between young people's and adults' views of violence influenced their understanding and normalising of violence. Young people generally viewed adult physical and non-physical violence as much more serious than the forms of violence in which they routinely indulged.

Extract from a mixed sex group interview with John (15 yrs).

Int: What about adults, do you think adults would call the fights violence?
J: No, cause adults are the worst around here, like, mostly on the weekends you always see adults fighting, with loads of police about all the time, every weekend. *Int: So you think they are worse than you younger guys?* J: Yeah.

Conclusion

Everyday peer violence in public space is an extensive and complicated phenomenon. In order to break down the complexity, and to understand the everyday experiences of

young people, it is essential to look across a number of dimensions. Seven key dimensions
have been discussed in detail herein, in order to explore what is commonplace, unusual
and different and absent in young people's violent encounters. As identified in the
Models, certain dimensions play a central role in what we have found. Therefore,
following the dissection of the violent encounter, these central features are used to
build up a profile of peer violence.

Gender is an important variable in peer violence, not only because the offending and
victimisation rates differ, but because boys and girls understand and interpret violence
differently and play different roles throughout different violent encounters. That said,
the *general violence* and pattern of events is experienced *similarly* by both girls and boys.
The type of combatants explains a lot about the type and level of violence used. In-group
and out-group perspectives on violence differ significantly although, again, the type
and pattern of violence is commonplace. Likewise, individual and collective encounters
follow a similar pattern which ranges from non-physical to serious physical violence,
however, the interpretation and consequence of such encounters is fundamentally
different. Lastly, the intent behind a violent encounter differs in terms of the situational
and personal influences at the time.

As an overview, a profile of peer violence in public space in Trewaun, Wales includes
predominantly older boys involved in violence which ranges from verbal exchanges to
punching and kicking and with girls involved in mostly non-physical violence or low-level
physical confrontations. Alcohol has a presence in most scenarios, while weapon carrying
and use is evident, though not prevalent in some encounters. The location is invariably
a 'hot-spot' where young people routinely congregate, with little adult supervision. The
encounters vary between individual and collective, with many combatants knowing
each other. The violent encounter is often *spontaneous*, in reaction to a perceived
'wrongdoing', and is (at least theoretically) overseen by a 'code' of conduct enforced
by peers.

6 Feedback and Consultation

As part of the research feedback and dissemination process, young people and experts
from the research locality were invited to attend a workshop. The main objectives of
the workshops were to disseminate the research findings of the Daphne project and to
identify recommendations for dealing with peer violence in public space.

Workshops' Description

The young people's and experts' workshops took place in July 2008 at Starmans Youth
Facility, which is located at the centre of the research location.

Nine (4 male and 5 female) young people aged 13 to 16 attended the workshop. The young people were recruited from the youth centre and through word of mouth (from other young people). The newly established youth committee in the centre was approached for permission to use the premises and to invite young people of the relevant age group to the workshop. The committee recommended organising a fun day and barbecue to coincide with the workshop and that the research team could supply BBQ food and prizes for the competitions that took place after the workshop (as an incentive and reward for attendance).

There were *three* objectives for the workshop: a) to gauge whether the research captured the full range of young people's experiences of peer violence in public space (validity); b) to collect details of young people's opinions of the research results; c) to collect young people's recommendations on preventative or reductive violence measures.

Although during the workshop there were a small number of disruptions due to members of staff and young people coming and leaving, in general participants were interested in the findings and in discussing the questions asked.

Four people (3 male and 1 female) attended the experts' workshop – including staff from the Valleys Race Equality Council, Crime Prevention and Youth Service. Apologies from four organisations were received the morning of the 18th (from the detached youth work team, school youth worker, mental health charity and victim support charity) and two further agencies failed to turn up, though they had said they would attend (including representatives from the local police). This was disappointing, though perhaps it reflects a gulf between the rhetoric of professional concern and the reality of professional commitment to the issues that were the focus of discussion.

The workshop was recorded and, like the young people's workshop, had *three* objectives: a) to establish whether the research findings (the models in particular) were helpful to the experts understanding of peer violence in public space; b) to identify what impact these findings would have for each agency/organisation; c) to collect experts' recommendations on what provision is required to help young people cope with and/ or prevent peer violence.

Reflections from the Young People's Workshop

Young people agreed that the research findings were a faithful account of their experiences of peer violence in public space. Overall they felt that peer violence was commonplace, but *excessive* in the locality. Boys, in particular, focused on the fact that it was a normal part of growing up in Trewaun. Weapon use was seen as unusual among their peers, but the current concern in the UK about young people's fatal weapon use had made them more aware of the *potential need* to use weapons in the future as protection from other peers.

Revenge and an enhanced reputation were seen as the main reasons for violence – and as such, needed to be carefully considered in any plans to reduce young people's peer violence. The impact of *alcohol* on the rate of fights and level of violence was the most unanimous discussion point. That said, the young people also unanimously concluded that it was 'impossible' to stop their consumption of alcohol – due to availability and the *cultural* norms surrounding alcohol.

By and large, the young people perceived peer violence to be a *normal* experience and so did not feel the need to understand or explain it.

Reflections from the Expert Workshop

The experts agreed that the research findings were an important first step to understanding and dealing with the problem of peer violence in public space. They felt that the characteristics and prevalence of peer violence was often hidden (or fell under the radar) from agencies (such as the police or youth provision) and adults in the community, which means agencies are not aware of the extent of the problem or providing young people with the resources they need to cope. The discussion focused on the breakdown in traditional cultural and social ties and controls in the locality and the need to build *bridges* between young people and their *community* again.

The apparent *lack* of adult awareness and control over the issue highlighted the importance of peer relations and opinions in forming young people's views and experiences of peer violence. Alcohol and boredom were seen as the main reasons for violence – and as such, were the focus of most recommendations to reduce young people's peer violence. Alcohol and its significant influence on the type, rate and levels of violence reported by young people, was repeatedly identified as an issue that should be urgently tackled in the short and long term.

In general, the discussion focused on the emotional, psychological and social *needs* of young people, rather than punishment and control as a means of dealing with peer violence in public space. That said, the former recommendations were considered to involve a longer, more expensive and joined-up (agency) commitment than the latter and so presented more challenges. The relatively few reports of weapon ownership and use were overwhelmingly viewed as the most positive finding of the research.

In Summary

Both workshops delivered a broad and in-depth discussion on the research findings. The variety of recommendations supported the research argument that peer violence in public space is a *complex* problem in the UK. The participants in both workshops expressed a difficulty in truly understanding *why* peer violence amongst young people was so prevalent.

The key motivators identified by each workshop were quite *different* – for example, young people identified status and respect, while the experts identified territory and the effects of external influences (such as alcohol, TV and games). It was interesting that young people felt that the findings were as expected; in contrast, the experts felt the findings identified an important hidden (unexpected) problem. This difference perhaps highlights the *distance* between young people and the adults in their community and their subsequent vulnerability to peer violence.

A small number of young people recommended a reduction in formal controls (and penalties) on violence to reduce its appeal to young people. In contrast, the experts' recommendations tended to focus on increasing positive social and psychological influences in the lives of young people, while decreasing the negative (e.g. alcohol). The limited *weapon* use amongst young people, while identified as a positive finding by the experts, was viewed as a negative one by young people as they expected it to become a more *significant* issue in the future.

In conclusion, the workshops successfully validated the research findings and provided comments on preventative measures and a link between research and practice.

7 Some Final Reflections

As pointed out by the experts above, this research provides a first step in understanding young people's experiences and interpretations of everyday peer violence. The *post-industrial* location provides an interesting backdrop to the research. In the final reflections, the local context with its fragmented communities, levels of poverty, social exclusion and unemployment, the dominant influence of a *masculine* ideology and the movement towards a more global identity is linked to the key findings.

In line with the *gendered* roles of masculinity, individual male and collective encounters are a core feature of everyday violent interactions between 13-16 year olds. Boys predominantly engage in traditional types of violence (fist fight) and avoid modern UK trends (such as the escalation of weapon use). Girls also play a largely *traditional* (background and low level) role in violence. However, their use of *technology* and numerous reports of participation in what is traditionally male violence may suggest girls are moving in line with general UK experiences of violence. Youth identity is largely established by young people within their community, through area loyalty and defence. Young people have grown up amidst community decline with a sense of social dislocation, which has isolated them from traditional means of gaining *status* and self-esteem. This issue has affected boys more than girls – as evidenced by the focus on area and group rivalries. The absence of serious weapon use or fatalities from violence is an important research finding. However, as detailed in the workshop, young people of both sexes are increasingly feeling the weight of external influences and the consequences this has on their experiences of violence.

Young people tend to *normalise* violent encounters. Taking example from their locality, young people compare adult violence and aggressive behaviour against their own experiences, which influences how they interpret and internalise the *'cultural* norms of violence'. As a result, young people turn to their group and self-direction, rather than adults or authorities to deal with everyday experiences of violence. This can have a significant impact on normalisation of violence – for example, physical encounters by girls are often reduced by peers to being insignificant, and 'funny'. Likewise, boys in groups are required to accept non-physical and physical violence on a daily basis as part of group *'fun'*. Social exclusion and unemployment isolate young people from environments where violence (of any type) is not the *norm* and there are supervisory arrangements in place to reduce victimisation.

In conclusion, young people's experiences, interpretations and ability to cope with peer violence in public space are greatly influenced and compromised by the *environment* in which they live, (an absence of) adult engagement and understanding and increasingly, the wider world.

Notes

1   Ethnicity was not focused on due to the uni-cultural nature of the research location.
2   Reference to a movie of the same name which documented a popular 'private club' where men engaged in serious violence to establish reputation and status.

References

Akwagyiram, A., (2008). Killing highlights gang culture. *BBC News*. Available from: http://news.bbc. co.uk/1/hi/uk/7232344.stm [Accessed: 9 May 2008].

Audit Commission, (2006). Rhondda Cynon Taff – Reconfiguring resource use. Available from: http:// www.audit-commission.gov.uk/neighbourhoodcrime/downloads/casestudies10.pdf [Accessed: 05 July 2008].

Balakrishnan, A., (2008). Girl jailed for filming 'happy-slap' killing. *The Guardian*. Available from: http:// www.guardian.co.uk/uk/2008/mar/18/happyslap.killing [Accessed 18 March 2008].

Barclay, P., (1995). *Income and Wealth. 1*. York: Joseph Rowntree Foundation.

BBC News, (2008a). Knives Affect 'one in 10 Youths'. *BBC News Online*. Available from: http://news.bbc. co.uk/1/hi/uk/7351207.stm [Accessed 16 April 2008].

BBC News, (2008b). Goth clothes 'prompted killing'. *BBC News Online*. Available from: http://news.bbc. co.uk/1/hi/england/lancashire/7291985.stm [Accessed 16 April 2008].

BBC News, (2005). Survey reveals high teen violence. *BBC News Online*. Available from: http://news.bbc. co.uk/nolpda/ukfs_news/hi/newsid_4372000/4372820.stm [Accessed 16 October 2007].

Bennett, T., Brookman, F. and Wright, R., (2006). A Qualitative Study of the Role of Violence in Street Crime. *Economic and Social Research Council.* Available from: http://www.esrcsocietytoday.ac.uk/ ESRCInfoCentre/ViewOutputPage. ata=v9XrjLJ6xhENpjnmO7XDg64E649yyd2SPfkFLlgpzg1gLRfjg6dTxnsVWfFDqp4Rtk8pIDd%2fVktIDGuB3 61TToXs1yn7V%2b6wijNCOof6ZOGc2wvKxqcVPqv17AOYsUm3wI8IlCfSU7c%3d&xu=&isAwardHolde r=&isProfiled=&AwardHolderID=&Sector [Accessed 18 February 2008].

Bennett, T. and Holloway, K., (2004). Gang Membership, Drugs and Crime in the UK. *British Journal of Criminology,* 44, 305-323.

Bullock, K. and Tilley, N., (2002). *Shootings, Gang and Violent Incidents in Manchester: Developing a crime reduction strategy.* London: Home Office.

Burman, M., (2004). A View from the Girls' Challenging Conceptions of Violence. *Sociological Review,* 13 (4), 2-6.

Casciani, D., (2008). Are our Girls getting more Violent? *BBC News Online.* 15th May 2008, Available from: http://news.bbc.co.uk/1/hi/uk/7401996.stm [Accessed 15 May 2008].

Cawson, P., Wattam, C., Brooker, S. and Kelly, G., (2000). *Child maltreatment in the United Kingdom: a study of the prevalence of child abuse and neglect.* London: NSPCC.

Children in Wales, (2007a). *Briefing Paper 3 - Child Poverty, National Assembly Elections 2007.* Available from: www.childreninwales.org.uk/7204.file.dld [Accessed 12 August 2007].

Children in Wales, (2007b). *Updating and Revising the Welsh Index of Multiple Deprivation, prepared by the End Child Poverty Network Cymru.* Available from: www.childreninwales.org.uk/4673.file.dld [Accessed 13 August 2007].

Dodd, V., (2008). Marginalised British youngsters leave adults living in fear, says US magazine. *The Guardian.* 29th March, Available from: http://www.guardian.co.uk/uk/2008/mar/29/ukcrime. children [Accessed 15 May 2008].

Doward, J., (2007). Britons Fear the Rise of the Yob. *The Guardian Unlimited.* 19th August 2007, Available from: http://www.guardian.co.uk/society/2007/aug/19/drugsandalcohol.crime [Accessed 19 August 2007].

Hills, J., (1995). *Joseph Rowntree Foundation Inquiry into Income and Wealth. 2,* York: Joseph Rowntree Foundation.

Jones, S. and Adamson, D., (2001). *The South Wales Valleys: Continuity and Change 2001.* Pontypridd: University of Glamorgan.

Kidscape, (2002). *Bullying Pays: A survey of Young Offenders.* Available from: http://www.kidscape.org. uk/assets/downloads/ksyoungoffenders.pdf [Accessed 30 October 2008].

Leapman, B., (2008). Violent youth crime up a Third. *The Telegraph.* Available from: http://www. telegraph.co.uk/news/uknews/1576076/Violent-youth-crime-up-a-third.html [Accessed 20 January 2008].

Maher, J., (2007). *Angels with Dirty Faces: Youth gangs and Troublesome youth groups in South Wales.* Unpublished Thesis. Treforest: University of Glamorgan.

Mulholland, H., (2007). ASBOs Encouraging more crime, Thinktank Claims. *The Guardian.* 10th December 2007, Available from: http://www.guardian.co.uk/politics/2007/dec/10/immigrationpolicy.ukcrime [Accessed 10 December 2007].

National Statistics, (2008). *Neighbourhood Statistics.* Available from: http://www.statistics.gov.uk/ [Accessed 05 July 2008].

National Statistics, (2001). *Census: The Census in England and Wales*. Available from: http://www.
neighbourhood.statistics.gov.uk/dissemination/AreaListMapSelection.do [Accessed 10 February
2008].

NCH and Tesco Mobile, (2005). *Putting U in the picture: mobile bullying survey 2005*. Available from:
http://www.nch.org.uk/uploads/documents/Mobile_bullying_%20report.pdf [Accessed 10
November 2008].

NSPCC, (2007). *Calls to ChildLine about sexual abuse*. Available from: http://www.nspcc.org.uk/Inform/
publications/Serials/ChildLineCasenotes/CLSA_wda53965.html [Accessed 10 October 2007].

Pearson, G., (1983). *Hooligan: A History of Respectable Fears*. London: Macmillan.

Pitts, J., Marlow, A., Porteous, D. and Toon, I., (2002). *Inter-group and Inter-racial Violence and the
Victimisation of School Students in a London Neighbourhood. ESRC Violence Research Programme*.
Royal Holloway University of London.

Sharp, C., Aldridge, J. and Medina, J., (2006*). Delinquent Youth Groups and Offending Behaviour: Findings
from the 2004 Offending, Crime and Justice Survey*. London: Home Office.

Strauss, A. and Corbin J., (1998). *Basics of Qualitative Research*. London: Sage Publications.

Taylor, M., (2008a). 40% rise in violent crime by under-18s. *The Guardian*. 16th May 2006 Available from:
http://www.guardian.co.uk/uk/2008/may/16/ukcrime.gender [Accessed 16 May 2008].

Taylor, M., (2008b). Gang chased youth, 16, and stabbed him to death, court told. *The Guardian*.
12th February 2008 Available from: http://www.guardian.co.uk/uk/2008/feb/12/ukcrime.london
[Accessed 23 March 2008].

Ward, L., (2008). Binge drinking fuels youth violence. *Society Guardian*. 23rd January 2008, Available
from: http://www.guardian.co.uk/society/2008/jan/23/youngdrinkers [Accessed 23 January 2008].

Welsh Assembly Government, (2006). *Communities First*. Available from: http://wales.gov.uk/topics/
housingandcommunity/regeneration/communitiesfirst/?lang=en [Accessed 30 October 2007].

Welsh Assembly Government, (2005). *Welsh Index of Multiple Deprivation [WIMD] 2005*. Available from:
http://wales.gov.uk/topics/statistics/theme/wimd2005/?lang=en [Accessed 30 October 2007].

Wilson, D., Sharp, C. and Patterson, A., (2006). Young People and Crime: Findings from the 2005
Offending, Crime and Justice Survey. *Home Office*. Available from: http://www.homeoffice.gov.uk/
rds/pdfs06/hosb1706.pdf [Accessed 30 October 2007].

Wood, M., (2005). The Victimisation of Young People: Findings from the 2003 Crime and Justice Survey.
Home Office. Available from: http://www.homeoffice.gov.uk/rds/pdfs05/r246.pdf [Accessed 30
October 2008].

Deprived Young People Struggling for Resources and Recognition in a Densely Built Quarter: Urbanitz, Austria

Johanna Blum and Ingrid Kromer

1 Introduction: Setting the Scene

Starting in the early 1990s the public discourse on the violence of young people rose in Austria. Gang-like and extremist forms of youth violence were highlighted first and attention subsequently shifted to violence in schools. Increasingly, youth violence was covered in the media, though it was certainly not a new phenomenon. Recent media coverage mainly reports on a significant increase of violence-prone girls and boys in Austria and – at the same time – reinforces the negative image of young people in the public eye. Headlines like 'Juvenile law of force'[1] or 'Wave of brutal juvenile violence in Vienna'[2] convey an inappropriate and appalling picture of youth in Austria and fuel discussions on the need for boot camps and tougher penalties. The source of violent behaviour of young people is often prematurely attributed to family background. The multifaceted roots of violence are rarely mentioned in the media and therefore a public debate on social, socio-economic and individual factors that influence violent behaviour is virtually non-existent. A lack of communication skills, pressure to perform well, competition, insecurity and an absence of alternative perspectives may all contribute to violence and aggressive behaviour but their impact is disregarded.

Media coverage is predominantly based on crime figures published by the police or courts although experts continuously stress that such data must be treated extremely cautiously because of changing reporting behaviour. Crime statistics have, however, 'revealed' a considerable increase in juvenile violence in Austria during the past decades (Beclin and Grafl 2000). In particular, drug crime and delinquent behaviour amongst girls grew during that period. According to police records the number of incidents rose about 15% in 2007 compared to the previous year. Most prevalent has been vandalism and damage of property, which increased about 29% from one year to the next. Bodily harm (17%) and theft (10%) has gone up too. The extensive use of official crime data to describe trends in youth violence is at least partly due to the absence of systematic empirical research in Austria. Research on youth violence concentrates on delinquency (mostly recorded crime) and violence in schools. Apart from that there is little research on the violent behaviour of girls and boys, despite the wealth of materials, project descriptions, handbooks, and training manuals for practitioners on the subject (see for example Akzente Salzburg and Salzburger Landesjugendbeirat 2007).

Though the delinquency of young people has been studied regularly since the 1960s (see for example Grafl 1995; Császár 1989, 1985; Steinert 1984; Pilgram and Rotter 1981; Császár 1978; Graßberger 1972; Schindler 1968) most of this research has been based on crime statistics and files. Only one recent study has surveyed adolescent self-reported delinquency (Stangl *et al.* 2006). Factors contributing to delinquency, such as attitudes towards crime, leisure time activities, peers, school and neighbourhood, were considered in this investigation. Grafl (2005) examined delinquency among young immigrants more closely, using data on convictions. There have also been several investigations into school violence (Atria *et al.* 2005; Haller and Stögner 2004; Klicpera and Gasteiger-Klicpera 1996) and racism and xenophobia (Karazman-Morawetz and Steinert 1995,1993; Pelinka and König 1993). As early as 1975 there was some research on peer violence in the public space conducted in Vienna: Tumpel and Edlinger (1975) examined youth crime rates in three different neighbourhoods in Vienna. They compared one disadvantaged area with two other quarters but found no differences in prevalence rates.

In Austria 20% of the 13-15 year olds have already been involved in a brawl (Stangl *et al.* 2006). Shoplifting (18%) and destruction of property (17%) are also recorded quite often. Furthermore Stangl *et al.* (2006) found that boys are more inclined to violence (42%) than girls (22%). Violent and criminal experiences alter with age: 26% of 13 year olds, 32% of 14 year olds and 36% of 15 year olds have committed a crime at least once. Young people attending lower secondary schools, junior vocational schools and polytechnic schools are more likely to experience violence than young people attending higher secondary schools. Neighbourhood and residential area also have a major influence on deviant behaviour. This is especially true for districts with more extreme socio-economic and cultural differences. Reported delinquency of young immigrants increased since 2000 (Grafl 2005). Furthermore, considerable regional differences were found, suggesting divergent reporting and conviction behaviour.

The locality study presented in this chapter allows a broad perspective on the everyday experiences of young people in public space. The chosen qualitative research approach – including interviews and workshops with 13-16 year olds and experts – facilitates a comprehensive view on violent behaviour that includes physical forms as well as non-physical forms.

2 Locality in Focus

Background Information

Urbanitz – the chosen disadvantaged locality in Austria – is a part of Vienna, which is the federal capital of Austria. As to the national statistics, in Austria live about 8,250,000 people, a quarter of them in the city of Vienna. Austria is characterised by a predominantly rural or semi-rural landscape. Only five more cities have population figures of more than 75,000 inhabitants. In Austria young people aged between ten and 20 years form 12% of the total population. Within the age group on whom the research focused, 13-16 year olds, there are 395,000 girls and boys, which is 5% of the total population. Since 1987 Austria has experienced an increase in population, because positive migration-rates have compensated for the declining birth rate. The percentage of people without Austrian citizenship is about 9%. In Vienna, the proportion of foreign citizens is highest at 16%. Due to the economic growth since the 1950s, Austria has been a favoured immigration country for migrant labourers and refugees (Statistik Austria 2007).

Two million people live in the metropolitan area; the municipality itself has 1.6 million inhabitants. Of all inhabitants about 80,000 are between 10 and 15 years old and another 85,000 are aged between 15 and 20 (Magistrat der Stadt Wien 2006). The city of Vienna is situated in the east of Austria and is divided into 23 districts. They are marked off by important streets and rivers. The inner districts are separated from the outer districts by a ring road, the 'Gürtel' (or 'Ring'). The Danube canal, the river Danube itself and the Wien River are distinctive borders too.

The locality finally chosen for the research is part of two outer districts of Vienna. Originally Urbanitz comprised three separate communities that were incorporated into the municipality of Vienna in late 19th century. In general both districts are dominated by residential and green areas. A large part of the two districts is within the green belt around Vienna. Within these districts Urbanitz represents a densely populated part of Vienna. The majority of the residential zones in the quarter have a density of more than 200 inhabitants per 10,000 sqm^3. Nowadays the locality in focus comprises five distinct quarters, each having one local centre.

Population and Socio-economic Structure

As Urbanitz is not defined by administrative boundaries but bounded by main roads, statistics for the area are not easily available. It was impossible to secure data about the locality in focus except for population figures[4]. Both of the districts to which Urbanitz is connected are inhabited by about 145,000 people and 12,500 young people aged 10 to 20 years live there (Magistrat der Stadt Wien 2006). Although the size of Urbanitz is a little less than a fifth of the two districts, it is populated by 60.000 people. All in all, 6,000 young people aged 10 to 20 years live there (Magistrat der Stadt Wien 2007).

On average the population of the one of the two relevant districts has achieved education levels a little lower than the total population of Vienna. People who finished only compulsory education are over-represented in this area. In contrast, the average education attainment of the population of the other district meets the average of Vienna. The data draw a similar picture on the current occupational status of the inhabitants of the two districts, with one district having a lower, and the other a slightly lower status than the city average. According to statistics available for the two districts, the area is one of the poorer neighbourhoods in Vienna. The average income of employees is lower than in most other areas of Vienna (Magistrat der Stadt Wien 2006). Summing up, in Urbanitz there live less educated people that are less often white-collar employees and more often unskilled labourers than in the rest of Vienna. Moreover, the inhabitants of Urbanitz have a lower average income.

Ethnic Diversity

On average one fifth of the Vienna's inhabitants are citizens of foreign countries. Taking into account those immigrants who have become Austrian citizens already, the proportion of those with a migrant background is higher. It is estimated that about 30% of the inhabitants have an immigrant background (Waldrauch and Sohler 2004). The biggest immigrant groups in Vienna are those from former Yugoslavia, Germany and Turkey. Data show that the offspring of migrant labourers (the so-called 'guest workers') have problems with educational advancement and are over-represented in low-income jobs in Austria. Many children and grand-children of these immigrants have been born and raised in Austria. Nevertheless, they still experience social inequality based on their origin and ethnic background (Waechter *et al.* 2009).

One of the main reasons for the choice of Urbanitz as the research locality is its diversity according to ethnic background of its inhabitants. The part of Urbanitz closer to the city centre is dominated by *immigrants* whereas the more distant part is inhabited primarily by native Austrian citizens. 30% of the young people in the locality in focus are *foreigners* (Magistrat der Stadt Wien 2007). We may estimate that the figures for young people with an immigrant background including second and third generation immigrants (those who were born in Austria and are already naturalised) are considerably higher.

Housing and Infrastructure

Urbanitz includes housing with a distinct mix of private, cooperative and public housing that is typical of Vienna. Within the inner part of Urbanitz there are mainly houses that were built about hundred years ago when Vienna was growing rapidly ('Gründerzeit'). In these buildings, which are owned predominantly by private persons, are particularly many *substandard* flats with housing standards strikingly lower than elsewhere in Vienna. Among all apartments 14% to 17% are not equipped with a toilet and may not have a water supply within the apartment. In the whole city only 8% of flats are assigned to this category (Magistrat der Stadt Wien 2006).

All in all, Urbanitz is a residential area where young people live but they leave the area when they go out. They meet in places elsewhere in Vienna, especially in the inner-city:

pubs, bars, cafés, cinemas, and shopping malls. In the interviews the young people told us about the different places they go to. They are very mobile, but for different reasons: some avoid social control through the community within their home district and others like the facilities in other districts more.

The infrastructure of Urbanitz is, however, manifold: public transport within the chosen area is operating mainly with tramways (six tramway lines, one bus line). At its edges there are two underground lines and one city railway line. There are plenty of ethnic restaurants, pubs and cafés and there is one big market that is the heart of the inner part of the locality. In the area around this market there is an annual modern art festival. There are several small shopping centres and shopping streets. A big shopping mall, that contains a cinema too, is situated very close in a neighbouring district.

A big park of about 50,000sqm is situated in the outer part of Urbanitz. Additionally there are a few other parks and small green areas with playgrounds and sometimes sport facilities. All in all, the small parks amount to 60,000sqm. Those with sport facilities are especially relevant for young people: Eleven out of 19 parks are equipped with children's playgrounds and nine with sport facilities.

Urbanitz has three youth centres. Two of these are doing mainly street work. During the warm seasons the youth workers spend their time outside in the parks of Urbanitz. There are 16 schools in the area: eight elementary schools, three general secondary schools, two higher secondary schools ('Gymnasium'), two secondary vocational schools and one private school.

Juvenile Delinquency and Violence

Figures from the Vienna Federal Police Department (Bundespolizeidirektion Wien 2007) on delinquent behaviour of young people show a considerable increase in offences from the younger (10 to 14 years) to the older (14 to 18 years) age group. In 2006, the younger group recorded 67 offences while the older ones committed 334. Two kinds of crime are reported more often than others: offences against the person and property offences. Of the 5,500 criminal offences by young people in Vienna, 401 were committed in the two districts where Urbanitz is situated.

According to the expert interviews conducted for this study, *parks* appear as focal points of peer violence in Urbanitz. Some violent incidents happen in the streets around two schools which seem to have an ongoing rivalry. Additionally hot spots of youth violence in Vienna are around discotheques and pubs young people visit on weekends. There, violent behaviour is usually connected with the consumption of alcohol. However, there is no such hot spot in Urbanitz. All in all, the interviewed experts suggested that there are no gang rivalries in Urbanitz and peer violence is mostly due to a lack of space that is available for young people.

3 The Approach Adopted

Identifying the Locality

The decision regarding the area in which the fieldwork took place was based on interviews with seven experts: a youth politician, a street worker, a youth worker, a city planner, two architects and a senior police officer (responsible for human rights affairs within the Viennese police). Four of them were women and three of them men. During the interviews, we discussed disadvantaged areas in Vienna and where peer violence occurs more frequently than in other areas. The discussions with the social worker and the city planner were particularly productive. The interview with the senior police officer was also extremely helpful to access information on youth crime. Additionally police officers in eight different regions of Vienna were contacted to get an impression of the differences between these regions.

The main criteria for choosing the disadvantaged locality were ethnic diversity, a rather low socio-economic status of the inhabitants and a rather high rate of juvenile violence. Young immigrants are an important population group in Vienna and we therefore wanted to include them in the study but not to focus only on them. This background – different ethnic and social groups who live together in one area and, amongst other things, use the same parks, squares, and means of public transport – seemed to be the most promising for gathering rich data about peer violence in a disadvantaged area.

In order to decide which sites to include into the study we made a site visit to the different parks and squares in Urbanitz. Finally we agreed on *five sites* within Urbanitz where our fieldwork should be carried out. The choice of the sites aimed at representing the diversity of the locality to 'catch' all forms of violent experiences. Some interviews were conducted in two youth centres and in one parish youth group.

The Fieldwork

Data collection was achieved through qualitative, semi-structured interviews. A topic guide was prepared, containing four different parts: leisure time activities, places and partners; violent encounters among young people in public space; coping strategies; and definitions of violence. Additionally we asked for personal details in the beginning of each interview. We prepared a leaflet with information on relevant helplines and advisory and counselling services for young people, to be handed out to respondents in case they wanted to seek help.

25 young people in the chosen area were interviewed. All interviewees were 13-16 years old. The sample comprised *21* single-interviews and two single sex group interviews with two friends each. The interviews took half an hour on average; the longest lasted 50

minutes, the shortest 15 minutes. All interviews were done between September 2007 and February 2008. They were conducted mainly during the afternoon and evenings – the optimum time to reach 13-16 year olds. The interviewees were contacted in public space or semi public locations by the interviewers and asked for an interview. We approached them by ourselves or with the help of street/youth workers. During some interviews it was difficult to establish a quiet and undisturbed setting, because our request produced a lot of interest and curiosity among the other young people who were around at the same time. However, after some minutes this interest diminished and a more relaxed situation was established.

One problem that occurred during the fieldwork was that almost only boys from *minority ethnic backgrounds* used the public space for leisure time activities. There were also some girls from minority ethnic backgrounds but they hardly ever gave their consent to an interview. It was challenging to find 'native' young people in public space. It would appear that minority ethnic and 'native' young people do not use the same facilities and, thus, do not associate with each other. On account of this difficulty we decided to do some interviews at two youth centres and at one parish youth group. In all, 15 young people were interviewed in public space – in parks or squares – and the other 10 young people at youth centres or youth clubs.

Finally, the sample comprised interviews with 15 boys and 10 girls. Eight respondents were 13 years old, two were 14 years old, seven were 15 years old and another eight were 16 years old. Additionally, mostly young people with migration backgrounds than without were included in the sample. 19 young people out of 25 originated from Turkey, Croatia or Serbia. Some of them already belonged to the third generation of immigrants: their grandparents had come to Austria. Six of the interviewed girls and 13 of the boys had a minority ethnic background. In contrast, however, six interviewees (four girls and two boys) had 'native' Austrian parents. Nevertheless, from this distribution of gender and ethnicity it is especially difficult to draw conclusions for boys *without* migration backgrounds.

Despite the sample's large proportion of immigrant youth all interviews were done in the German language. With a few interviewees this was particularly challenging because of their lack of language skills. During fieldwork it became clear that some words (e.g. slap) had different meanings for young people due to the fact that they had a mother tongue other than German. During analysis these differences were taken into account.

The interviewees typically grew up in big families: half had two or more siblings and the other half had only one or no brother or sister. With regard to the educational situation of the interviewees they were mainly pupils: eleven attended a general secondary school, eight attended an academic secondary school and two attended a vocational college. Four interviewees did not attend school anymore; they were looking for an apprenticeship or a job. Most of the sample felt affiliated to groups based on friendship and kinship. Only in four cases was membership of a gang reported: The gangs had names like 'OTK', 'City Terror' and 'Scorpion Nike'. These gangs were different from other groups insofar as they had a leader. However, during the interviews the importance of the gang for experiences of peer violence was not emphasised.

Analysis

All interviews were recorded and transcribed. The analysis of the interviews is based on the grounded theory method (Strübing 2004; Strauss 1998; Strauss and Corbin 1996). Since we were interested in locating new phenomena (foremost a typology of everyday violent encounters) rather than testing already established theories, this method seemed to be an appropriate interpretation strategy. Central to the analysis was the 'coding paradigm'. First, we applied a bottom up approach and started with open coding. Later we focused axial coding - to analyse codes in-depth in order to identify features and dimensions of a certain phenomenon. Finally, we concentrated on a core category that emerged as essential for violent interactions and built up a typology based on that (selective coding). After concentrating on single violent encounters in the initial analysis we continued by including more cases and working in a comparative way until the analysis was 'saturated' (i.e. we did not expect any new dimensions to occur). The analysis was accomplished in an interpretation group of three people. We analysed the data through the software package for qualitative analysis Atlas.ti.

One problem that arose during the interpretation process was that of social desirability. Some of the narratives presented by young people seemed to exaggerate the nature of violent incidents, the frequency of offences, and the use of weapons. In order to interpret these sequences we took this into account insofar as it was an important feature of the young people's social system, where over-reporting (and sometimes underreporting) may be desirable. Furthermore, we solely interpreted narratives of violent encounters that they themselves had been engaged in and therefore reconstructed their role as, for instance, combatant, defender, supporter or witness. Stories about violent behaviour they had only heard were not taken into account in the analysis, even though such stories can also influence the behaviour of young people.

4 Models of Peer Violence

One of the main aims of the study was to provide a typology of violent encounters among young people. Therefore, the different dimensions of violent encounters were related to the various intentions – that emerged as a key category during analysis – and *seven models* were found. However, the analytical separation of the intentions behind violent behaviour was no simple feature as intentions are multiple and overlapping.

'That's My Park!': Occupation of Territory

Some young people reported in their stories that certain parks were 'occupied' by others and were seen as their property. Conflicts arise from disputes over who has the actual privilege or 'right' to spend their leisure time there. Other young people who want to use the same facilities were excluded. Either access was completely denied or young people were displaced. This model of violent encounters is rather typical and occurs regularly and routinely. Sports facilities such as 'ball game cages' are especially important; they are typically the arena of conflicts.

> Extract from an individual interview with Ivica (13 yrs).
>
> *Int: Has it happened to you?* I: More than once. *Int: Tell me what happened?* I: Some, if you don't leave the park they hit you. *Int: Really? How does it start?* I: One says, for instance when we play on one goal, and then they say, 'Get out! We want to play a match.' When we don't get out, then they hit you and push you, like that. *Int: Really? Do you defend yourself, how does it go on?* I: Then there are more coming.

The 'park occupiers' challenge other young people to leave the territory: they are called names and are prompted to leave. If they refuse or respond in any way, this will possibly lead to physical violent behaviour. Respondents typically reported incidents of pushing and jostling, but physical injuries were not mentioned. However, the conflict is not always acted out explicitly. Sometimes power is demonstrated in other types of behaviour. For example, one boy claimed the ball of another to play with it and subsequently the ball was destroyed. If power is not acknowledged but instead is questioned, then the risk of violence escalation is high. To avoid further escalation, strategies of ignoring and reactive behaviour were mentioned. The threat of physical violence, which is implicit in an order, causes many young people to 'obey': they leave the park without comment or retort. Repeated experiences of that kind result in the avoidance of a certain park by other young people. Young people sometimes also mentioned examples of more peaceful and creative solutions to these kinds of conflicts. For example, there had been a football match or 'Paper-Scissors-Stone' to decide who may use a place for a certain time.

It is characteristic of conflicts about parks for one group to be in 'occupation' of the park. They have established the prerogative to play in that park. As a result, other young people have to leave as soon as this group enters. Typically, the interviewees associate different parks with specific ethnic groups who remain rather homogenous. This becomes obvious when racist verbal violence, whether used by young people from minority ethnic or 'native' backgrounds, is applied in order to control the access to parks. Such ethnic group ascription of parks therefore causes intentional avoidance of those parks by other groups, whether from their own direct experience or simply by the reputation of a place.

Moreover, *younger* boys and *girls* are displaced more often. Girls are predominantly involved in verbal violence (conflicts between boys and girls rarely escalate into more physical exchanges). The expelled feel inferior to those young people who occupy the park and, hence, do not resist. Besides age and gender the *number* of people involved is crucial for the development of a conflict. If a group is smaller in number they tend to withdraw or avoid physical violent behaviour. Moreover, larger groups are usually not challenged. Generally, there is a hierarchy in the use of parks with regard to age and gender that also varies according to group size. Therefore, group membership becomes crucial for leisure time activities as soon as one group claims a park for themselves.

The young people involved are mostly not friends but they tend to know each other by sight. Reported violent encounters predominantly occurred during the day. This is because younger boys and girls spent their leisure in parks only at that time of day.

> Hasan (13 yrs, in an individual interview) reported that he was playing with a friend in a park when a boy who they did not know approached them and wanted them to give him their ball. He reasoned that the boy commanded him because he thought that the park is his. Hasan refused to give the ball to him because he feared that he will destroy it as he had made this experience earlier with other boys. To avoid this he decided not to obey this time. However, the boy did not accept his denial and threatened Hasan.
>
> H: Yes, one time, there it happened, I was back in that park. I was there, and a Turk, he is, I had the ball and he said: 'give the ball to me' and so on, like 'give me the ball' and 'otherwise I hit you' and so on. He got on my nerves. Then ... he pushed me. I said: 'I leave' but he said to me something and I hate it when somebody insults my mother. Then I approached him and hit him. After that his friends came, my friends came too. I don't know, then a woman passed by and she said: 'stop it' and we left. *Int: Yes.* H: My friends helped me. *Int: Was he older than you? What was it like?* H: I don't know, I don't know him at all. He was so tall, surely as tall as me. *Int: Does he take your ball?* H: No, the ball of my friend, but we wanted to play and he did, he pushed us around only because he is in his park. *Int: Are there young people who think the park belongs to themselves?* H: Yes. 'That's my park. That's my wall' and so on.

'I'll Show You!': Bravado

Some young people tried to gain prestige through violent behaviour. That means they tried to enhance their own social position at the expense of other young people. Even though this is one model of violent interaction on its own, it is not the most important type in our sample.

Usually this type of violent action begins with an intended provocation. The interviewees insulted someone without any reason or they interpreted actions of other young people, like jostling (pushing and shoving), deliberately as offensive. Non-physical behaviour escalates quickly and is then replaced by physical violence. In this model of violent encounters very crude forms of violence, including the use of weapons, occur.

Young people who reported on interactions like that sought violent conflicts by provoking others, for instance by insulting young people they do not know. Even the interview situation was used to 'present' and project the status of the respondent: earlier encounters of this kind, in which they had been involved, appeared to be embellished and exaggerated. Besides their proactive stance this also seems to indicate that violence is apparently perceived as a normal, even positive thing. Thus violent behaviour is seen as means to gain social recognition. The narratives are, however, also contradictory and ambivalent. On the one hand they presented themselves as the ones who started the dispute; on the other hand they presented themselves as innocent, having 'had' to react to perceived provocation. The conflict is usually terminated by use of weapons or by an intervention from other people: friends or relatives support the boys or girls. Finally, these strategies are commonly justified by an inferior position. Thus they demonstrate the power to defeat others and, therefore, enhance their status.

With regard to the characteristics of those involved in this kind of violence it seems essential that the young people are strangers. No interviewee reported on offending or assaulting friends or acquaintances for the sake of status enhancement. However, they did mention that they attacked younger individuals. That means that rules of fairness that are valid for other models of violent encounters do not apply for the form of bravado. The distant relationship of the participants is a main reason why the violent interactions take place in the public space.

Young people who intend to enhance their status through violence experience conflicts with other young people more frequently. Those conflicts arise between two individuals as well as between groups. Furthermore, these specific interactions are of short duration: The conflict arises very abruptly, escalates and comes to an end. Typically consequences are not mentioned.

Dejan (14 yrs, in an individual interview) characterised himself as big-mouthed because he liked to annoy and ridicule other young people. He actively and regularly launched conflicts through verbal forms of violence without any reason. When an escalation to the stage of physically violent behaviour had taken place he phoned his older cousins in order to support him. He was aware of the strength of the group he was affiliated to, because he knew that they ought to shelter him. It was exactly this back up that allowed him a proactive approach toward violence. When he started a conflict he was sure to win.

Int: Why would somebody want to hit you? D: Well, because I'm big-mouthed. *Int: You are big-mouthed. What is it that you say?* D: Oh nothing, I pull at their legs and so on... *Int: For instance?* D: 'What's wrong with you?' *Int: You only say 'What's wrong with you'?* D: Yes, and I call them asshole and so on. *Int: How does it go on? What does the other one do?* D: And then when he hits me, then I call my cousin. *Int: Does this happen sometimes?* D: Yes, often. *Int: When has it happened the last time?* D: Last week. *Int: Can you describe me, what happened last week?* D: Well, I pulled the leg of someone. I was taking a walk with a friend and in the street there were four 'Schwabos' – Austrians. They then pushed us, then we pushed them, then we got some slaps and then I called my cousins. And then they came and they hit them.

'Don't You Dare!': Affront to Identity

A characteristic form of violent encounters among young people takes place in order to restore one's own integrity. Respondents often told about being annoyed by others. This encapsulated non-physical violence like ostracising and innuendo as well as name calling and insulting. The intention of this kind of violence could be understood as a reply to an affront to identity. That said, the reaction often includes a pre-emptive element: they want to prove their strength and deter the possibility of further assaults. When the girls and boys tried to keep their face the escalation to the stage of physical violence is described as self-defence in the narratives. The legitimation of the behaviour is a common means of dealing with the incident as in this interpretation the blame for the violence is placed elsewhere. Typically, the reaction to an incident follows immediately without chronological delay. If an attack is indirect (e.g. rumours while being absent) the conflict can escalate at a later point in time.

Interviewees talked about innuendo, e.g. because they were left by their girlfriend or boyfriend. Jealousy in friendships also had a place in verbal attacks. The underlying reasons of feeling irritated stayed vague or were not mentioned. In the interviews it becomes clear that the incidents apparently often had a previous history: in most cases the non-physical violence and symbolic forms like gesture are repeatedly experienced over a long period. However, in some cases the interviewees were (perhaps unintentionally) jostled or pushed only once. In such a conflict situation the young people first try to stop the dispute by ignoring or demanding the other to quit. They may also 'return' the offence (verbal or physical violence) in order to stop being bullied.

It was typical for girls that earlier violent encounters had often preceded the episodes that were described during the interviews. Girls' experiences with this form of peer violence is significantly characterised by relational violence, which means conflicts emerge between friends. If innuendo and insults last over a lengthy period the outcome is often an escalation in violent interaction. For boys, however, this seems to be different. They make use of physical violence even after non-recurring incidents to keep their face. With respect to gender, more distinctions can be made. Boys refrain from punching or slapping girls when they feel annoyed. They tend to let it rest or do not attach that much importance to it.

All young people said that they were particularly upset about insults referring to their mother. Presumably, this is perceived to be strongly connected to their personal identity or integrity. Moreover, racist and xenophobic insults pose a serious affront to identity. Typically, such insults trigger shifts to physical violence very quickly. The young people pull someone's hair, slap, push, punch or kick each other. Sometimes they even use weapons. In cases when they resort to physical violence the conflict generally ends there. Consequences like injuries (sometimes fractures) or penalties were mentioned. One interviewee had even got a criminal record, having been prosecuted for violence. Penalties imposed by teachers, like suspension, as well as sanctions by parents were also mentioned.

This physical violence takes place in public, usually among two opposing individuals who generally know each other. Some are classmates or friends. This close relationship explains the importance of an apology. Whether or not reconciliation is possible depends on the strength and impact of the violence used. When physical injuries occur, even if a dispute has died down, reconciliation seems especially unlikely.

This kind of interaction reveals different types of attitudes toward violence. Young people vary in their perception of what kind of behaviour is perceived as an attack on their integrity. For those young people who are generally proactive in their quest for conflict, someone else looking 'stupid' is reason enough. Fadime had a conflict with a female schoolmate of her cousin.

Extract from an individual interview with Fadime (15 yrs).

F: Well, for example, at my cousin's school – there is a girl, who is in her class. And she had a boy-friend who was in a higher class. He is 18 or so ... they all attend a business school. And, I was with my cousin, I picked her up, when he fell in love with me. And then he talked about me a lot with my cousin while his girlfriend is present and listened. The she said to my cousin 'Call her, call your cousin!' But my cousin did not want to call me because she knew what would happen then. Though I wasn't guilty, I had a boyfriend back then and I would never ever cheat him. Then it happened that she hit my cousin and my cousin did not phone me. After I heard of that I went there alone and she came to me and said 'you bitch' and like 'my boyfriend fell in love with you. It's your fault that he doesn't love me anymore.' I told her, that this not my problem and that I came to pick up my cousin. And that was all, I did nothing. And then she almost hit my nose with her fist. *Int: Yes?* F: Then I grasped her hair and pulled at her. I used my knee and hit her in the stomach and then she fell down. *Int: Really?* F: Then I phoned my cousins, of course, and they came immediately. Then I told her that she shouldn't bother me anymore because I didn't do anything. Then she was afraid.

'We'll Back You Up!': Peer Support

This type of violent encounters arises when young people arrange a *battle* to continue a conflict in another place. The arrangement implies a local shift, e.g. from school to a park and a chronological expansion of the conflict. The time between the incidents varies: It can be some minutes or a longer period of time. However long the interruption is a chronological break is established. The opponents may use this break to prepare for the anticipated situation. Typically the young people show up with a group of supporters at the agreed place, so that two groups face each other. The two sides continue the dispute with verbal attacks or, if the conflict escalates, with pushing or hitting. The intention of an appointment at a certain place and a certain time is the continuation of a conflict by the means of physical violence. The conflict may end before that because one group feels inferior and leaves the scene. Sometimes one party to the conflict does not appear at the meeting place and therefore, by 'default', loses the dispute. The menace of physical violence if one group is likely to be outnumbered may be the reason. The anticipation of the use of weapons (such as baseball bats) may be another: young people are especially afraid of weapons and, if one side is not equally well equipped, they will leave the location to avoid physical injuries.

Besides the two groups of combatants, there are often 'supporters' who are also involved. The mobilisation of this group is usually carried out via mobile phone: the message of an arranged battle usually spreads very fast inside a circle of friends and acquaintants. The underlying intention to arrange a battle is often to establish the possibility of restoring someone's integrity. This may be for oneself or for a friend but, beyond the direct combatants, the function of the supporting group is to provide additional safety and encouragement: they cheer for them, support them in circumstances of inferiority and arguably have a deterrent effect on the other side. Such peer support is essential for cohesion and solidarity between friends and a reassurance of their group affiliation. The stories of the young people reveal that a victory against an outnumbered group is accorded great importance within their peer group. At the same time the violent encounters offer excitement and tension to the supporting peers. Furthermore, among the supporters there are some watchers and onlookers who want to have fun.

Gender plays a role concerning the group of supporters. If there are more boys among one group it is seen as especially strong. This may cause fear amongst the more actively antagonistic young people involved and lead to retreat and retraction by the opponents. There were also boys among the supporting group even when conflicts emerged between girls, though their narratives indicate that they took the situation less seriously, because they were more like onlookers.

The analysis suggests that supporting young people experience violent encounters more often. They reported that such incidents occurred regularly. Those who took part in arranged battles were predominantly young people who interpreted violence as behaviour that inflicts physical injury. The use of weapons was perceived as *brutal*, which points towards a relation between violent encounters and violence perception: those who regularly experienced violence subscribed to a narrow definition of violence. The data also suggest a more active attitude towards violence among young people who frequently take part in a supporting group.

If conflicts actually occur between groups, adults often have to intervene or the police are called. The arrival of the police then ends the conflict and subsequent consequences may include judicial or other penalties.

> Melanie and Yvonne (both 14 yrs, in a single sex group interview) spoke about an incident that happened to their friend. They all were classmates when a girl continuously offended Melanie and her friend. Insulting, name calling, innuendo and ostracising were used. The cause was a rivalry for a best friend. One day the conflict escalated to a physical stage when their friend's mother was insulted. The supporting groups, which Melanie and Yvonne belonged to, were cheering their friends and some of the boys filmed the fight with their mobile phones.
>
> Y: Well, I was in her class for four years. She continuously was mean to me and my friend. And, well, my friend did not have a family any more and that girl always insulted her family. That hurt my friend deeply. We said, after school, 'take your friends, we call ours'.' And then they were 20 and we were six or so. They arrived in front of the school and then they hit us. And then the police came. M: But the others lost. *Int: Yes?* M: That was the best of it. Y: Because they said that they had a knife even if they did not have any. We were lucky, that they told that. M: Then they were screwed up. *Int: That means, once again, you met in the park and then you hit another?* Y: Well, we waited for them because they didn't come first. She called her friends 1,000 times and then they arrived by tramway. Then we stood there and began to speak and so. She hit first and then everybody had a go at her. Then her friends intervened. She was bleeding and crying and then she

said that we were like a kindergarten while she was crying. That was funny. M: Very funny. Y: Yeah. Then somebody from the tobacconist's shop called the police and they arrived immediately. Well, then all of us were recorded, well. Then it was over.

'I'll Pay You Back': Revenge

Revenge is a delayed reaction: the conflict temporally expands and consists of different sequences. From an everyday situation like a foul in a football match a conflict arises, which then escalates. Finally, the young people slap and shove each other – or more. If one involved party loses a dispute and has to withdraw they sometimes want and seek revenge. So they look for a chance to pay back. In contrast to arranged battles, revenge is carried out one-sided: one party to the conflict bides their time and prepares for a 'counterstrike'. This is probably a reaction to the disgrace or humiliation initially experienced and the subsequent aim to re-establish or re-assert their 'face'.

The number of young people involved may change. The individual who wants revenge determines to be 'stronger' next time and therefore calls friends for support. The narratives suggest that the young people involved often do not know each other. If groups are seeking revenge they are usually only friends among themselves.

Revenge takes place at the same place as the first incident. The young people, looking for satisfaction, return to the place assuming to meet the others again. In the case of revenge to repay having been offended, both individual and groups of young people may be involved.

Ivica (13 yrs, in an individual interview) told about a violent encounter that happened during a football match. Because of playing foul a conflict emerged and finally escalated. Ivica and his friends were outnumbered and had to withdraw. However, since they did not want to lose their face they decided to return to park the next day.

Int: Have you asked somebody for help once? I: Yes. Int: For instance? I: Well, my friends, when the others hit us, then we walked there the next day to pay it back. Int: How often has this happened to you? I: Only once. Int: What did happen then? I: Well, they hit us. They played unfair and then they insulted us and then we replied, 'What's up?' and then they began to hit. We defended ourselves and on the next day we went there again and then we bashed them. But not all of them, only one.

'Hands Off!': Protection of Girls and Younger Teenagers

Two different interactions lead in this type of violence: Firstly, a girl is sexually harassed and secondly, a – mostly male – friend or relative intervenes and tries to protect the girl. The interviewees predominantly describe the second form as violent action and the first one as underlying cause or reason for the use of violence.

A male friend or relative protects the girl by threatening the boy not to harass the young woman again. Typically he is threatened with physical violence. If the boy continues to harass the girl the conflict escalates and leads to violent physical action. An immediate violent reaction may occur, especially if sexual violence against the girl is perceived. However, a prerequisite for an intervention is that the young people have to comprehend sexual harassment as something negative or violent. Therefore it has to be clear that the girl rejects the behaviour of the boy. That means if the *protectors* lack this perception an intervention is not considered as necessary. For this form of violence it seems to be crucial that the girl and the *protector* are familiar with each other: usually it is a relative (brother) or a friend although, in some circumstances, it is possible for strangers to come to her defence.

Typically, boys from minority ethnic backgrounds try to protect girls from sexual harassment.

> Extract from an individual interview with Fadime (15 yrs, Serbian background).
>
> F: Once I had a boyfriend who I dated rather long. Then he wanted me to marry him but I wouldn't. We had a long-distance relationship, he lived in Germany and I lived here in Vienna. On weekends he came to visit me and we phoned every day. But then he wanted to marry me and I told him 'no, thanks, it is too early'. /.../ Then he slapped me and my cousin hit him, my cousin struck back.

The paramount reason for protecting the girl is to preserve her virginity. The point of her defence is not in fact the protection of the girl herself or the avoidance of pain, but the reputation of the girl (and, indeed her family and her culture). This assumption is supported by the close relationship between the girl and the protecting boy. Moreover, the narratives of the young people emphasise the social consequences but not the emotional or physiological hurt that is caused to the girl.

> Yvonne (14 yrs, native Austrian background, in a single sex group interview) reported that she was once in a cinema continuously harassed by a young

man. He was stalking her and looking at her in a disturbing manner. She
was accompanied by a couple of male friends who told the young man that
he should stop. Nevertheless he continued the sexual harassment. Finally,
they went all outside to the parking lot and the young man was pushed,
punched and kicked by the girl's friends. When they stopped he was lying
on the floor.

'I don't Dare!': Feeling of Powerlessness

One model of violent encounters among young people is characterised by the feeling of
powerlessness. The young people intentionally avoid any reaction in order to prevent
the incident or situation becoming even worse. *Two different phenomena,* robbery and
sexual harassment, can be subsumed within this model and are explained below.

Robbery

Some of the boys and girls reported that they were victims of thefts. A very dramatic form
is taking valuables under threat of violence. Typical of this form of violence is a rather
passive and helpless role of the victim. In addition to physiological and psychological
injuries, in this model of violent encounters the young people suffer from material loss.
Besides losing, for instance, their mobile phone the fear of further offences remains.

Typically respondents were asked for the time before the robbery. After they had looked
at their mobile phone to read the time they were told to hand it over. Sometimes
physical violence was used immediately: They were held and punched. Weapons were
sometimes also used to threaten the victims. In such a situation young people face
the choice of being slapped or to hand over their belongings. Any way of resisting in
order to keep one's valuables seems impossible and useless. Normally such incidents
cannot be narrowed down in space or time. Young people may be tracked over time
and eventually subjected to the robbery. The data suggest that violent encounters like
this occur often. One interviewee had been robbed several times. It seems that certain
parks are associated with the taking of belongings: to avoid such an incident those parks
are best avoided.

The young people involved in such violence tend not to know each other. The victims
are usually alone, or in pairs, or at least in an inferior (physical) position. The interviews
report that even young people who usually showed a proactive attitude towards
violence refrained from resistance in such a situation. This illustrates the point that the
use of violence strongly depends on the specific situation and its conditions. Despite
that, more girls and boys who can be characterised as 'deactive' tend to anticipate and
avoid the situations where this kind of violence is most likely to occur. Goran described

a violent encounter in which his mobile phone was stolen. Without any chance to resist he handed over his belongings.

> **Extract from an individual interview with Goran (16 yrs).**
>
> G: There are some tall guys, for instance, they hit you sometimes without a reason... the take my mobile, that happened already three times to me, that my mobile and my mp3-player were stolen. *Int: Who did that and why?* G: I don't know them. I walked that way and they asked 'can you tell me what time it is?' and I said: 'yes' and when they see your mobile, they let you walk for a couple of metres but track you. Then they hold me and take everything.

Sexual Harassment

The feeling of powerlessness can be caused by verbal attacks or an aggressive, harassing look. It was when these words and looks were considered to have a sexual motivation that girls saw it as sexual harassment: for them, it was a very common form of non-physical violence.

Sexual harassment can trigger the feeling of helplessness in the face of someone's verbal or symbolic violence. The young women who spoke of such incidents described themselves as powerless yet not passive: they actually and actively decided to avoid any (re)action because they feared an escalation of the situation. They were afraid that any response might worsen the situation and because of the superior position of the aggressors they perceived no chance to address the matter on a more equal basis. For this reason the girls continued to do what they did when the sexual violence began. This demonstrates that the girls were in a position where there was no obvious way to solve the situation on their own. Hence their feeling of fear and insecurity is a constant one. Some girls try to protect themselves with a pepper spray or warning hooters and also reported phoning a friend in unpleasant situations which made them feel safer.

Other Forms

Other forms of non-physical offences can lead to similar experiences. Some young people reported being excluded of certain places – especially parks – by insults and threats of physical violence. Once again, it entailed the avoidance of certain places. Again, exclusion may be associated with gender, ethnicity and language issues. Normally the young people involved are not familiar with each other.

Melanie and Yvonne (both 14 yrs, in a single sex group interview) reported that they were insulted and threatened when they were walking through a park because they had entered the turf of the boys' group. The girls said that they behaved in a de-active way in order to avoid any escalation: they kept walking and left the park as soon as possible. This kind of violent encounter happens quite frequently to them.

5 The Character of Violent Encounters

Above, some of the essential dimensions of violent encounters between young people were used to describe the models: the type of behaviour, intentions, consequences, those involved, time, place, conditions and interpretation of violence. The aim of the study, however, was not only to develop a typology of violent encounters but to look at the dimensions of violence across the different models. Therefore, different patterns – according to the different dimensions – that have emerged during analysis are discussed in this section.

Types of Violent Behaviour

The young people interviewed provided accounts of symbolic, gestured, verbal or physical forms of violence. Although the principal range of violent behaviours does not differ substantively between girls and boys, the frequency of the appearance of these behaviours is gender related. Boys are more likely to use physical violence whereas it is more typical for girls to engage in non-physical violence.

- Girls: Rumours and gossip, ridicule, insult and innuendo, insult of third persons (e.g. relatives), racist and xenophobic insults, stalking, ostracising, giving a look, hair pulling, pushing, hitting, kicking, using blunt weapons, using prepared and unprepared weapons (such as knuckle-duster, or belt)

- Boys: Rumours and gossip, ridicule, insult and innuendo, insult of third persons (e.g. relatives), racist and xenophobic insult, stalking, giving a look, spitting, pushing, tripping, hitting, kicking, groping, using blunt weapons, using prepared weapons (knuckle-duster), taking (robbery)

Usually more than one of these various types of violence was used in an encounter, verbal attacks being strikingly regular in their occurrence. The data reveal *escalation cycles*: There are typical stages of violent behaviour from the beginning of a conflict to the end. Less dramatic forms of violent behaviour are used at the outset. Typically verbal, symbolic or gesturing forms of violence precede physical offences. In some models of violent encounters it is the *prospect* of escalation, rather than the actual use of severe forms of violence, that poses the threat to young people.

The main kind of escalation cycle starts with an incident like staring or looking at somebody or pushing somebody in a manner that is understood as offensive. Sometimes an intended provocation like insulting or calling somebody names leads to a more severe form of violent behaviour. They might interrupt the argument and continue it at a later point in time; typically they make an 'appointment' for that.

The escalation can be a part of a longer lasting and more complex conflict: Then the violent encounter takes place over a period of time and comprises of a couple of single violent actions that happen at different points in time. However because these single incidents are not solved they add up to a complex conflict. Finally, one relatively minor violent interaction can lead to more severe forms of violent behaviour. The analysis shows that complex violent interactions are more typical with girls: Rumours, innuendo and ostracising among friends happen repeatedly and eventually, perhaps inevitably, some conflicts escalate to a stage of physical violence. But usually girls' conflicts end at a symbolic or verbal stage. Among boys the escalation takes place immediately after the first violent action in many cases.

Transitory Violent Behaviour

The violent behaviour of young people seems to change with age. For example, one male interviewee reported that he had learned that girls do not like groping, so he stopped doing it himself. Moreover, he said that he now protects girls (who he knows well) from being sexually harassed. A female interviewee recounted using verbal violence until one incident that changed her mind: she realised that she caused hurt to the other and stopped doing it. These narratives show that the perception of what violence is changes over time. Consequently these reinterpretations influence their actual behaviour and they cease using certain kinds of violence. One important influence on young people finally changing their behaviour is the awareness that they hurt somebody else and the development of greater empathy for the situation of their protagonist.

Strategies of Conflict Resolution

Even though conflicts come to an end (or are put on hold), most are not solved in a conclusive sense. The narratives of young people suggest that they do not know how to deal with the situation in a constructive way and with the possibility of resolution. Their skills to 'solve' a conflict seem to be restricted to the exertion or menace of physically violent behaviour which furthermore means that this comes to be seen as a legitimate means to settle an argument. Alternative strategies of conflict resolution therefore are not commonly used: the 'choice' is whether to avoid violent encounters or to fight verbally or physically.

Another way to end violent encounters that the interviewees gave account of is an intervention from 'outside'. Apart from the young people themselves adults intervene and try to stop the conflicts. According to young people, this can be a powerful strategy: Young people often phone their friends or family members for help. When they arrive the argument is often settled only because of their presence. Sometimes even an instruction by a passer-by is sufficient to stop a violent interaction.

The processes of de-escalation and conflict resolution vary across gender and education. Girls try to stop or solve conflicts in a verbal way more often. On the contrary boys typically end conflicts by the means of physical violence which means that they just stop and do not resolve conflicts. Physical supremacy legitimates one's social position and power.

Multiple and Overlapping Intentions

The data revealed seven main types of intentions that lay behind engagement in violent behaviour. As the intention to act violently is a core category to understand everyday violence among young people, a strong emphasis was placed upon this in the analysis (see also the section on models above). The number of varying intentions found in the data demonstrates the *multifaceted* causes of violence. However, the intentions underlying violent encounters are multiple and at times contradictory. In relation to gender there are two typical forms. On the one hand, the interviewees reported that only boys occupy and defend a territory: appropriation of space and dominant behaviour in public space by boys tends to exclude girls from public space. On the other hand, conflicts in friendships are the girls' domain: gossiping and jealousy among friends emerged as characteristic.

Usually different actors do have various intentions in the conflicts. For instance those who occupy a park verbally threaten the *intruders* in order to defend their *turf*. Most of the young people who are excluded from the park resist and do not give in immediately. However the crucial violent behaviour that leads to an escalation are often the verbal insults that follow: the excluded young people do not want to lose face through being insulted and so react in a violent manner. There might be more than one overlaying intention as well: a female interviewee gave an account of a violent encounter with another girl, who blamed her for poaching her boyfriend and, additionally, that girl hit the interviewee's cousin a few days before (see the cameo in 'Don't You Dare: Affront to Identity' in the section on models above). In the incident she described she did not only defend herself against the personal insults but also took revenge on behalf of her cousin. Overlaying intentions are more typical in complex violent interactions than in short and simple ones. Multiple intentions can eventually lead to a rapid escalation and increase the severity of violent behaviour: actions then can become exceptionally violent.

The special form of *fighting for fun* occurs between friends only and rarely causes hurt to anyone. It is not therefore described as a distinctive model of violent encounters. In rare cases of escalation, the situation then fits into one of the other types that emerged from the data.

Justification as Self-defence

In general the young people cognitively know that violence is criminal and deviant. They know if an incident is reported to the police the one who started the assault could be prosecuted. Although this knowledge does not impact significantly on young people's violent behaviour they draw one important rule from this: they should not to be the first to hit because then one is guilty. This was often alleged against those boys and girls who intentionally sought conflicts that were characterised as brutal, who were seen as not 'playing by the rules', whereas self-defence was invariably described as legitimate in the narratives. The young people apply the notion of self-defence for almost every violent encounter. Typically the interviewees argued that they had to respond to an offence despite not really wishing to have a conflict with anybody. That young people reconstruct their behaviour mostly as self-defence seems to be a coping strategy – a technique of neutralisation – since, through this reasoning, they try to reconcile their actual behaviour with prevailing social norms.

Penalties and Hurt

In the interviews the young people reported different consequences that can be subsumed within the following types: (a) physical injuries like bruises or fractures, (b) mental hurt, (c) penalties from parents, teachers and the police, and (d) the impact of violence on interpersonal relationships (e.g. loss of friendships).

There were some *gender* differences in the narratives: Whereas girls mainly talked about wider social penalties, boys talked about the immediate consequences like physical injuries (such as bruises, nosebleeds, fractures). The analysis suggests that this is due to traditional gender roles. Girls are subject to pressure to adapt to social norms and values of femininity. For instance, when girls hit somebody they do not conform to the gentle and weak image of women and, therefore, it is often interpreted as a more serious misdeed than if the same behaviour was perpetrated by boys. For boys, violent behaviour is a part of their gender identity insofar as they have to be strong and powerful. To boast of physical injuries inflicted on others stresses one's physical strength and dominance. Moreover, a boy's violent behaviour is excused as pubertal more often, whereas girls who act violently are usually sanctioned, thus explaining further their emphasis on penalties.

Summing up, those respondents who have exercised physical violence on other young people did not feel responsible for the hurt they caused. They were more or less unconcerned about the consequences of their behaviour even if they were caught and sanctioned. Strikingly *not one* interviewee mentioned the pain they caused by physical violence. Regarding their own feelings they mentioned that they were usually irritated and furious. They described the situations as unpleasant and frightening but generally the young people struggled to express the feelings they had during certain violent encounters. Emotions and hurt seemingly played no big role in their narratives. This reflects the point that young people were not accustomed to baring their feelings in their everyday social environment.

Avoidance of Incidents

One important reason why young people avoid violent encounters is that they usually have no alternative approaches at hand to solve a conflict. Therefore, the most important strategy to cope with violent encounters is avoidance. *Three* different approaches to avoidance could be identified: Ignoring offensive behaviour, avoiding certain sites, and avoiding being alone in public space.

First, the ignoring of offensive or provocative behaviour by other young people is by far the most important way to avoid conflicts. Young people do not listen to (they appear not to hear) verbally violent behaviour; they go away and sometimes even run away to evade a prolongation of the situation. This strategy can also be seen as one means of ending a conflict, because some violent behaviour has actually already happened. Nevertheless the decision depends on whether one judges they are 'better off' fighting or running away. If the others are older or appear to be stronger or they are greater in number a retreat is more likely. Another factor contributing to whether or not this approach is chosen is the young people's attitude toward violence. Insofar as they see violence as a legitimate means of power they are less likely to avoid a violent encounter.

The second type, avoiding certain sites, is a true strategy of avoidance. The young people told us about different parks and other places they did not go to because of bad experiences. Moreover, stories they were told or the (bad) reputation of a park influenced the mobility of girls and boys and served as a mechanism of (self-) exclusion. Incidents from their own experience or second-hand information on places are equally important to this avoidance strategy. However, it is more common among younger teenagers and girls to avoid parks and specific places. This fact illustrates that these groups tend to be excluded from the public space more often because of peer violence.

Third, young people prefer to be accompanied in public space. Many respondents reported that they had never gone for a walk or had played alone in the parks because of a possible attack. When they are accompanied by one or more friends then they have some supporters. Another way of mustering such support, commonly used by girls, is talking with friends on their mobile phones when they are walking home at night. Through the phone call they feel safer because there is somebody present who could call for help if something happens. Whereas girls reported that they ensured such support more typically at night, boys said that they never stayed out alone at all, fearing the possibility of violence at all times.

Roles of the Young People Involved

Different groups of participants in violent encounters can be identified. Apart from the *combatants* there are *supporting groups* to the combatants. The different roles are fluid and may change during the violent interaction, for instance when a supporter becomes a combatant. The supporting groups consist of a couple or more young people who are watching the brawl and ready to intervene if necessary. At minimum, they cheer for one of the combatants.

Usually the combatants in a simple violent encounter know one another but they are not close friends. More complex violent encounters are more likely to involve friends or schoolmates – on either side. Rather predictably, the relation of combatants and their supporting group is strong: they are usually either close friends or relatives. Among young people from minority ethnic backgrounds it is characteristic that family members such as siblings or cousins support each other. The data suggest that family ties play a more important role among minority ethnic youth. The closer the degree of kinship the more obligatory is the support. If the violent interaction is put off to a later point in time, there are often other friends and acquaintances among the supporting group too.

The severity of the violence meted out and its consequences are pivotal to the future relationship of combatants. If friends seriously injure another they are unlikely to remain friends afterwards. However, if there are no physiological injuries they presumably continue to be friends - apology and reconciliation are still possible.

Code of Conduct

There is a tacit knowledge among young people about a *fair conflict* which comprises a set of rules. Foremost, there have to be around the same number of combatants on each side of the conflict. One against one is the most common case. Though gang rivalries are not mentioned in the interviews an escalation of a violent encounter can lead to an expansion of the numbers involved. The supporting group is both a referee and a second to the combatants: they judge whether the violent interaction complies with the code of conduct and – if not – they intervene.

Additionally the code of conduct sets up *taboo groups* that are not acceptable targets for physically violent behaviour. Girls and younger individuals in particular belong to these groups. Therefore, conflicts arise mainly among young people of the same age. Younger ones are exempted because they are supposed to be weaker and have to be sheltered. The same goes for girls. Boys mainly use physical violence – except in the case of sexual harassment – against other boys. When girls interact violently they usually fight other girls. The data suggest that the taboo groups are more typical amongst *minority ethnic youth* because the idea of sheltering the young and women is more predominant within their cultures.

However, the analysis shows that these taboos do not exist with regard to verbal violence. Girls reported nevertheless that they do not verbally offend boys because they fear physically violent reactions. Such observations from the data point out the fact that there is a divergence between declared 'rules' and the actual behaviour of young people in conflicts. There are breaches of the code of conduct which supports the hypothesis that girls and boys, younger and older are bargaining for respect and shelter – and there is 'conditionality' on whether or not they receive it. If, for instance, girls align to traditional hierarchies and accept the superiority of boys they earn their shelter and protection. However, if young teenagers continuously offend older ones and do not show sufficient and expected respect to them, then eventually an escalation of the conflict takes place. Hence, conflicts can arise if the hierarchy according to age and gender is not honoured. Moreover this code of conduct secures a reproduction of social structures: young people that subordinate themselves to others who are older expect the same behaviour of younger ones when they themselves grow older.

The Journey of Violence

Violent encounters 'move' through public space and take place at different sites. One essential journey of violence can be found in the data: young people's violent interactions often start at school and eventually shift into more public space. This relocation is due to less social control in the parks and streets. If the girls and boys use physical violence in school they fear penalties from teachers. Additionally, there is a high probability that parents and the police will be informed about the incident. Thus, young people interrupt and delay a violent encounter in order to continue it beyond the school. This represents a relocation of the conflict both in space and time: the conflict is postponed but not abandoned. Such shifts mean that stronger regulations at school do not necessarily prevent violent experiences among peers, but simply cause a relocation to more unwatched and unsupervised places.

Displacement and Exclusion of Girls from Public Space

Girls do not spend as much time in the parks and streets as the boys do. When they described their leisure time activities there were not only pastimes to enjoy but also tasks to fulfil, such as baby sitting or food shopping. This finding shows that parents influence young people's use of, and capacity to use, public space considerably. Additionally, the data suggest that girls who attend a higher secondary school spend their afternoons more often at their own or their friends' homes and in organised free time activities like music lessons or sports clubs. Furthermore, the phenomenon of the displacement of girls from the public space is closely linked with the strategies of avoidance of violence. First, it is boys only who are occupying infrastructure meant for all young people in parks – one reason why teenage girls switch to children's playgrounds. Secondly, girls seek to avoid conflicts more often than boys. Female youth typically reported avoiding certain places or on leaving a place in case of conflict. Consequently both dynamics add up to an exclusion of girls from public space. Boys appropriate space more dominantly than girls, who give way easily. The tacit code of conduct that defines girls as an ineligible target of physical violence does not diminish the fear of being subjected to such violence, because if girls in any way undermine the predominance of boys the code of conduct ceases to apply.

Approaches towards Violence

The way young people respond to a prospective violent situation can range from avoidant to pro-active behaviour. How they act in a specific encounter depends, not least, on situational conditions (especially the number of friends they are with) as well as on psychological aspects. The narratives show that having a bad day or feeling stress can promote a more pro-active stance towards violent behaviour. Also young people in a group tend to get more actively involved in conflicts whereas young people being alone are more likely to rely on avoidance.

Some types of violent encounters seem to tie in with specific strategies. For instance in cases of robbery the interviewed victims always reported that they did not defend themselves but accepted the situation. In contrast, bravado in the peer group is characterised by a more pro-active approach toward violence: violent behaviour is seen as a legitimate means in order to enhance one's status.

Definitions and Interpretations of Violence and Crime

The *a priori* definition of violence constructed by this research project is quite *different* from the young people's comprehension. Typically the interviewees interpreted violence tightly: almost only physical forms of behaviour were referred to. We surmise that this gap is due to two factors: *age and education*. The data revealed that a *dynamic* view of the interpretation of violence is necessary as definitions alter with the age. Some of the interviewees reported that when they were younger they did not think of some types of behaviour as violent whereas they do now. As a result of this shift in perspective their behaviour has changed as well. Crucial for the change in mind was the awareness of causing hurt to others. Additionally, the data suggest that there are differences according to education. Teenagers in higher secondary school more often included any behaviour that causes hurt.

Girls' violence is not seen as serious as violence perpetrated by boys - from the boys' perspective. Boys act more as onlookers in girls' conflicts: they do not intervene, as supporters in other encounters sometimes do. It is more like an entertainment than a demonstration of allegiances. Apart from this, however, there were no other obvious gender differences in the meaning attached by young people to violence.

Depending on their own experiences, the meaning of violence varied: on the one hand, young people with experience of more frequent and severe violent encounters tended to have a narrow definition that included only – as the interviewees called it – "true violence", producing physical injuries and involving the use of weapons. On the other hand, girls and boys with less violent encounters interpreted a wide range of behaviour – including verbal actions – as offensive.

The interviewees sometimes mixed up the notion of violence and crime when they were asked for the meaning of violence: for instance, they referred to drug abuse and prostitution. Moreover, violence is seen as something criminal that you could be convicted for. Hence, some drew the conclusion that unless you could get sanctioned for the behaviour you have not exerted violence. Yet paradoxically, according to young people's own code of conduct, a breach of the rule of *fairness* is sometimes interpreted as violent. The tight connection to crime points out, however, that most young people perceive violence as something really negative and socially undesirable. Their own experiences, nevertheless, are not always classified by them as violent which may be interpreted as efforts to justify and rationalise, as well as cope with them. When they downplay their violent encounters it is easier to deal with it. Consequently, the young people's understanding of violence is characterised by its distinction from 'normal' behaviour: 'violent' in contrast to 'normal' behaviour is extraordinary and exceptional in its severity. Although the young people describe violence in contrast to normality the experience of violent behaviour among peers in everyday interactions is widespread.

6 Feedback and Consultation

Aside from the interest in understanding the violent encounters of young people, it was the aim of the study to get feedback on the research findings as well as to gather information how peer violence in public space may be avoided. Therefore the results of the qualitative analysis were presented and discussed in a workshop with young people and in a workshop with local experts. Both workshops took place in June 2008. In each workshop, the research team participated, guided the discussion and made notes. In addition, the workshops were recorded.

Young People: "There is nothing you can do about it."

Regarding the workshop with young people a local youth centre was chosen as the venue. A flyer was distributed and youth workers of different youth clubs in the chosen area were asked to promote the workshop and invite young people. However, the majority of teenagers were recruited spontaneously for the discussion. They were given movie tickets as an incentive. Finally, six adolescents aged 13 to 16 years (one boy, five girls) took part in the workshop. All of the participants had *minority ethnic backgrounds* and none of them had been interviewed for the initial fieldwork.

The workshop was structured as follows: the Daphne project was introduced and the main results – the models of violent encounters – were presented, in order to stimulate thinking and discussion of recommendations on preventive measures. Two questions were designed to produce a wide range of recommendations: first, what would you advise your friend, if she/he is involved in a violent encounter; and second, if you were a politician, what would you do to prevent violence among young people?

Interestingly, from the perspective of the young people in Urbanitz violence is an adequate and acceptable strategy of *communication*. As one girl from the neighbourhood said: "talking does not help, it does not change anything among us young people". However in the discussion they mentioned the dilemma of further escalation when violence is used to 'answer' an attack. If nothing else helps they suggested ignoring as the only possible way out. Summing up, the girls and boys emphasised that this rather frequent use of violence is tightly connected to teenage lifestyles and youth culture. They expect themselves to be calmer and more settled once they are older which implies that violent behaviour is not socially recognised anymore. Therefore, they define their own behaviour as transitory and see no need for prevention.

Almost all the young people who participated in the consultation expressed in general their *distrust* of preventive measures because they did not believe that conflict resolution was possible once a conflict had started. In their opinion violence is 'normal' and usually helps settling a conflict. The girls and boys mentioned different options for action when they are attacked. First they came up with the idea to call the police; however this is only possible when serious physical violence is used. Secondly girls and boys told about running away or ignoring provocation in order to avoid an escalation of the situation. Thirdly a course in self-defence may help to prepare for future conflicts. Apart from these three indirect strategies they accepted that there was often a need for direct involvement in violent conflicts in order to 'deal with' them.

Notwithstanding these perspectives, some concrete preventive measures were proposed by the young people that might deter them from violence or that address the source of conflicts. They suggested fines, video surveillance and a differentiated use of parks. Evidently young people would prefer a separation of age groups in the parks whereas city planners are keen to integrate different groups that use places in different ways. The young people stated that there are no facilities that are available specifically for 13-16 year olds – they have to choose between playgrounds for children and sports facilities which are mainly used by older groups. As a consequence they are often constrained in their activities. For this reason they suggest a *regulation* of the access to parks according to age and time of day, and that such provision is supervised by an adult. Ideally facilities for 13-16 year olds are built in parks so that each group has its own area.

Experts: Participation, Democracy and Empathy

The workshop with the experts took place at the Austrian Institute for Youth Research and was carried out after the workshop with the young people. The local experts were contacted personally and invited to the session. Six experts participated in the workshop: Among them were one youth worker, one street worker and one social worker, all of whom work in Urbanitz. Additionally, there was one police officer who is concerned with youth violence in the Vienna Police Department, one lawyer of the Vienna Children and Youth Advocacy and a city planner who works in a local counselling office. Three of the experts were women and three were men.

After a general presentation of the project, the data and findings were used as the basis for a discussion to develop recommendations and measures. The following questions were examined during the workshop: What resources do young people need in order to prevent or to cope with violent encounters among peers? In which policy areas do preventive measures have to be implemented? An open atmosphere facilitated the discussion of various problems and ideas.

In contrast with contemporary dramatic media coverage on youth violence the experts asserted unanimously that there have been few significant changes over the past decades. Young people are always confronted with the task of the adaptation of socially recognised norms and values, and this can lead to tensions and incongruities. However they acknowledged that offensive provocation which implies a pro-active approach toward violence is a more common phenomenon among young people nowadays.

The experts mentioned prominently that the lack of public space for young people is an important reason for aggression between peer groups. The inbound part of Urbanitz is characterised by little space that can be appropriated by young people. The advancing commodification and commercialisation of public space reinforces such problems: young people who usually have limited economic resources are restricted more often because consumption is made obligatory in ever more spaces available to them (such as shopping malls, cafes). The experts therefore suggested the provision of more youth cafes or youth clubs. Moreover, indoor sports facilities should be opened on weekend so that girls and boys can use them. However, though measures to increase young people's access to facilities were considered to be necessary, it was also important that young people are also provided with 'unstructured' space they can shape themselves. They need the freedom to explore and to experiment.

The negative media coverage in Austria of youth in general is perceived as particularly problematic. Firstly it fuels a labelling of young people as ever more violent despite empirical findings[5] that do not support this perspective. Moreover this campaigning against young people is partly responsible for their behaviour as it can produce a self-fulfilling prophecy in that young people feel the need to act aggressively. Therefore the experts called for a media coverage that is more balanced and does not only highlight bad news. It is necessary that media acknowledge their impact not only on the image of young people but their actual behaviour as well.

Furthermore, gender has to be considered in the prevention of violence. Up to now masculinity and femininity have not been sufficiently taken into account. The experts state that attitudes toward violence of girls and boys tie in with gender roles. However due to the ongoing change of gender roles in Austrian society, girls are more prone to engage in violent and criminal behaviour nowadays, which is true for native Austrian girls as well as for girls with a minority ethnic background. Therefore gender sensitive approaches in formal and non-formal education should provide more opportunities to better support young people in adolescence.

An important topic during the discussion was that of *traditional* sets of values that prevail among young people from *minority ethnic backgrounds and among socially disadvantaged young people*. According to the experts difference instead of equality is increasingly emphasised in societal discourses. The enhancement of specific rights and the particularity of single groups jeopardise democratic values and equality of people. As authoritarian and hierarchical structures are primarily conveyed in families violence prevention has to include parents. It is important to pass on values of emancipation, equality and democracy. This is challenging because youth and family workers have to establish a dialogue about those values without imposing them on others. Therefore it is not necessary to persuade young people by the means of good arguments but to enforce the capabilities of reflection and critique with the help of empathy.

The experts called for preventive measures that start as early as *in kindergarten*. Furthermore preventive measures need to be linked to each other. The experts saw a lack of coordinated work on prevention because of the limited resources allocated to this task. Many of the implemented projects are due to personal commitment of social workers, teachers and other professionals. Foremost in youth work more resources are needed to establish continuing relationships with young people that enable good support. Low threshold activity – notably street-based engagement – is especially important to prevent violence among young people. Additionally, training for teachers should be provided as they are often faced with violent behaviour amongst pupils. The experts suggested that the structural 'violence' (in the form of hierarchical authority) that is inherent in the Austrian educational system is a main source of school violence.

In their opinion a more participatory educational system may help to prevent violence. Apart from youth work and the educational system, social work with parents and families is necessary to decrease youth violence. Offers of parental and family work have to be more easily accessible in order to reach families with *low socio-economic status* and *from minority ethnic backgrounds.*

Summing up, both experts and young people did not recognise the alleged alarming increase in youth violence portrayed in contemporary media coverage. Nonetheless both groups, young people and experts, called for measures to prevent violent experiences among young people. However the suggestions differed significantly from each other. Young people favour strategies that produce and protect separation, and dedicated, supervised provision, and they are more likely to agree to *law and order* politics like control and surveillance. Experts place more emphasis on the development of *participatory* and democratic spaces for young people. Then supervision is not necessary to control young people; instead youth workers should try to establish relationships with young people. The discrepancy between these suggestions indicates that training in social and communication skills is important in order to empower young people to express their own interests and to cope with heterogeneous and differing interests in public space.

7 Some Final Reflections

In Austria, politics and social science currently do not focus on juvenile delinquency in general and youth violence in particular: they are neither focussed on in policies nor are they frequent research topics. The aim of this study is to provide empirical findings that encourage and enable an open and sound debate on the issue without exaggerating the problem.

The chosen disadvantaged area is a part of Vienna which is characterised by low socio-economic status and a densely built environment. Its residents are people whose trajectories and perspectives are deprived, many of them having a minority ethnic background. Therefore young people with a minority ethnic background comprise a large proportion of the sample of interviewees, not at least because it is mainly these young people that spend their leisure time in the parks and streets. Native young Austrians, who live in the area, do not equally use the public space and can be hardly encountered there. Nonetheless the interpretation of the data did not lead to the conclusion that most of the findings are specific for young immigrants and related to their minority ethnic background. It rather appears that the experiences of the interviewees are typical for young people with a low socioeconomic status. As could be shown in the analysis, the cultural background was mainly relevant with regard to gender roles as young male immigrants tend to be more conservative in this matter. Interestingly, despite the minority ethnic background of the interviewees, racism was hardly a characteristic of peer violence in the chosen area.

The neighbourhood impacts considerably on the everyday life of young people, both positively and negatively. The physical environment decisively influences the way young people communicate and interact with another. It grants them different scope for mobility and their use of public space varies according to age and gender. 13 and 14 year old boys and girls, being at the point of transition from childhood to youth, are particularly affected by the lack of appropriate space. There are built facilities for children and there is leisure infrastructure that is occupied by older teenage groups, but there are no specific provisions for girls and young people in the middle age range. They are too old for playgrounds, but too young and too weak to command space, sports fields or in sports provision within parks. Competing with the other groups their interests do not prevail and hence they are likely to be displaced from public space. Girls face this predicament for even longer because they are typically more restricted in mobility by their family.

In the study, several models of peer violence were detected: occupation of territory, bravado, affront to identity, peer support, revenge, protection, and powerlessness. These models are built on different intentions underlying decisions whether or not to use violence. Depending on the specific situation, young people act on a continuum from avoidance to active trouble seeking behaviour, aiming to find an appropriate strategy in dealing with everyday conflicts. In complex conflicts those involved may switch roles repeatedly, the roles of perpetrator and victim being intermingled and interdependent. The narratives of the young people further demonstrate that the perception and interpretation of a specific situation may not only be different but even contradictory between those involved, especially with regard to the initiation of a conflict. Sometimes conflicts seem to unravel without anybody actively having started them. Apart from the combatants themselves, more peripheral participants fulfil several roles: they support their friend(s), who are directly engaged in the conflict or may intervene if necessary.

Evidently there are gender differences in violent behaviour in Urbanitz. Boys are more likely to use violence to gain access to or control of resources. On the contrary it is typical of girls that peer violence occurs with regard to conflicts about friendships and relations. Furthermore, girls are more likely to resign or retreat from violent behaviour deliberately because of feeling powerless. Yet, not only girls but also younger individuals tend to use avoidant strategies to cope with peer violence. They mentioned eschewing certain places to 'not being bothered' whether or not they used them. Moreover they favoured spending their time in public space in the company of one or more friends, because of the support this provided if conflicts arose. Finally, peer violence is conceived as *transitory* by the young people themselves and also the findings indicate violent behaviour changes according to age.

Young people in Urbanitz also reported a movement of violence through space and time. Conflicts are postponed and dislocated mostly to avoid social control and possible penalties. Appointed conflicts take place in parks characteristically and the number participants who are present in those follow up encounters is usually bigger than when the violent encounter was first initiated. Moreover the data reveals that an escalation during violent encounters is not unlikely as violent behaviour triggers increased violence. Typically verbal or gesturing forms precede physical forms of offensive behaviour. In the course of escalation the seriousness in terms of violence used and consequences rises. However, the simple fear of an escalation may itself lead to an end of the conflict before any more serious confrontation in fact takes place.

After all, peer violence seems to be typical of *adolescent* use of public space in Urbanitz. To prevent peer violence in disadvantaged areas, it has to be taken into account that there is not one single category of 'youth'. Different ethnic backgrounds, living conditions and life courses are important structuring elements of everyday violent experiences among girls and boys. Preventive measures have to start with recognising those differences among young people. By the means of respect and dialogue it is particularly necessary to enhance the living conditions and perspectives of deprived young people through efficient and effective policies.

Notes

1 original: "Jugendliches Faustrecht", in: Die Presse, 26.04.2008
2 original: "Welle brutaler Jugendgewalt erfasst Wien", in: Österreich, 18.08. 2008
3 see http://www.wien.gv.at/stadtentwicklung/forschung/karten/images/ewdicht01.gif
4 Population figures for the area could be obtained through a special analysis of the population registry (Magistrat der Stadt Wien 2007).
5 Media coverage of youth crime and youth violence is usually based on statistics on vandalism, bodily harm or robbery. If more incidents are reported to the police the level in the statistics rises no matter if criminality actually increases (Kromer and Hatwagner 2008).

References

Atria, M., Strohmeier, D. and Spiel, C., (2005). Bullying und Viktimisierung: Jede Klasse ist anders [Bullying and victimisation: Each class is different]. *In:* Ittel, A. and Salisch, M.V., eds., *Lügen, Lästern, Leiden lassen. Aggressives Verhalten von Kindern und Jugendlichen.* Stuttgard: Kohlhammer, 204-236.

Beclin, K. and Grafl, C., (2000). Die aktuelle Entwicklung der Jugendkriminalität - Anlass zur Sorge? [Current trends in juvenile delinquency – cause for concern?]. *Österreichische Juristenzeitung 2000*, 821-832.

Akzente Salzburg and Salzburger Landesjugendbeirat, ed., (2007). *Gewalt und Konflikte. Impulse. Handbuch für Jugendarbeit. Band 3.* Salzburg: Akzente Salzburg.

Bundespolizeidirektion Wien, (2007). *Sonderauswertung der Kriminalstatistik 2006 [Special analysis of the Vienna criminal statistics 2000].* Vienna: Bundespolizeidirektion.

Császár, F., (1989). Rückfall nach Jugendstraftaten [Backslide after youth crime]. *In:* Melnizky, W. and Müller, O. F., eds., *Strafrecht, Strafprozessrecht und Kriminologie – Festschrift für Franz Pallin zum 80. Geburtstag.* Vienna: Manz.

Császár, F., (1985). Karrieren delinquenter Jugendlicher [Delinquent carriers of young people]. *In:* Bundesministerium für Justiz, ed. *Strafrechtliche Probleme der Gegenwart,* Vol 12., Vienna.

Császár, F., (1978). Kinder- und Jugendkriminalität in Wien [Children and youth crime in Vienna]. *Österreichische Juristenzeitung 1978,* 62-70.

Grafl, C., (2005). Sind ausländische Jugendliche krimineller als inländische? [Are foreign young people more delinquent than Austrian?] *In:* Bundesministerium für Justiz, ed. *Straftaten ausländischer Jugendlicher und junger Erwachsener.* Vienna, Graz: Neuer wissenschaftlicher Verlag, 9-31.

Grafl, C., (1995). Entscheidungsgrundlagen für strafrechtliche Reaktionen bei Jugendlichen – Eine empirische Untersuchung am Jugendgerichtshof Wien [Foundations of decision making of penal reactions of young people – an empirical study at the Youth Court Vienna]. *Monatsschrift für Kriminologie und Strafrechtsreform,* 1995, 69-83.

Graßberger, R., (1972). Die Jugendkriminalität der Gegenwart [Juvenile delinquency nowadays]. *Österreichische Juristenzeitung 1972,* 229-233.

Haller, B. and Stögner, K., (2004). *Gewalt gegen Kinder in der Schule [Violence against children in school].* Vienna: Institut für Konfliktforschung.

Karazman-Morawetz, I. and Steinert, H., (1995). *Schulische und außerschulische Gewalterfahrungen Jugendlicher im Generationenvergleich – Ergebnisse einer Repräsentativumfrage bei Jugendlichen, Erwachsenen und Lehrpersonen in Österreich [Young people's violent experiences inside and outside of school with regard to generation – results of a survey among young people, adults and teachers in Austria].* Vienna: Institut für Rechts- und Kriminalsoziologie.

Klicpera, C. and Gasteiger-Klicpera, B., (1996). Die Situation von „Tätern" und „Opfern" aggressiver Handlungen in der Schule [The situation of perpetrators and victims in school]. *Praxis der Kinderpsychologie und Kinderpsychiatrie,* 45, 2-9.

Kromer, I. and Hatwagner, K., (2008). *Wie kriminell ist unsere Jugend heute? Jugendkriminalität in Österreich – ein Seismograph für gesellschaftliche Entwicklungen [How delinquent are young people nowadays? Juvenile delinquency in Austria – a seismograph of societal trends].* Unpublished Report. Vienna: Bundesjugendvertretung.

Magistrat der Stadt Wien, (2007). *Sonderauswertung aus dem örtlichen Melderegister, Stand 31.12.2006 [Special analysis of the Vienna population registry].* Vienna: Magistrat der Stadt Wien.

Magistrat der Stadt Wien, (2006). *Statistisches Jahrbuch der Stadt Wien, Ausgabe 2006 [City of Vienna Statistical Yearbook, Issue 2006].* Vienna: Magistrat der Stadt Wien.

Pelinka, A. and König, I., (1993). *Jugendgruppen und Gewalt [Youth gangs and violence].* Vienna: Institut für Konfliktforschung.

Pilgram, A. and Rotter, M., (1981). *Jugendkriminologie in Österreich. Materialien zur Kriminalitätsentwicklung und -theorie [Youth criminology in Austria. Trends and theory].* Vienna: Ludwig Boltzmann Institut für Kriminalsoziologie.

Schindler, S., (1968). *Jugendkriminalität – Struktur und Trend in Österreich 1946-1965 [Juvenile delinquency – structure and trends in Austria 1946-1965].* Vienna: Österreichischer Bundesverlag.

Stangl, W., Hager, I., Kromer, I. and Stummvoll, G., (2006). *Jugenddelinquenz in Österreich. Ein Beitrag zur zweiten internationalen „Self-Report-Delinquency Study" [Juvenile Delinquency in Austria. The ISRD_2 study in Austria].* Vienna: Institut für Rechts- und Kriminalsoziologie und Österreichisches Institut für Jugendforschung.

Statistik Austria, (2007). *Statistisches Jahrbuch Österreichs. [Statistical Yearbook of Austria.]* Vienna: Komm.

Strauss, A., (1998). *Grundlagen qualitativer Sozialforschung: Datenanalyse und Theoriebildung in der empirischen soziologischen Forschung [Qualitative analysis for social scientists]*. München: Fink.

Strauss, A. and Corbin, J., (1996). *Grounded Theory: Grundlagen Qualitativer Sozialforschung [Basics of Qualitative Research: Grounded Theory Procedures and Techniques]*. Weinheim: Beltz.

Steinert, H., (1984). *Jugendkriminalität unter den Bedingungen einer anhaltenden Wirtschaftskrise. Disziplinierungsdruck, Ausbruchsversuche, Soziale Reaktion. [Juvenile delinquency during continuing economic crisis. Pressure to discipline, attempts to breakout, social reaction.]* In: *Kriminalsoziologische Bibliographie*, 43/44, 96-107.

Strübing, J., (2004). *Grounded Theory. Zur sozialtheoretischen und epistemologischen Fundierung des Verfahrens der empirisch begründeten Theoriebildung*. Wiesbaden: VS Verlag für Sozialwissenschaften.

Tumpel, M. and Edlinger, G., (1975). *Kriminalität in Wien – Jugendkriminalität in Stadtrandsiedlungen [Delinquency in Vienna – youth crime in periphery apartment blocks]*. Vienna: Ludwig Boltzmann Institut für Kriminalsoziologie.

Waldrauch, H. and Sohler, K., (2004). *Migrantenorganisationen in der Großstadt. Entstehung, Strukturen und Aktivitäten am Beispiel Wien [Immigrants' organisations in cities. Development, structures and activities at the example of Vienna]*. Frankfurt am Main, New York: Campus.

Waechter, N., Blum, J. and Scheibelhofer, P., (2009) *Social capital as key for successful school-work transitions? Analyzing migrant youths' trajectories and social networks*. In: Brooks, R., ed., *Transitions from Education to Work: New Perspectives from Europe and Beyond*. Basingstoke: Palgrave (in press).

Looking across the Localities: Commonalities and Differences in Peer Violence in Public Space

Jennifer Maher, Barbara Riepl, Johanna Blum, Helena Helve, Kadi Ilves, Ingrid Kromer, Veli Liikanen, Judit Strömpl, Howard Williamson

1 Introduction

The previous chapters presenting the locality studies suggested a number of situational and cultural *differences* in the context of the research undertaken, as well as some variation in the research methods adopted. This chapter presents a *combined portrait* of the empirical *cross-national* data collected in each of the research localities, using central themes to go some way to establishing a *general picture* of peer violence in public space across Europe. The possible impact of differences on the findings is identified below, followed by a more detailed comparative focus on the empirical findings.

Young people's experiences in Järvikaupunki and Trewaun vary from those in Perkova and Urbanitz in terms of the significant population differences reported in each site – with Urbanitz being the largest urban site and Järvikaupunki the smallest. Economically, young people in Trewaun and Järvikaupunki have experienced significant upheaval as a result of de-population and post-industrialisation. However, despite the relatively more *disadvantaged* economic profile of these regions in general, samples from both countries included young people from quite diverse socio-economic backgrounds. Essentially, the low population *density* supports hot spots of youth convergence, bringing together teenagers from different kinds of neighbourhoods and families. In contrast, the youth profiles in Perkova and Urbanitz portray almost exclusively young people of *low economic* status. Comparatively, the *uni-ethnic* and uni-cultural nature of Trewaun differed from the other three localities where both national and ethnic *diversity* affected the peer violence experienced by young people. The predominantly *immigrant* status of young people in Urbanitz is also noteworthy when trying to understand the prevalence and severity of peer violence.

However, although the *contexts* and research *methods* were to some extent different in each of the four localities studied, the findings emphasise that European young people's general experience of peer violence in public space is, in many though not all respects, strikingly *similar.*

2 Towards a Typology of Peer Violence in Public Space

One of the main aims of the study was to create a more solid basis for forthcoming *comparative* research on the issue. Therefore, a typology of general models of peer violence in public space should be developed, reflecting the initial research question:

What different types of violent interactions and engagement amongst 13 to 16 year olds can be commonly *found in public space in four studied localities?*

Following this question, peer violence has been divided on a number of levels in previous chapters in order to identify the different types of everyday violence experienced by young people. In the locality reports on Järvikaupunki and Trewaun the models focus primarily on dimensions such as *number* and *type* of participants in the violence. In the locality report on Perkova, however, the diverse models of violence were instead identified through characteristics, *interpretations* and meanings from their respondents' point of view and in the locality report on Urbanitz through the *motivations* reported by young people.

The models of peer violence presented in this chapter take this *diversity* of approaches into account. *Each* model is described on the basis of central dimensions, highlighting especially those that are specific for the model. The descriptions only refer to the findings in the interviews and do not provide any additional interpretation by the research team. This means that they use the depictions and interpretations of the young people in order to point out the *young people's perspective*, especially with regard to intentions and impact. For example, likely consequences of a specific violent encounter that were not mentioned in the interviews would also not be included in the model description.

The dimensions that were used to characterise the models are: type of behaviour, combatants, time, place, conditions, intentions and consequences. Reflecting on these dimensions, *nine types* of violent encounters were elaborated by the international research team, based on common discussions.

Though these nine types are based on the analysis and the models in the locality reports, it is important to mention that they nevertheless are not identical with models described in the locality reports. Therefore, references to models in the locality reports cannot be made as this would rather lead to misinterpretations than to better understanding. Yet, the typology listed below (see Figure 1) is not at all disconnected with the locality studies as it brings together all the different findings and puts them into a new structure.

Figure 1: Types of violent encounters and their occurence in the locality studies

	Järvikaupunki	Perkova	Trewaun	Urbanitz
Provocation, defence and revenge between individuals or small groups	x	x	x	x
Rivalries between larger groups	x	x	x	
Sanctions for breaches related to group norms		x	x	
Bullying and cyber-violence	x	x	x	
'Playful' violence between friends	x	x	x	
Sexual harassment from boys to girls	x		x	x
Girls' physical violence towards boys	x		x	
Boys' physical violence towards girls	x		x	x
Robbery and material acquisition				x

These general models can also be captured within three main categories:

- Group related models including: Rivalries between groups; Sanctions for breaches related to group norms; 'Playful' violence between friends;

- Individual related models including: Provocation, defence and revenge between individuals or small groups; Bullying; Robbery;

- Gender divided models including: Sexual harassment from boys to girls; Girls' physical violence towards boys; Boys' physical violence towards girls.

Provocation, Defence and Revenge between Individuals or Small Groups

Provocation, defence and revenge are closely connected. They represent one of the most commonly and frequently found models of peer violence in public space. Different expressions and roles of involved young people are very fluid and *flexible*. Sometimes it seems to be difficult to distinguish the *perpetrators* and the *victims* since young people, for example may already start to 'defend' themselves, even though a provocation may not yet have taken place; it was just anticipated. *Provocation* usually starts at a non-physical level with displays of superiority like innuendo, teasing, threats or insults, either verbally with yelling, name-calling and gossiping or with hand signs, looks and behaviour like laughter; in some cases it may also begin with low physical violence like pushing, shoving or taking something from someone. Violent encounters of this kind may end at that stage if the attacked person or group draws back. If unresolved at this point, a quick escalation is likely and the conflict may lead to more serious violent behaviour like punching, slapping, kicking and holding down.

The involved young people are typically young people who *know* each other but are not friends. Often they go to the *same* school or have some other common history. Violent encounters of this type usually take place *between individuals* or *small groups* when they happen to meet in the streets. Most often the clash will occur in front of friends or a crowd of peers who may become more involved during the fight.

All in all, the *offending* young people feel superior for different reasons: Typically they are *older* than the offended young people and, as mentioned above, often they are backed up by friends or a group. Of course 'displays of superiority' can also be part of racist violence when native young people offend young people with migrant background. As to the gender of the young people, most common are single sex conflicts: Boys to boys and girls to girls.

Provocation can happen any time during the day or evening when young people are out in public space. Regarding the frequency, single incidents were found as well as repeated offending by the same person/group in different situations. Places are also not specific but at hot spots of youth congregation the likeliness of these specific violent encounters is higher. With respect to the situational conditions it is evident that under the influence of alcohol provocation occurs more often and tends to become physical more quickly.

Basically, young people offending through displays of *superiority* view violence as a legitimate means to establish status and position. Often perpetrators explain that they did it for fun or because they dislike a person or just for no good reason. In other cases they refer to earlier insults or mention jealousy.

Concerning the impact, most victims report that they get annoyed but draw back if the superiority of the perpetrators is obvious. Sometimes, even when there is no self-defence, the conflict ends with broken belongings and physical hurt, ranging from minor harm like bruises to more severe injuries like bleeding and broken bones. The psychological hurt varies between a general feeling of having *lost face* to more concrete humiliation if specific aspects of an individual's character are ridiculed. As a consequence, victims usually try to prevent further confrontation with the perpetrators and therefore avoid places and situations where the conflict could be repeated. However, there are also victims who defend themselves right away or seek for revenge together with friends. Adults like police or parents are normally not involved. However, the young people also reported conflicts where police intervened and mediation was necessary afterwards.

Characteristics of *out-group provocation, defence and revenge* are:

- both non-physical and/or physical violent behaviour

- combatants usually know each other

- individual/small group to individual/small group

- mostly boys to boys and girls to girls

- to establish or defend status and position

Rivalries between Larger Groups

In most cases confrontational groups of young people have a well established *long-term* rivalry, established through conflicting interests in the neighbourhood or through different *sub-cultural* or *ethnic* backgrounds. In some cases the involved young people are *strangers* to each other. The rivalry is then usually based on the fact that one group in some way felt offended by the other, for example by entering the group's territory. Sometimes the 'rivalries between groups' are triggered by preceding conflicts of single group members.

Group rivalries may start and end with verbal provocation. This is not unlikely as young people usually remain anxious about the impact that a physical fight between groups can have. However, verbal insults and other non-physical provocative behaviour can escalate quickly to more *serious* physical violence like punching, kicking and stamping. At that stage the use of weapons such as knives or other objects that are available in the situation may exacerbate the conflict even further.

The size of groups in conflict with one another does, of course, vary: big fights between groups seem to take place rarely. They seem to be something that young people may have heard of but that they did not usually actively witness. Smaller group fights, involving only few young people, seem to be more common. Regarding the age, combatants in group rivalries are rarely 13 to 14 but *rather 15- 16 years old* (or older). However, if there are younger members in a group, they will also take part in fights. Though group rivalries often take place between young people from different ethnic backgrounds, this is not a rule. Yet, *racist* conflicts are quite common.

The main reasons for rivalries between groups were *defence* and *revenge*. If group members feel offended, insulted or provoked, they need to 'defend' the area (neighbourhood), specific facilities (such as a park), the group's honour (which could be the honour of an ethnic minority) or specific group members (especially girls). Sometimes current conflicts are the legacy of past ones: stories of previous encounters are handed down and, though older members of a group may leave, newcomers continue the same conflicts against the same opponents.

All in all, it is most likely that boys fight against boys and girls fight against girls, with group rivalries between boys being more common. Similar conflicts between girls tend to be rather non-physical or lower levels of physical violence are used. Mixed sex group fights were more likely in large group encounters but even then boys usually target boys and girls target girls. Whereas sometimes all the present group members are involved in the fighting, it is also quite common that only one young person from each group is fighting and the others are watching, ready to get involved if it seems necessary. During boy's same sex encounters girls may support them by acting as encourager, look-out, and weapon carrier - or at times have a more calming influence.

Rivalries between groups can take place any time and any place, wherever the different groups may encounter each other. *Weekends* and *evenings* (or later in the nights) seem to be quite typical times as alcohol consumption promotes the likeliness that group rivalries become physical. For the very rare serious fights though, which are usually arranged in advance, the involved young people tend to use darkness and remote places.

As to the impact of rivalries between groups, it was found that members of the inferior group may try to avoid being recognised as a member of that group in the future. Furthermore, they avoid places and occasions where they might meet members of the other group and especially the group as a whole. The physical hurt caused in group fights includes severe injuries like broken bones or noses and deep cuts. Larger group conflicts and more *severe* rivalries tend to produce adult involvement: Typically the *police* will be called and penalties of different kinds may follow (e.g. arrest, school exclusion or youth club ban). As a consequence, police presence may be increased in certain locations at certain times to enhance neighbourhood safety.

Characteristics of *rivalries between groups* are:

- both non-physical and/ or physical violent behaviour

- group to group, sometimes each group being represented by an individual

- mostly boys to boys and girls to girls, even in mixed sex groups

- rather 15 to 16 year olds

- to defend resources or seek for revenge

Sanctions for Breaches Related to Group Norms

Groups of young people often aim to sanction individuals or smaller groups (both within and beyond their own group) for perceived or invented transgressions of either established or only assumed group norms. These breaches or transgressions vary broadly: examples from the study include being *drunk*, being *homosexual* or being *an informant*. The sanctioning is usually a single intervention directly related to a specific incident. In the case of actual or perceived 'inappropriate' behaviour by people outside the group, individuals are 'punished' because their behaviour does not accommodate the approved norms of the group and is therefore seen as a provocation. Victims may be quite unaware that they are doing something that could be viewed as a provocation by a group to which they have absolutely no connection.

The violent behaviour towards the *victim* includes ignoring, ostracising, insulting, mocking, verbal threats, shoving, pushing, hitting, beating, kicking and using weapons. Though some of the conflicts already start with severe violence, 'sanctions' are likely to start verbally. If not ended at that stage, the conflict then develops quickly to severe physical violence. More serious situations with *excessive* violence seem to arise among older young people. Regarding gender and migration backgrounds, the data suggest that this kind of violence seems to be most typical for native boys, with young immigrants often the victims. Even though the entire group may be present in the conflict, it does not necessarily mean that all the young people are involved in the physical attack as they are sometimes just backing up one member who takes the lead. The places and times of sanctions of group norms do not seem to be very specific. However, the punishing of group members appears to be more calculated and tends to happen during evenings and in more hidden locations, whereas out-group conflicts are more situational and often reinforced by *alcohol*. Witnesses often do not dare to interfere in the group-on-one violence as they are afraid to become victims as well. The physical and psychological hurt from such sanctioning depends on the severity of the fight. However, the psychological harm inflicted seems to be more essential, both for the perpetrators as well as for the victim. In-group fighting can end with the affected young person permanently leaving the group.

Characteristics of *sanctions for breaches related to group norms* are:

- both non-physical and/ or physical violent behaviour

- in-group and out-group

- group to one/small group, sometimes one to one (with the group backing up the perpetrator)

- mostly boys to boys

- to 'punish' transgressions of group norms

- a single intervention directly related to a specific incident

Bullying and Cyber-violence

Bullying is characterised by the fact that an individual becomes a *victim* of mostly non-physical aggression which is exerted by another individual or a group. In some cases there may be two victims, usually friends that are addressed by the perpetrators. Even if there is only one individual proactively bullying, he or she is backed up by a group of other young people who observe the bullying and display interest and support for what is going on. In case the victim is an acquaintance and well-known (in most cases from school) to the perpetrators, bullying usually takes place repeatedly over a longer period of time. If the affected young person is a stranger who just became a victim by chance, the bullying is likely to remain a single incident. Friends of the victim may happen to be included in the bullying if they are present.

Typical behaviours in all studied localities are *verbal* insults, giving looks, slander, spreading rumours or innuendo. Physical offending is mostly taking away things and not giving them back or pushing, shoving and bumping into. Very rarely, more severe violence like 'happy slapping' may take place.

Different from all other types of peer violence in public space, this kind of violence uses *new media* to spread information, rumours and threats. For example, it is quite common to open an account on the *Internet*, where humiliating information is posted. Also *mobile phones* are used for that aim. In *'happy slapping'* the victim is beaten up, with the encounter being recorded and placed on the Internet or passed on via mobile phone.

Age and ethnicity do not seem to play a specific role in this type of violent encounters though it can be stated that older young people tend to be more critical about bullying. Regarding the *gender* of victim and perpetrators, it is obvious that boys usually bully boys and girls bully girls. However, there are a few examples of mixed sex bullying.

Besides the new media, there are no specific places or times for bullying. It is rather typical that bullying takes place anytime and everywhere the victim and the bullies cross paths. Alcohol or the availability of *weapons* do not seem to be of importance for this type of peer violence. Bullying is less based on conflicting interests than on an unequal power relation that allows offending the victim without fear of consequences. According to this, young people usually do not explain the bullying in terms of conflicting interests, defence and revenge but rather with the wish to fight *boredom* and *have fun*. They object to the way a particular individual behaves and 'lose patience' with them. Typical issues that are given as reasons for bullying are someone's dressing style, weight or mental and physical abilities.

Severe consequences for the victim are the *loss* of self-esteem and the constant fear of recurrence of the bullying. This can lead to the avoidance of places and people and in some cases to the involvement of adults. However, bullying in public space is generally rather invisible to adults.

Characteristics of *bullying* are:

- mostly non-physical with the exception of 'happy slapping'

- group to one or one to one (usually the perpetrator being backed up by a group)

- mostly boys to boys and girls to girls

- over a longer time period, except 'happy slapping' which usually affects the victim only once

- use of new media (Internet and mobile phones)

- to 'have fun'

- rather invisible to adults

'Playful' Violence between Friends

What is often defined as a 'play' between friends by young people themselves does not always mean fun for all of those involved. 'Playful' violence stands for *making fun* of someone, wrestling, shoving, pushing around, holding down and not too hard punches between friends. The intention is to establish or test the (informal) group hierarchy and to create solidarity. Often, the 'play' is also used to flirt and impress group members of the opposite sex. Whereas physical violence between boys and girls and among girls is uncommon in this context, it is routine especially between boys at the age of 13 to 14 years. Some girls explained that they would never tolerate physical violence from another girl.

Playful violence occurs between *two* friends only as well as in *bigger* groups of friends. Usually there are only two people involved, often with other friends both of same and opposite sex watching or cheering. At the same time, the group as a whole acts as mediator to ensure no one gets seriously hurt. Under the influence of *alcohol*, however, the 'play' is likely to become more rough and serious but weapons were not mentioned at all. Violent encounters of this kind are usually very short. Yet, they happen often and specifically in groups, almost any time and any place a group of friends gathers. The physical hurt of 'playful' violence is *not* severe though accidents may lead to bruising and cuts. And sometimes the conflict *escalates* into a *real fight* if the offended person gets too upset and irate. Most important, perhaps, is the psychological hurt experienced by the victim, which is often not sensed by the perpetrators.

Characteristics of *'playful' violence* are:

- both non-physical and/ or physical violent behaviour

- in-group

- one to one (with the group backing up the perpetrator)

- especially 13-to 14 year olds mostly boys to boys

- to establish or test the (informal) group hierarchy and to create solidarity

Sexual Harassment from Boys to Girls

Sexual harassment was not a big issue within the age group of 13 to 16 year olds. In most reported cases, older boys harass *younger girls* by staring at them in a sexually motivated way or with rude sexual *comment and innuendo*. Sometimes it may include groping which is usually harmless with regard to physical hurt but may cause psychological hurt because it is unwanted and ignores limits. If at all, physical sexual harassment takes place between younger ones and often is not recognised as such by the perpetrators – it rather seems to be a transitory behaviour aiming at testing social rules. Whereas non-physical sexual harassment seems to be more common between strangers, groping is rather an in-group behaviour. As to places and times of sexual harassment, these are not specific though it seems to be more likely during the evenings. The number of individuals involved in the sexual harassment varies: there are cases of one boy to one girl, a small group of boys to one girl or a small group of boys to a small group of girls. Sexual harassment does not usually affect girls with a *Muslim* background. However, if these girls are being harassed, intended or not, this may lead to the physical defence of these girls by their boyfriend or relatives like brothers and cousins. All in all, sexual harassment is seen as an *unpleasant* experience by the affected girls that they sometimes talk about with friends afterwards. It may lead to *discomfort* and *fear* of being alone in public space at evenings and girls learn to avoid such situations.

Characteristics of *sexual harassment from boys to girls* are:

- mostly non-physical

- both in-group and out-group

- one to one/small group to one/small group to small group

- boys to girls

Girls' Physical Violence towards Boys

The specific violence from girls towards boys is characterised by physical behaviour like a single *slap* in the face or a *kick* to the balls. Biting, scratching and sometimes punches were also mentioned. Typically it is only a short and single intervention, mostly in answer to a preceding rude or inappropriate behaviour from the affected boy or 'just for fun'. Just like the physical sexual harassment from boys to girls, it seems to be more common *between the 13 to 14 year olds*, than between the 15 to 16 year olds. In some cases, the violent behaviour of the girl is directly connected to sexual harassment from boys within a mixed sex group. In some places, girls' violence towards boys is considered to be quite *'normal'* behaviour from both girls and boys and frequently takes place. However, girls use such physical violence towards *boys* only if there is no serious conflict and if they can be sure that the boy will not defend himself. Though violence of this kind usually does not cause any injuries, it does hurt physically. Affected boys therefore may get annoyed but, as mentioned before, do not fight back because this would be considered *unfair.*

Characteristics of *girls' physical violence towards boys* are:

- physical

- mostly in-group

- one to one

- girls to boys

- short and single intervention

- responding to preceding rude or inappropriate behaviour

Boys' Physical Violence towards Girls

Physical violence from an individual boy towards an individual girl seems to be very *uncommon* in public space. If a boy attacks a girl in public space, the conflict is usually very severe, and so is the violent behaviour. It may range from threats of physical violence to hitting, slapping, beating up and can even include the use of a (blunt) weapon. The involved boy and girl are usually in a relationship or are relatives. As to the age, it seems that this kind of violence is more likely the older the boys are. Though it is quite common that violence within a relationship is not restricted to a single incident, it is usually *not showing up in public space* but rather in more *hidden private places*. So even if it is prolonged and repeated, it may seem to be sudden and simple in public space. Specific *situational* conditions like the consumption of *alcohol* can influence the severity and the place of the violent behaviour. The trigger for a boy's violent behaviour towards his girlfriend or a close relative is a disagreement in which the boy does not manage to control his anger. The consequences of boys' violent behaviour towards girls are quite severe. Besides bruises and bleeding, the affected girls need to cope with psychological hurt and the fear of repeat, particularly when they do not intend to 'split' from the male perpetrator or, if they plan to, fail to do so. In some cases, family or friends become involved which may on the one hand stop the victimisation, but on the other hand the conflict sometimes becomes even more violent. Despite the severe consequences, there is usually no involvement of police or social workers.

Characteristics of *boys' physical violence towards girls in close relationships* are:

- physical

- one to one

- boys to girls

- boy and girl usually have a relationship or are relatives

- during a conflict

- less evident and more concealed in public space

Robbery and Material Acquisition

A small group of young people encounters another young person they do not know, sometimes after they have tracked them for a while. The prospective victim may be *asked for the time* in order to find out more about their mobile phone or other belongings. If it seems to be worth it, the young person is held by the perpetrators, threatened and asked to hand over everything they are carrying: mobile phone, mp3-player or money. The threatening can be either verbal or also with a weapon like a knife. Once victims have handed everything over, the group just lets them go. The robbed young people do not defend themselves in order not to be hurt.

Age and ethnicity of the perpetrators and victims do not play a role in this type of peer violence. As to *gender,* only *boys* were reported to rob boys. Sometimes two friends both become victims if they walk along together. The robbery takes only a very short time and is most likely to occur in streets and parks with not many adults around. The consequences of the robbery are the loss of property as well as the fear of becoming a victim again. However, reporting the incident to the police does not seem to be common.

Characteristics of *robbery* are:

- physical violent behaviour

- perpetrators and victims do not know each other

- group to one/two

- boys to boys

- a single encounter

Concluding Remarks

Some models include all types of the peer violence identified in the study, but not all types were found everywhere. In other localities some specific models might have been found. *Group related* models of violent encounters appeared to be the most 'popular' and attractive among teenagers: having their own group and acting within it, being defended and supported by it. Such peer group affiliation may, for many reasons, be very significant for young people at this age – in marking youthful independence, self-determined norms (hence the punitive stance towards those who 'break the rules') and collective solidarity. In comparison, more *individual* models are rather more 'messy', in terms of their style, structure, origins and consequences. Finally, *gender derived* models look less socially 'desirable' in the eyes of peers interviewed for this particular study.

3 The General Characteristics of Violent Encounters

The *key* similarities and differences described below offer a *general* picture of peer violence and assist a deeper understanding of the issues. The findings presented are a response to the following *research questions*: How do young people describe violent encounters? How do they experience and interpret these violent encounters? What is the impact of direct or indirect involvement in these violent encounters? In which ways do gender and ethnicity mediate experiences and understanding of such violent encounters?

Definitions of Violence by the Young People

Definitions of violence vary greatly between young people of different ages, gender and ethnic backgrounds, and yet a common understanding of violence is evident across the localities. All young people made a distinction between non-physical and physical violence, playful and non-playful violence and boy(s) and girl(s) violence. When defining violence, emphasis was first placed on *serious* physical forms –such as murder, rape and gun crime. This type of violence was considered to be 'real' violence. Additional emphasis was placed by some young people on the outcome (physical harm), the number of combatants and the presence of weapons in defining an encounter as 'real' violence. However, as young people began to discuss their experiences and interpretations of violence, reports of non-physical and low-level physical violence accounted for a large proportion of their experiences of violence. The emotional and psychological effects of this 'lesser' violence was also evident in each site. Girls, for example, were most likely to identify verbal abuse as violence and were more fearful of being a victim of this type of violence.

Both boys' and girls' *soft* physical or non-physical (usually in-group) violence was often defined as *play* or *'fun'*. Young people in each locality emphasised a difference between non-playful (real) and playful violent encounters – which were generally defined by the non-hostile nature and non-malicious intent. This was in contrast to the serious intent associated with more physical forms of 'real' violence. A notable exception to this divide is girls' violence towards boys, which was not considered real violence whatever the nature of intent and behaviour. That said, Järvikaupunki boys clearly had less tolerance for violence initiated by girls – as they were most likely to complain about this type of violence.

The types of physical and non-physical violence experienced by boys and girls were similar – including verbal insults to punching, stamping and, very rarely (it is important to stress), weapon use. Yet the differences in severity and prevalence of violence reported by boys and girls made *gender* a noteworthy divide. While girls were likely to define boy's behaviour (including some boy-on-boy 'play' violence) as violent, boys failed to define most girl-on-girl encounters as violence.

Overall, it appears that non-physical and low-level physical violence is so 'ordinary' and routine that young people were hesitant to define it as 'real' violence. Also, as noted by young people in Trewaun, the adult violence witnessed on quite a regular basis (which was often serious) is often the measure against which they define their own violence. Although, initially, there was a *contrast* between young people's definition of violence and that proposed by the study (due to young people's focus on 'real' violence), it is now evident from the locality studies that *non-physical* and *low-level physical* conflict is the most prevalent and everyday type of violence experienced by young people.

Some young people reported some *positive* impacts of violence as a result of the ending and resolution of conflicts. They suggested that there were also some psychological 'benefits' in resorting to violence, such as increased excitement replacing depressive moods, the end of bullying and intimidation leading to an appreciation of ex-enemies or finding new friends, greater respect from peers and an enhanced reputation). However, the perceived and alleged positive aspects of peer violence in public space requires rather more exploration and elaboration.

Different Participants in Violent Encounters

Young people categorised encounters according to the type and number of young people involved: male or female, individual or collective, in-group or out-group and central or peripheral participants. As explained above, a gender divide was usual in all localities, with single sex – especially boy-on-boy encounters being the most prevalent. One-on-one and group collective encounters were most commonly reported, with group-on-one being the least common - or acceptable. The relationship between participants was central to identifying the type of violent encounter. *Most commonly* young people described the severity and intention of *in-group* violence as different from *out-group* violence. In Urbanitz, out-group violence was mainly targeted at gaining and defending resources (e.g. facilities or territory). Violent encounters among friends were usually less severe and typically aimed at 'saving face'. In Perkova, similar reports of in-group violence were made, with the exception of punishment for 'extreme' deviation from the group norms (e.g. *homosexuality*). Young people reported different types of out-group rivalries, specific to: *area* (Trewaun, Urbanitz, Perkova); *ethnic* group (Urbanitz, Järvikaupunki) or *sub-cultural* affiliation (Trewaun, Perkova). In Järvikaupunki, while there were indications of ethnic rivalries, most encounters related to *personal* histories (e.g. badmouthing) or random encounters with strangers. The identification of specific groups as *'gangs'* was specific to young people from Trewaun and Perkova. Where mentioned, encounters with random strangers usually involved the most serious types of violence (e.g. 'happy slapping' and other unprovoked attacks in Trewaun).

During conflicts both *central* and *peripheral* participants were reported. Central participants were those involved in the actual encounter. Peripheral participants were witness to or played a secondary role: they included, for example, family, friends, peers or other adults in the roles of spectator, supporter, guard, referee, instigator and mediator (if necessary). Central and peripheral roles were often identified as dynamic, especially in collective encounters. For example, in collective violence young people may move from being spectators to central combatants and vice-versa. In Järvikaupunki and Urbanitz, these roles appeared more static - interviewees reported changing roles from spectator to combatant, but very rarely the other way around. Many girls reported distancing themselves from boys-on-boy combat and/or trying to intervene by calling for help (phoning friends, family or the police - with the exception of Perkova girls). In Trewaun, girls were more likely to try to physically stop their boyfriends from fighting or to seek help for them by informing other group members of the encounter.

Dynamics of Peer Violence through Places and Time

Peer violence in public space most often took place in locations and at times that were most likely to be devoid of adult and social controls (e.g. parks, dark lanes, city centre streets during the weekend and evenings). Both poor weather and daylight reduced the frequency and severity of peer violence – with significantly fewer encounters during the winter months when compared to summer months. Hot spots of peer violence were often locations where large numbers of young people congregated or isolated areas specifically chosen for organised violence. In Järvikaupunki, the *marketplace*, sports fields and parks in the town centre were prime areas for serious conflict between native boys, mainly during weekend evenings and nights. It is, however, worth noting that these encounters were often witnessed rather than participated in by the young people interviewed.

Low-level and *playful* violence was more likely to take place in or near schools, youth centres and playgrounds. Conflicts involving immigrant teenagers and between girls were more varied in timing and location. In Urbanitz, *parks,* during the afternoon and evening, were the main setting of peer violence; these were the most unsupervised settings within the urban context. Violence between Trewaun boys often took place in *isolated* areas (such as dark side streets, parks and sports facilities), while girls' encounters were often more public (outside youth clubs, shops and schools). Collective encounters were more likely to take place in more isolated remote areas (planned) or very late at night in the city centre (unplanned). Young people in Perkova were more likely to ignore each other and avoid locations where they might meet rival groups, resulting in less public fighting between large groups. Verbal attacks were most likely to characterise large rival group encounters. Small spontaneous rival fights were more common and occurred in various locations (including the city centre).

Young people generally portrayed a dynamic *movement* of peer violence through *space*. Schools were routinely identified as key settings for everyday peer violence by young people and both schools and youth clubs were linked to violence in public space. Conflicts that began indoors were often continued outside, and relationships established in these places were used to organise encounters (away from adult supervision). In Perkova, most reported conflicts were connected with school relationships. School bullying (verbal or non-verbal) could develop into a physical encounter elsewhere (e.g. parks, yards, empty buildings or on their way home from school). And girls especially used the Internet to continue bullying. The dynamic journey and escalation of violence (especially among native boys) from less public spaces to the hot spots where young people gathered in town centres - during peak hours at weekends and during the *evenings* - was apparent in both Urbanitz and Trewaun. Additionally certain locations were identified as arenas for the organised physical resolution of simmering conflicts.

The actual *length* of an encounter depended on the type of violence and participants – collective organised fights took the longest time (up to an hour) and were *repetitive* (over a number of years), female non-physical encounter were usually repetitive, but of shorter duration, while physical (especially female) one-on-one encounters were the shortest. Girls' violent experiences were often repetitive - escalating over time, whereas boys' violent interactions were typically one-off conflicts. Both simple (*one-off, short*) conflicts and complex (*prolonged, repetitive*) encounters characterised all four localities. In Trewaun, the site location facilitated both types. Due to the small population size, it was easy to spread gossip, but difficult to avoid peers, thereby making more complex encounters more probable. Yet, conversely, the *confined space* in which peer mobility took place also inhibited the escalation of female physical violence, as girls were afraid of losing friendships or being ostracised by local groups.

Situational Conditions: Alcohol and Weapon Use

The excessive consumption of *alcohol* was strongly linked to peer violence in Perkova and Trewaun, especially at night and on weekends. In Trewaun, boys reportedly drank a specific brand of strong alcohol (lager) to prepare themselves for conflict (reference to the brand itself was associated with being very drunk and ready for violence). Trewaun girls were less likely to 'prepare' for conflict, but were evidently more argumentative and prone to engage in verbal and physical violence under the influence. Likewise, alcohol consumption was central to Perkova youth culture. For boys, alcohol was a crucial influence in physical violence, but not so for the girls.

In addition to consuming alcohol to prepare for violence, *intoxicated* young people were more likely to lose control of their behaviour and overstep group norms (e. g. make stupid remarks to peers, react aggressively to a joke or provoke aggression among friends). In Järvikaupunki, alcohol use was linked with physical encounters between boys rather than girls. Alcohol often influenced boys' conflicts as it reportedly affected the combatants' judgement. In Urbanitz, however, alcohol consumption did not play a role in violent encounters. This was due mainly to both the high number of immigrant young people in the sample, whose faith prohibited alcohol consumption and the locality in focus which was mainly a residential area and lacked social facilities such as pubs or nightclubs. Access to alcohol was readily available to young people in Perkova and Trewaun - purchased by themselves, older friends or family from shops and large supermarkets (which, in Trewaun, have been publicly criticised for the sale of very cheap alcohol).

Weapon ownership was reported in all localities. Weapon *use*, although very uncommon, was nevertheless a feature of Trewaun and Perkova peer violence. In all localities, however, it is important to register that interviewees were often reporting on friends' experiences or hearsay, rather than their direct experiences. The weapons used were more likely to be found during an encounter (e.g. bricks, bins) rather than carried into it. During organised group conflict, weapons (e.g. bats, bottles, sticks, knives and other blunt objects) were more likely to be brought for the purpose of the fight. Weapon use was largely the prerogative of boys. In Urbanitz and Järvikaupunki, a few examples of the use of prepared and found weapons (e.g. knuckle-duster, belt, helmet) were mentioned. The young people in every site perceived weapon use during combat as exceptionally violent. Encounters involving weapon use received special attention and significance by young people in all localities.

Use of Contemporary Media: Fun, Buzz, Revenge or Status

Contemporary violence reported in the research sites largely involved the use of the *Internet* (email and chat rooms) and *mobile phones* (texting and calls). Young people used technology to organise violent encounters and/or to engage in non-physical bullying. In Perkova and Trewaun the use of Internet chat rooms to bully peers was clearly in evidence, though specific to girls. Internet bullying usually took the form of nasty commentaries in web communities. Perkova girls focused on appearance by placing deformed pictures of the victim anonymously on a site. This type of bullying was recognised as particularly 'dirty' and resulting in deep emotional upset for victims.

Mobile phones were used to text insults and bully peers, in addition to more serious violence such as organising group fights (Perkova, Trewaun) and *'happy slapping'* (Trewaun). These types of encounter – especially 'happy slapping' were often motivated by the desire for fun, buzz, revenge or status. In Järvikaupunki and Urbanitz, there were few reports of modern media being used in violence, despite extensive use of mobile phones and the Internet.

Escalation of Violence

Young people regularly reported the escalation of violence during violent encounters. One of the most common consequences of violence was yet *more* violence. This is particularly true in terms of out-group and collective conflict. The escalation of violence predictably produces the escalation of seriousness in terms of the violence used and its consequences. Violent encounters rarely began with serious violence. The most common violent encounters were low-level non-physical violence, yet within an encounter verbal violence may escalate to more abusive verbal violence, followed by low-level physical violence or scuffles. Escalation was informed by the intentions of the combatants and their supporters, in what could be likened to a game of chess – each move producing a counter move until one side succeeds in stopping, stalling or repelling the opponent. It is important to note that violence can also de-escalate and diminish over time. For example, Trewaun young people mentioned that during the build up to a large organised rival fight, emotions could de-escalate (if it took too long to organise), which resulted in the encounter being abandoned.

Rules and 'Fairness'

Young people in each site identified with rules and an implicit code of conduct when participating in certain types of violence. A clear distinction was made (except in Järvikaupunki) between 'a fair fight' and 'a bad fight'. A fair fight consisted of a violent encounter where participants were equal – in terms of the number, age, gender, fighting ability and organisation of the fight. For example, in Trewaun a group on one person, an older on a younger person, a boy on a girl, a large strong boy on a weak boy, and the use of certain weapons or the use of a weapon in a previously organised non-weapon fight were all considered 'unfair'. The 'reasonable' (non-excessive) use of force was also an important condition of 'fairness'. Fair fights were most often seen in individual encounters or organised group encounters. *Unfair* encounters reported most often in out-group situations were identified as 'ugly', 'crazy' or simply 'out of line'. The general principle that "men do not hit children [e.g. young members] and women" (cited in Perkova) was upheld in the other locations. Thus, neither girls nor the youngest were targets of 'real' boys' violence. That said, girls may fall into one of two categories: 'bad girls' who fight with boys and 'good girls' who do not fight with anyone - this rule may only apply to the latter when they accept the hierarchy and respect of the boys in exchange for defence and protection. In this respect, peer violence creates and stabilises social and gender structures.

The importance of having a *fair fight* is largely ingrained in the motivation for the fight; the need to enhance masculinity and status, establish a reputation and control. It is difficult to establish status or masculinity otherwise. In fact, it can be favourable to have the odds against you - victory; in the face of a bigger enemy, was the basis (whether true or otherwise!) of many boys' accounts of celebratory serious violence. On the other hand, violence that was not triggered by questions of personal status and was motivated by revenge, self-defence or robbery had little regard for fairness.

When defending oneself or a friend, rules on fair play were seldom adhered to (with the exception, perhaps, of boys hitting girls). *Defence* often involves a collective encounter as friends are drawn into the conflict, and the type of violence used (both physical and non-physical) is usually more serious. The use of weapons was largely avoided except in the case of self-defence. In most localities (except Trewaun) group support was cited as very important, yet young people supporting a friend rarely engaged in physical encounters. Defending a friend in non-physical conflicts was a more common personal experience.

Reasons for Involvement

Young people consistently reported similar reasons for violent encounters, such as the existence of a *previous* history between young people or groups, and feelings of being provoked or pressured into playing a violent role. In Urbanitz, for example, provocation often involved insults, unfair play in sports or gossiping. In Perkova reaction to insults was a traditional motive for violence, which could result in defending a group member, the group norms and values or some ideology. Both girls and boys described becoming violent as a result of a *look, noise* (whistle) or *physical gesture* made towards their partner by a member of the same sex. Jealousy over resources (e.g. girls or use of certain facilities) accounted for a good deal of the boy-on-boy and girl-on-girl violence experienced by young people in Urbanitz and Trewaun. Commonly, young people feel they are a 'victim' defending themselves or their group, not the violent instigator. It is not, however quite so simple: some of the most 'active' violent individuals in Trewaun argued that they never looked for violence, but only defended themselves against other young people. Essentially, their definition of self-defence and provocation was egocentric and extreme (a quick reaction to any perceived affront).

'Fun', or the alleviation of boredom, was also identified as a reason for violence among some young people. The perpetrators of violence and their peripheral supporters often held the perspective that certain violence was only 'fun'; a view not necessarily shared by their victim. These young people failed to recognise the harm this behaviour caused to the victims. In contrast, victims often failed to understand the 'fun' intended, instead emphasising the harm caused. The random and spontaneous 'happy slapping' identified in Trewaun is an extreme but crisp example of this contrasting and conflicting perspective among young people. In Järvikaupunki and Urbanitz 'buzz' or 'excitement' were seldom reported as reasons for physical violence. In contrast, in-group violence was often referred to by both the victim and perpetrator as 'fun' or play fighting. As friends mediated the encounters, boundaries and limitations were adhered to (most of the time) and the behaviour was deemed to be harmless. Although inflicting harm for fun was not socially desirable among most young people, especially friends, these violent encounters could still escalate (demarcated by causing hurt) which resulted in the original reason - fun' – transforming into something else. For example, Perkova interviewees identified the need to establish hierarchical relations inside the group as the reason for violent group fun. This introduced a further issue: *why do young people become violent* (e.g. provoked) and what do they intend to achieve from their violent behaviour (e.g. revenge or to enhance reputation in and outside their group)? The rationales lying behind very similar violent acts can be very different.

Intentions and Motivations

Young people reported a similar range of intentions underpinning peer violence. Self-defence, group defence, control, enhanced identity and status, retaliation for disrespect or verbal abuse, revenge, protection and the desire for fun or buzz were the dominant motivations expressed in the each site. Control is a good example of a common intention; it could involve dominating younger groups or group members or gaining control of a location or facility. In Trewaun and Perkova, control was also seen as a motivation for both in-group and out-group violence. The fact that 'gangs' were located in these localities maybe linked to this need to establish control. In Urbanitz defending or gaining control was a motivation for out-group violence only. The *absence* of the intention to control in Järvikaupunki could arguably be linked to the loose structure of groups (perhaps due to the low and fragmented youth population) and the lack of competition for public space (due to an abundance of public space).

Violence for *financial* gain was recorded in Urbanitz alone. The absence of financial motives in other localities may be the result of under-reporting due to varying definitions of violence and reasoning for violence. Many young people portrayed their violence as *moralistic* (to defend something) rather than *predatory* (for revenge or to actively gain something).

The classification is used *loosely* here; based on young people's explanations and interpretations of the violent encounter and personal approaches to violence (proactive, active, reactive, de-active). It is important to note that any *true* classification of intent or motivation is difficult as young people often justify their behaviour with hindsight, using classical criminological 'vocabularies of motive' and 'techniques of neutralisation', as they lack the insight or honesty necessary to identify the 'true' or *deeper* intentions that lie behind their violent behaviour (see next section).

Justifications and Interpretations

It is noticeable that the reasons and intentions reported may be not consistent with the *original* reasons and intentions – *self-defence* is a good example of this. When some young people spoke about self-defence, they described a sequence of events leading to and during the encounter that appeared to be proactive, retaliatory, or status enhancing. For example, it was commonly reported in Perkova that young people used physical violence 'in defence' against an arrogant person or a verbal insult. Equally, carrying a weapon was justified as self-defence, though it is more likely a proactive, aggressive strategy in at least some cases, especially in areas where weapon use is not commonplace.

The approach taken by a young person to *justify* violence is closely linked to the personal approaches to violence already identified. Some of the regularly violent boys in Trewaun who described actively seeking or happily engaging in violent conflicts resisted the need to justify their violence: it was simply what had to be done. Other active personalities tied violence to 'losing patience over insults' and 'setting things straight'. However, the most common approach reported by young people was the reactive approach. This is integrally linked to the recurrent reports of self-defence on the part of young people. Girls or younger boys most often articulated a deactive approach. As discussed above, this is often more complex than taking young people's reports at face value (e.g. *'just for fun'* violence may be active, while punishment violence may be pro-active). The findings suggest that the personal approaches are dynamic. Depending on the characteristics of the violent encounter – such as the type of violence, the number and gender of young people involved and internal conditions (e.g. personal mood or intent) – different strategies are adopted.

The interpretation of violence may also be dependant on the *position* (victim, perpetrator or witness) of the *narrator* and the *form* of interview. Young people *individually* interviewed were more able to explain their experiences as victims, which contrasted with the absence of personal victimisation reported during group interviews. Perkova *perpetrators* (like their Trewaun peers) often presented themselves as *defenders* of the group, norms and values. This included cleansing the neighbourhood of outsiders or drunken people and defending those perceived as weaker and needing protection. When violence moved beyond acceptable boundaries, the 'blame' (or justification) often focused on alcohol consumption. Ironically, Perkova young people were very critical toward drunken people, both outside and inside their friendship groups.

Avoidance

A number of avoidance *techniques* were identified in the different localities. Girls and boys reportedly avoided violence escalation by *ignoring* provocation and avoiding certain locations or being alone in public space. This impact represents a form of (deactive) *coping* with the further consequences of experienced violence or the *anticipation* of prospective violence. In Urbanitz the avoidance of certain public sites results in the exclusion of specific groups – especially girls - from public space. Boys, in contrast, tried to ensure they were with peers when in public space, to avoid being targeted by unknown teenagers. In other localities (Trewaun, Perkova) young people identified territory (e.g. bus station, park, steps) that was de facto allotted to certain groups – meaning that other groups avoided these places, especially at certain times of the day, so as not to provoke an encounter. These avoidance strategies were not always informed by personal experiences of violent encounters with the said groups. Instead, hearsay and local mythologies largely informed young people's understanding, interpretations and manoeuvring around peer violence.

Harm and Hurt

The direct *consequence* of peer violence was psychological and/or physiological hurt. Young people discussed feeling fear, anxiety, paranoia, anger, and helplessness, in addition to experiencing bruises, concussion, bloodied noses, and fractures. *Boys* were more hesitant than girls in identifying hurt or harm, especial non-physical harm. This may explain why reports emphasised the non-physical: largely *emotional* hurt – such as losing friendship or feeling fearful in public space. In Järvikaupunki, older interviewees, especially boys, reported physical consequences more often than the younger boys or girls. The same applied generally to the report of psychological consequences – which is consistent with their differing levels of violent engagements. Perkova young people were more afraid of psychological violence, as it caused deeper prolonged hurt.

Young people generally suggested physical hurt to be less serious when compared with the psychological trauma sustained. Across the research localities, few *serious* injuries were recorded resulting from peer violence. This may be surprising given the range and sometimes severity of violent encounters reported. Many of the accounts of serious physical injury happened to acquaintances of respondents rather than respondents themselves. Although serious group fights were reported, albeit rarely, some girls suggested this violence did not have a significant impact on the combatants.

Sanctions and Penalties

Young people seldom experienced serious sanctions or penalties, though there were some interventions made by friends, parents, teachers or police officers. For example, Urbanitz girls and boys mentioned temporary 'house arrest' by *parents,* suspension from *school*, and fines and criminal convictions meted out by the *police* and *the courts*. Girls largely reported receiving penalties and sanctions regarding violent behaviour, whereas boys did not. Perkova young people's accounts were characterised by a complete absence of adult penalties and sanctions, with no mention at all of positive adult intervention in peer violence encounters. The presence of the police and other adults nevertheless tended to hinder, for a number of reasons, young people's capacity and opportunity to use violence in public space. As a result, young people reported strategies for avoiding prospective penalties (e.g. arrest, detention, expulsion) by engaging in violence away from adults in their community.

Peer *sanctions* were most often referred to by Trewaun interviewees. The *loss* of friendship was commonly reported by girls, and occasionally by boys. This links to the casual attitude many of the boys had to engaging in violence. In-group violence, although motivated by friendship, attraction or fun, rather than malice, was reported to result occasionally in significant harm. Young people reported negative outcomes in terms of (accidental) physical and emotional injury and the break-up of friendships, when the violence overstepped the boundaries of friendship (often due to excessive alcohol use). The loss of friendship among boys was most likely when serious physical or deep 'personal' hurt was caused. Boys were more likely than girls to report a favourable outcome to an encounter or an escalation in violence (exacting revenge or settling a score).

Concluding Remarks

This section on general characteristics of peer violence has endeavoured to draw together a number of *recurrent* themes that arose during the research study and to comment on the similarities and differences between the four localities. It is clear that, despite certain differences arising from sampling procedures, the characteristics of the areas studied, and broader issues to do with *historical* and *cultural* specificities, there are some striking *similarities* in the ways in which young people anticipate, perpetrate, explain and rationalise their violent behaviour. Those similarities in turn suggest that there is a shared *platform* for understanding peer violence in public space that permits some common responses and interventions to be developed.

4 The Role of Age, Gender and Ethnicity

Changes Coming Along with Age

In Järvikaupunki, most peer violence reportedly took place between similarly aged individuals. Conflicts between older and younger teenagers were mostly non-physical. When physical, encounters were often initiated by the older combatant. Younger peers, generally, reported less serious physical consequences and expressed less concern over violence. Some Perkova interviewees described encounters where older girls responded violently to the 'bad behaviour' of younger peers. Although older young people in Trewaun suggested that it was unfair to target younger peers, this was not the way younger individuals saw it: they reported being targeted by older peers. This inconsistency reflects a discrepancy in motivation and intent; for older interviewees rationalised these encounters as 'just for fun' or to 'teach them a lesson' (assert control), which was not perceived as 'real' violence. As illustrated in Järvikaupunki, younger boys' interpreted physical violence and its consequences somewhat differently from the narratives of older boys.

Regarding the fairness of an encounter, *equality* of the size of combatants was in fact a more common measurement than equality of the age. Avoidance strategies were expressed by younger respondents as a way of *coping* with peer violence that could lead to their displacement and exclusion from certain public spaces. Young people in Urbanitz felt they were too vulnerable in public space occupied by older teenagers and it was easier to use children's facilities in parks or stay at home.

A *change* in the approach to and interpretation of violence was evident as young people got older. Commonly, young people of both sexes explained that their feelings changed towards certain types of violence – when they were younger they did not identify some types of behaviour as violent. According to this shift in attitudes, their behaviour and use of violence also changed. Young people also expressed a change over their *teenage* years towards the use of less aggressive methods to solve problems.

The Role of Gender

Gender differences were apparent in each locality in terms of young people's participation in, attitudes towards and reports of the impact of violence. Most peer violence was between combatants of the same sex. Violent conflict was interpreted as *normal* and expected by most boys, while girls viewed it as a type of behaviour they only engaged in for specific reasons. Girls tended to express concern at the level and rate of violence perpetrated by boys, while boys largely viewed girls' violence as insignificant or less 'real', more entertaining or childish. Violence between girls was often viewed by both sexes as less 'real' or 'serious'. In particular the premise that boys were physically superior to girls and the labelling of certain forms of violence (e.g. face slapping, hair pulling or biting) as 'feminine' was used to lessen girl's experiences of violence.

Girls reportedly used *'feminine'* moves that were sometimes considered "amusing". When Järvikaupunki girls openly abused boys, even using kicking, slapping and punching, it was seldom identified as 'real' violence in the interviews. Yet, the experts in the workshop perceived girls' overt violence as much more sinificant than the young people themselves (which may be related to differences in the understanding of gender roles between adults and young people). Gender differences were noticeable in Urbanitz according to the intentions underlying violent behaviour. Boys were more likely to use predatory motivations, for example, violence was used to gain access to or control of resources (e.g. status enhancement, territory, property). In contrast, girls were more likely to report defensive intentions arising from conflicts over friendships and relationships.

The influence of *traditional* gender roles was evident in each site in terms of the rate and type of violence boys and girls engaged in. In direct opposition to the violence amongst boys that was linked to being a 'real man' and expressions of masculinity, a complete desistance from violence was expected amongst girls in Perkova who wished to create and leave a good impression (e.g. as a 'good girl' or 'real woman'). However, not all girls wished to create such good impressions - for these 'bad girls', this meant deviating from established notions of 'femininity' and adopting a more masculine role which normalised their violence with both girls and boys. Thus, 'bad girls' are less bound by the conventions of being 'good' and so can participate in a widespread repertoire of violent behaviours. Girls in Perkova and Trewaun generally engaged in the *same* types, but lower rates, of violence as boys and appeared more violent than those in the other localities. During *collective* encounters girls would not usually fight boys in the opposing group; instead they would take on opposing girls, carry weapons or assist their male counterparts as supporters at one remove from the direct encounter. Although girls were less violent in Järvikaupunki their efforts to *oppose* boys physically was, for some, an acceptable way to construct their identity as an active, independent and strong Finnish woman.

Violence between boys and girls was identified as a *serious*, but *uncommon* and largely *hidden* type of violence. Only a few serious cases of violence in boy-girl relationships were reported by the young people, including both verbal (e.g. name-calling and harassment) and physical (e.g. punching and kicking) behaviours. Boy's sexual harassment of girls was an issue for some of the interviewed young people in Urbanitz. Interestingly, *girls' sexual harassment* of boys, which sometimes bordered on bullying or assault, seemed to be a more acceptable behaviour that largely went unnoticed. In Perkova interviews with 'good girls' suggested they used covert means to abuse boys (e.g. gossip and personal slights). Sexual violence was identified as 'real' violence by Perkova young people, although no personal experiences were recorded.

The Minority Ethnic Dimension

Järvikaupunki migrant respondents had many experiences of racial conflict with native peers (but rarely with other migrant groups). This type of violence was not customarily identified as in-group, as it predominantly involved strangers. Having a *distinctive* ethnic appearance had a profound effect on the violent experiences reported; essentially they were more likely to be involved in serious types of violence. *Migrant* interviewees seldom reported the types of violence common to native young people – such as playful or cross-gender violence. While the attitudes of native Estonian and ethnic Russian young people towards violence were quite similar in Perkova, their separate identities clearly divided them. The ethnic differences between Estonian and Russian young people were expressed most commonly in everyday verbal encounters; essentially their distinct languages identified them as protagonists.

Additionally *'identity'-led* conflicts were evident in Perkova, between Estonian S*kinheads* and ethnic Russian teenagers. Ethnic Russian Skinheads were also identified in Perkova which, paradoxically, exacerbated identity conflict as Estonian Skinheads refused to acknowledge them as true followers of Skinhead culture. The resulting encounters between these groups were reportedly *serious* in nature and often involved a group of Estonian Skinheads attacking one single ethnic Russian Skinhead. Accounts of violence between opposing *sub-cultural* groups (e.g. Emos, Chavs, Goths) were identified in Trewaun. Overall, violence between young people and what they perceive as *'outsiders'* was often reported as the most serious type of violence – in terms of the level of violence used (usually more serious), the use of weapons and the number of young people involved (usually out-group, collective). This violence was largely motivated by revenge, (self) defence, anger, resentment, the need to establish identity and control and the desire for fun.

Doubtlessly, the *lower* levels of violence reported in Urbanitz, when compared to other localities, were influenced by the *large* minority ethnic sample informing the findings. The identification of unacceptable targets (e.g. girls and younger people) in Urbanitz can be explained by the wider *cultural* values on age and gender held by these minority ethnic populations. According to their ethnic *masculinity* it is the duty of males to take care of and protect younger peers and women. Therefore, violent intentions (e.g. 'protection', 'sexual harassment', 'bravado') found in Urbanitz are shaped, and arguably constrained, by certain specificities concerning cultural norms within the sample interviewed.

Concluding Remarks

Gender is pivotal in the research and marks the most important division of teenagers' behaviour. Violence, as all previous research has demonstrated, is *predominately masculine*, a territory of males' practices. What is different nowadays appears behind the diversity of senses, motivations and intentions, as illustrated in the four locality reports. However, if in the contest for resources and power was predominantly the driving force for youth violence, the same cannot be said quite so categorically today. We have a very colourful portrait of motivations, from (self)-defence and 'just for fun', like in sport, through 'for self-affirmation' among the peers (typical for adolescence) to 'for self-realisation', for communication and expression for the oldest interviewees. Even girls seem to be more *willing* from a very young age to participate in violent encounters, though in many cases they do so as *supporters* of their boyfriends and class-mates.

Ethnicity looks *less important* within peer violence in the present study. Socio-economic conditions, local context and facilities, and sub-cultural backgrounds predominantly structured the models and forms of peer violent encounters in disadvantaged neighbourhoods. In the case of young people, ethnicity as an analytic category looks out of date and can be translated internally into two major sub-dimensions:

- young people searching for their 'roots': the *culture* of origin, values and traditions of their parents and grand parents;

- *identity* quests, including multi-level questionings and perspectives (orientated to many forms of difference, including diverse racisms)

An overall conclusion of this chapter is that unravelling the form and content of peer violence in public space is complex and challenging: it weaves and 'melds' (mixes and welds) in ways that combine multiple and sometimes contradictory categories within young people's particular realities. Yet, looking for commonalities as well as for differences between the four – quite different – European localities meant to contribute to this unravelling by highlighting different aspects that may otherwise not have been perceived in this way.

Conclusions: Reflections and Recommendations

Barbara Riepl, Judit Strömpl, Helena Helve, Johanna Blum, Kadi Ilves, Ingrid Kromer, Veli Liikanen, Jennifer Maher, Howard Williamson

1 Theory and Method

Theoretical Perspectives of the Study

Testing an already existing theory on youth violence was not the aim of this study. The theoretical framework for the study is a social constructionist approach. On this assumption we focus on relations that arose from the narratives in which young people represented their experiences of violence in public space. The following theoretical perspectives emerge from this study of peer violence in public space in four different European countries.

Peer violence is culturally and context related. In terms of the context, it is important to recognise both broader (i.e. European) and more local contexts. There are clearly moments in which the European common youth culture is reproduced. However this common picture evolves from local contexts that may be quite heterogeneous with regard to structural as well as social dimensions (such as socio-economic background, and the role of gender and ethnicity). Within these contexts, *youth culture* is established as a sub-culture separate from the adult culture (Corsaro 2005; for more on the concept of construction of childhood and youth see also Nayak and Kehily 2008; James and Prout 1997). Though the youth culture is a space that is to some extent separate from the adults' world, it responds to the well-established dominant values and norms in the adult culture through reinterpretation as well as reproduction, based on its own experiences and understandings.

The values and norms of youth culture or youth groups are protected by sanctions similar to the proceedings in the adults' world. However, the execution of sanctions may differ with regard to means and severity if young people do not agree with or do not have access to the kind of sanctions that are used by adults. The locality studies demonstrated that peer violence was argued to be *'needed'* in many cases in order to defend personal and group safety, to take revenge or to establish respect. Within these violent exchanges and encounters, youth culture's norms are being established (Gordon and Lahelma 2003, Thorne 1993). Deviation from group norms is also sanctioned with violence, using different techniques of neutralisation (Sykes and Matza, 1957). The source of protection for victims is mainly through other peers, such as friends or relatives, since conflicts taking place within the youth culture are usually not even noticed by adults. Socially excluded young people who are not supported by others are particularly vulnerable not only to physical hurt but also to the psychological harm caused through violent actions perpetrated by other young people.

The study further draws attention to the fact that youth violence is *gender related*. Young people talking about their experiences with violence reproduced traditional gender *stereotypes* of masculinity and femininity in all of the localities. And it was also confirmed that young men are more likely to use physical violence than girls. The fact of belonging to the male world arguably assumes some violence (Connel and Messerschmidt 2005; Hearn 2004). Hearn defines genders as social categories and emphasises men as the dominant one. The dominant status gives to the men category a set of characteristics: *"Men are members of a powerful social group and a social category that is invested with power. This has the consequence that membership of that group or category brings power, if only by association. As with other powerful groups, dominance is maintained and reproduced in a wide variety of ways, including persuasion, influence, force, violence, and so on"* (Hearn 1998: 35).

In this context it is interesting that such a widespread pattern as boys' violence against girls (Klein 2006; Aaltonen 2002; Lahelma 2002; Tallavaara 2002) was hardly mentioned by young people in this study. Albeit the gender roles connected with femininity, such as vulnerability, sensibility, and need for protection, was audible both in boys and girls' narratives. The cases of physically violent girls that are presented in the media tell more about girls' deviation from feminine behaviour and are not generally accepted by young people. Young people talking about their experiences of violence in public space reproduce, rather than subvert, traditional gender stereotypes of masculinity and femininity.

Ethnic or racial affiliation provides another basis for young people's identity work and related perceived differences may lead to conflicts between young people. The study showed that even where there are no representatives of ethnic minorities or different racial groups, racism exists. The locality where ethnicity seemed to be least relevant was the one where the interviewed young people from an ethnic minority spent their leisure time quite separated from the 'native' young people: though both groups exist in the area there are hardly any reasons for getting in touch with each other.

Ethnicity is conceptualised by Fernando (1991 cited by Singla 2004) as relational and as a sense of belonging in interaction with the broader context. It is perceived as having two components – a stance of self-categorisation and a style of cultural adaptation. To some extent these components resemble the division of ethnic identity into complementary internal, subjective and external, objective dimensions. In another dimension, ethnicity is viewed as 'primordial', predicated on original aspects like colour and descent; and 'instrumental', predicated on social processes. Furthermore, in agreement with Ålund (1999 cited by Singla 2004), in an analysis of ethnicity's multiplicity, ethnicity is considered as a dynamic phenomenon intertwined with gender, race and class.

Racism is simply a way in which one constructs the differences between 'us' and 'them' by asserting that 'we' are superior to 'them' in certain respects, although according to Miles (1993 cited by Singla 2004) contemporary racism is built on ideas of culture, not so much on biological differences. It is accepted that when we study experiences of racism among young people with ties to some of the so-called third world countries, we are dealing with racialised social relations and hierarchies, since ethnicity is perceived in relation to experiences of race (Singla 2004).

All in all, the results of the study *underlined* what is also theoretically being discussed: that the question of belonging is an essential one for young people, be it related to youth culture and youth groups, to gender or to ethnicity and race.

Methodological Perspectives of the Study

The choice of a qualitative methodology in this study derives from the theoretical framework of the study. The value of qualitative methodology is that it makes possible not only the production of rich data, but also to develop communication with young people in different ways. During schooling, organised leisure time activities and home upbringing the adults' responsibility, control and powers of decision-making are emphasised. The situation is different in research communication when young participants are responsible for the information they give to the researcher. The focused interest on the opinions of young people in this form of communication gives them a feeling that their experiences and perspectives are important and respected. That does not mean that in schooling, organised leisure or home upbringing the opinions of young people cannot be taken into account, but it is not the primary aim of those settings. In the case of qualitative research it is the aim itself.

On the basis of experiences in this research we have analysed the positive and negative sides of collecting data in both group and individual interviews.

In the group interviews we followed the participants' social relations in more or less the 'natural' settings. Through this we had an excellent opportunity to get an insight into youth discourses on peer violence (Strömpl *et al.* 2007, Eder and Fingerson 2002), at least as far as the young people were willing to reveal it. We were aware, however, of the fact that the group interviews were not a good opportunity to gather information about harmful individual experiences, for personal reasons as well as due to the hierarchy within the group. When dominant young people describe violent encounters within a group interview, the voice of victims is unlikely to be heard. Furthermore, it was important to keep in mind that some of the information given by a participant within a group interview may be lead to sanctions after the interview from the other young people, no matter whether participants are friends or strangers to each other. A group interview is definitely more suitable for mapping young people's collective ideas, but when studying individual experiences with sensitive topics, individual interviews yield deeper information: in an individual interview young people can provide more details of violent encounters and what they actually meant to them.

In summary, there is a set of specific issues attached both to group and to individual interviews. With regard to the group interviews these are:

- Participants have a more powerful position in the interview situation when they are backed up by a group.

- Youth discourses are reconstructed within the interview.

- Young people get the opportunity to present youth culture to the adult world.

- Themes that young people may be reluctant to address in other settings, due to the unequal power relations in everyday life, can be discussed on a more equal relationship basis within a group interview (e.g. violence from adults to young people in institutional settings, see Pösö *et al.* 2008 and Strömpl *et al.* 2007).

- Some topics can harm some of the participants without the harm becoming evident in the interview situations.

- In the course of the interview, conflicts may arise among the group members.

With regard to the individual interviews these are:

- Individual interviews may cause more stress to the interviewed young person.

- More extensive information about young people's individual experiences can be gathered.

- If the interviewed young person feels comfortable with the interviewer, more confidential information will be given than would be divulged in a group setting.

- Less forthcoming young people, who would remain outside or on the edge of the discussion in group interviews, get the chance to express their views (Helve 1993).

- It is easier for the interviewee to ask for help, if needed, and for the interviewer to offer support and advice if this seems to be necessary.

- Because of the unequal power relation between young people and adults, the interviewee may tend to give the 'right' answers but an open-ended interview situation does allow for an issue to be explored from a number of angles, opening up the possibility for the interviewees to be more confident and assertive in articulating their views.

The experiences from this study on peer violence lead to the conclusion that it is very helpful to combine and connect group and individual interviews when studying a sensitive topic such as this. We would suggest starting with some group interviews during which the most common youth interpretations of the studied phenomenon would be discussed. On the basis of those data a topic guide for the individual interviews could be prepared carefully. The individual interviews would be carried out with the same young people who participated in some group interviews. These young people can then comment on the preliminary findings of group interviews and also add some more personal information about their experiences. In such a process the researcher will not be a stranger to the participant and the pressure and presumed expectations are likely to be less intensive than in those cases when the interviewer is seen for the first time.

This kind of research also permits more intensive communication between the researchers and young people when it comes to discussions with young people on more policy-oriented questions regarding how to change the situation of peer violence in public space. In other words, such repeated contacts and communication form stepping stones to more effective participatory work, which is especially needed in the context of what is frequently a lack of trust in and suspicion of adults amongst young people. It almost certainly also adds to the reliability of the research.

From the beginning the international research group discussed the question how to invite young participants to take part in the research. The question arose because of the sensitive topic on the one hand and the context of the stigma attached to naming disadvantaged neighbourhoods, on the other hand. Eventually it was decided to introduce the study to young people as being about young people's leisure time in public space and about relations between young people in public space, including friendships and conflicts. This was seen as a sensitive and incremental way of informing young people, as the issues mentioned explicitly actually were the topics to be dealt with in the study. However, it was rarely said at the very start of contact with young people that the focus of the study was on peer violence, not least because we did not want to 'direct' young people too directly to violence. This would have very much restricted the outcome of the inquiry, for young people would have just reported on conflicts that according to their own definition were violent. The aim of the study was to learn more about all kinds of conflicts amongst and between young people, including those that young people themselves would not call violent (e.g. the 'playful' violence as it was described in the study). We acknowledge that this approach to engaging young people in the study may be viewed by some as ethically contentious, as some participants might not have given their consent to participate in the study if they had known the focus right from the beginning. The broader methodological (and ethical) issue therefore is how precisely one should present difficult topics of inquiry to young people to enable them to make an informed choice as to whether or not to take part, while at the same time not deterring them prematurely from participation.

Another important methodological aspect is to design the study in a way that not only 'uses' young people but that it also is *of use* to them. This may be no more than the fact that adults show an authentic interest in youth matters by carefully listening to the voice of young people, or on a more policy-oriented level by using study results as a basis for initiating improvements for the situation of young people. In any case it is important that questions are not too strictly prepared so that the interviewer still has the chance to react and respond to what is brought up by the young person during the interview.

With regard to the analysis, we need to realise that information gathered from interviews with young people cannot be treated as facts and figures. The narratives provide explanations of motives and consequences by young people, interpretations that can be used to learn more about their youth culture and the role peer violence plays in it. This needs to be kept in mind when reading the models of peer violence as well as the description of the characteristics in this book. Yet it seems to be the only way to get an insight in a phenomenon mostly hidden to the adult world. A questionnaire using concepts and categories developed from an adult perspective could never provide the same in-depth information.

2 Policy and Practice

Previous chapters in this book have portrayed peer violence in four 'disadvantaged' European localities. The variety of findings from these localities, on the one hand, emphasises the *complexity* of the issue. On the other hand, the many commonalities clarified that peer violence is a *relevant* topic across Europe. Yet, though it is an existing phenomenon that should not be under-estimated, it also became clear that most interviewed young people defined some forms of peer violence (such as that described as 'playful' or 'sport-like', or 'just for fun') as not real violence. It was not seen as much of a problem in their everyday lives that needed much done about. To consider this specific point of view, which differs somewhat from that of researchers and adults, seems to be important, particularly when thinking about suitable and effective prevention/ intervention measures. In contrast, it needs also to be borne in mind that young people also identified some other forms of violence as severe and requiring urgent attention and intervention.

The implications of the research for policy and practice were not only considered within the European project team, but also within workshops with young people and experts in each of the localities. The recommendations resulting from these reflections are presented below, though not all of them are of the same relevance for each locality.

Established Principles behind the Recommendations

Based on the discussions, principles for the development of the recommendations were defined in order to point out the perspective and underlying guiding aim to prevent and reduce peer violence in public space. These were as follows:

- Reflecting the *diversity* of young people through *comprehensive*, as well as *specific* approaches.

- Respecting the *equality* of all young people through approaches that do not reflect or reinforce existing inequalities (e.g. gender or socio-economic inequalities).

- Promoting *empowerment* of young people through providing an appropriate and adequate framework of space and means.

- Securing *long-term* changes through sustainable approaches.

- Replacing negative behaviours through *positive* formal and non-formal, and recreational experiences.

Prevention Measures

Generally, policy measures against violence can be differentiated in *many ways*. One possibility is to consider the moment of intervention/preventions: With this in mind, *primary* prevention aims to prevent peer violence before it occurs, *secondary* prevention deals with the immediate consequences of peer violence, and *tertiary* prevention focuses on the longer term consequences of peer violence.

Another grouping of measures distinguishes between universal and selective interventions. Whereas *universal* interventions aim at the population in general or at population groups without regard to individual risk or need, *selective* interventions focus on those considered being at risk or more significantly in need.

Furthermore, interventions can have different *target* groups. Some approaches are focused on the individual; some approach specific settings in which young people are located, like school or youth work; others approach more general social contexts.

The following measures are not grouped according to any of these conceptual distinctions, as they cut across and through them all. However, it remains helpful to keep the distinctions in mind when reading the recommended measures in order to realise that, *in operation*, they may give different weight and be differently positioned within this theoretical prevention framework.

Raising Awareness of Violence

When seeking to counteract peer violence, a first step is to raise awareness of violence in general. Both adults and young people should pay *more* attention to violent behaviour, even if it is considered as not severe. Young people who consider violence as a 'reasonable' way to resolve conflict situations (because, to them, it may seem to be the only 'solution' they have) appeared likely to be involved in more serious violence at a later stage. To *sensitise* adults to the often 'hidden' use of violence in everyday life is relevant also with regard to their function as role models. In addition, *prejudices* with regard to gender and race/ethnicity need to be tackled in order to recognise them as another important aspect contributing to peer violence. Though it is important to draw attention to violent behaviour amongst young people, which is often underplayed by those involved and often ignored by others, peer violence should equally not be taken out of perspective and over-exaggerated. From the young people's propositions and points of view, peer violence generally should get rather less public attention in order to reduce its 'glamour' and attractiveness. A careful and sensitive balance needs to be struck but it is essential to raise awareness that *non-violent* behaviour benefits society in general: it not only improves the quality of life for young people, but of the community as a whole.

Promoting Respectful Relationships

Respectful relationships between young people as well as between young people and *adults* secure social bonds that allow individuals to feel comfortable and safe and to support each other. Adults' respectful and non-violent behaviour toward children and young people is an especially important basis for young people's understanding of relationships and approaches to conflict resolution.

Planning and Providing Programmes and Services

Combating peer violence means to develop *tailor-made* programmes, services and training for young people and their families. More traditional and successful forms of youth work need to be complemented with more *innovative* initiatives and projects. The challenge is to provide *attractive* programmes and services in the 'right' places at the 'right' times (especially late evenings, weekends and school holidays).

Securing the Availability and Attractiveness of Public Space

In contrast to common practice, public space does not necessarily have to be divided into specific places and facilities for specific *age-groups* as this tends to separate them. Instead a manifold and *multifaceted* use of public space is recommended. What is important for young people is that they are allowed to use public space according to their needs and that they are treated as equally important as other groups. Young people also need to respect the interests and activities of others.

Encouraging Youth Participation

Young people need to be encouraged to contribute to the planning of public space, of leisure time facilities, as well as of programmes and services directed to them in an open *dialogue*. That also means the broader involvement of young people in decision-making processes on matters that affect their lives. To integrate the ideas and wishes of the users contributes to the realisation of better outcomes and greater acceptance of the ultimate decisions. What is also important is that young people should not just be involved in decision-making processes of *low* relevance (e.g. where to put the bench in the park). It needs to be more widely acknowledged that young people as a population group are, though often indirectly and therefore less obviously, affected by a plethora of political decisions governing what they can and cannot do in public space – and therefore they should be given greater opportunity to contribute to those debates.

Improving the Living Conditions of Young People

Young people may be viewed as a marginalised population group struggling with their transition to adulthood, suffering from the breakdown of traditional social and cultural ties, and encountering disproportionate risks of poverty and exclusion. Reducing violence among young people therefore also means restoring their belief in the *future*, through addressing the deprivation and disadvantage in their everyday lives, which can often represent the socio-economic basis for at least some of their violent behaviour. Policies therefore need to fight income *inequality*, to take care of institutional reforms of the educational system and establish credible vocational training and job creation programmes for young people.

Establishing Multilevel Networking and Co-operation

To secure a pluralist, holistic, multi-agency and interdisciplinary approach to peer violence, one first important step is to initiate a dialogue and create co-operation between different professional actors in the broad arena of youth violence: formal and non-formal educators; the youth education sector, the police, the health care system and others working in public space. There also needs to be improved dialogue between research, policy and practice. Of specific importance is the further step that lies in the establishment of communication and exchanges between all these actors and young people themselves. Young people cannot be treated solely as the recipients of professionally determined measures of intervention, but must be considered as *equal* partners in the development and implementation of strategies for youth violence prevention.

Gathering Data and Disseminating Information

Data related to peer violence need to be *available* and *accessible* to the public to monitor developments. In addition, *research* on causes and impact is needed, as well as *evaluation* of measures and the distribution of information on best practice. It is further of specific relevance to provide easily accessible information on services and programmes to young people.

Intervention Levels

The measures listed and described above need to be implemented at the *local* level in a range of different settings, at the *national* and *European* level, or at both levels, depending on the respective responsibilities and aims. Interestingly, young people themselves mentioned mainly measures at the *individual* level. They described what they could do themselves to prevent becoming a victim through avoiding specific places, situations and young people.

At the *local* level some examples of measures are as follows:

- Providing regular and effective youth work.

- Establishing mentoring and peer-education programmes.

- Designing education programmes against discrimination and for more tolerance.

- Delivering training in social skills and *non-violent* conflict resolution techniques.

- Combating drug and alcohol use and abuse.

- Developing specific parenting programmes.

- Rehabilitation of young (violent) offenders.

- Improving the school setting including teaching practices.

- Offering unsupervised and consumption 'free zones' to young people for leisure time activities.

- Integrating young people in decision-making processes.

- Creating a safe and attractive environment for all ages.

- Promoting the networking and cooperation between relevant institutions and services.

At the national level, examples of measures are as follows:

- Defining the prevention of violence as a political goal.

- Securing long-term funding for programmes and services.

- Promoting the development of new concepts, programmes and services.

- Assuring funding for research and programme evaluation.

- Providing a holistic and concerted approach to youth policy, across the different political sectors with respect to the United Nations Convention on the Rights of the Child.

- Setting up a European 'Clearing House' to exchange relevant information.

- Building a positive picture of young people in the public discourse.

From an international perspective, national policies are backed up through European resolutions and political strategies. Furthermore, *cross-national* research in the field of the social sciences and the revisions of national policies would appear to be an extremely important issue in pursuit of a stronger understanding of youth violence and the prevention of such violence as a social phenomenon in the contemporary world.

The aim of the present study was to provide all relevant professional groups with some evidence on which to base their work – be it in policy, in education or in other fields. The study is intended to foster new (or renewed) public debate on a matter that appears to command considerable media attention yet limited political response. It is hoped that the findings will lead to relevant practical action, and to a recognition of the importance of research in assisting the understanding of peer violence in public space. Of most significance perhaps is the way in which this study has distilled a range of similarities and differences through its four locality inquiry, that has thrown into relief both local specificities and those issues that merit attention at both national and European levels.

References

Aaltonen, S., (2002). Told, Denied and Silenced. Young People's Interpretations of Conflicts and Gender in School. In: Sunnari, V., Kangasvuo, J. and Heikkinen, M., eds., *Gendered and Sexualised Violence in Educational Environments.* Oulu: Oulu University Press, 129-141.

Connel, R. and Messerschmindt, J., (2005). Hegemonic masculinity. Rethinking the concept. *Gender & Society,* 19 (6), 829-859.

Corsaro, W. A., (2005). *The Sociology of Childhood*. London: Thousand Oaks, New Delhi: Sage Publications.

Eder, D., Fingerson, L., (2002). Interviewing Children and Adolescents. In: Gubrium, J. and Holstein, J., eds., *Handbook of Interview Research. Context & Method*. London, Thousand Oaks, New Delhi: Sage Publications, 181-202.

Gordon, T. and Lahelma E., (2003). Vuorovaikutus ja ihmissuhteet informaalissa koulussa. *In:* Lahelma, E. and Gordon, T., eds., *Koulun arkea tutkimassa. Yläasteen erot ja erilaisuudet*. Helsingin kaupungin opetusvirasto, 42-58.

Hearn, J., (2004). From hegemonic masculinity to the hegemony of men. *Feminist Theory.* 5 (1), 49-72.

Hearn, J., (1998). *The Violence of Men*. London: Thousand Oaks, New Delhi: Sage Publications.

Helve, H., (1993). *The Worldview of Young people. A longitudinal Study of Finnish Youth Living in a Suburb of metropolitan Helsinki*. Helsinki: Academia Scientiarum Fennica.

James, A. and Prout, A., eds., (1997). *Constructing and Reconstructing Childhood: Contemporary Issues in the Sociological Study of Childhood.* 2nd ed., London: Falmer.

Klein, J., (2006). An Invisible Problem. Everyday Violence Against Girls in Schools. *Theoretical Criminology.* 10 (2), 147-177.

Lahelma, E., (2002). Gendered Conflicts in Secondary School: fun or enactment of power? *Gender and Education.* 14 (3), 295-306.

Nayak, A. and Kehily, M.J., (2008). *Gender, Youth and Culture*. Hampshire, New York: Palgrave Macmillan.

Pösö, T., Honkatukia, P. and Nyqvist, L., (2008). Focus groups and the study of violence. *Qualitative Research.* 8 (1), 73-89.

Sykes, G. M. and Matza, D., (1957). Techniques of Neutralization: A Theory of Delinquency. *American Sociological Review,* 22 (December), 128-132.

Singla, R., (2004). Youth Relationships and Ethnicity: A Social Psychological Perspective. *Young,* 12 (1), 50-70.

Strömpl, J., Selg, M., Soo, K. and Sahverdov-Zarkovski, B., (2007). *Eesti teismeliste vägivallatõlgendused.* [Interpretations of violence among Estonian teenagers] Sotsiaalministeeriumi Toimetised 3.

Tallavaara, A., (2002). Irritation − A Glimpse of Gendered Violence. *In:* Sunnari, V., Kangasvuo, J. and Heikkinen, M., eds., *Gendered and Sexualised Violence in Educational Environments*. Oulu: Oulu University Press, 25-37.

Thorne, B., (1993). *Gender Play: Girls and Boys at School*. New Brunswick, NY: Rutgers University Press.

Contributors

Johanna Blum

research associate in the Austrian locality study

currently works as a researcher at the Institute for Social Research and Analysis (SORA) in Vienna. Prior to this she was a research associate at the Austrian Institute for Youth Research from 2005 to 2008. She studied Sociology and Political Science at the University of Vienna and the University of Copenhagen. She has researched in the field of young people in education and work and is interested in transitions in the life course with a focus on ethnic and gender differences.

Contact: Johanna Blum, SORA, Linke Wienzeile 246, A-1150 Vienna, jb@sora.at

Helena Helve

co-ordinator of the Finnish locality study

is currently research professor at Tampere University and adjunct professor at Helsinki University. For the Daphne project she had a contract with Kuopio University. She has been a visiting research fellow at the Centre for Longitudinal Studies, Institute of Education, University of London, a coordinator of the Nordic youth research of the Nordic Council of Ministers, president of the Finnish Youth Research Society 1995-2005 and president of the International Sociological Association, Research Committee of Youth Sociology 2002-2006. Recent publications include co-authored and co-edited books on *Youth and Social Capital, Contemporary Youth Research, Local Expressions and Global Connections* and *Mixed Methods in Youth Research*.

Contact: Helena Helve, Tampere University, Dept. of Social Work Research, 33014 University of Tampere, Finland, helena.helve@uta.fi

Kadi Ilves

research associate in the Estonian locality study

is researcher and doctoral student of sociology at the University of Tartu, Estonia. She received her Master's degree from the University of Tartu in 2006. Her main research interest is the sociology of violence. Her Ph.D. research focuses on youth violence culture and peer violence among teenagers.

Contact: Kadi Ilves, Institute of Sociology and Social Policy of Tartu University, Tiigi Str. 78, 50410 Tartu, Estonia, kadi.ilves.001@ut.ee

Ingrid Kromer

co-ordinator of the Austrian locality study

is research associate and project manager at the Austrian Institute of Youth Research in Vienna. She joined the Institute in 1993 when she finished her studies in educational science. Before that she had many years' experience of youth work in youth organisations and in youth centres. Her research and publications focus on the transition from childhood to youth, young people's values, gender and identity, ecological activism, participation and socio-political commitment of young people, youth work, youth delinquency and deviant behaviour.

Contact: Ingrid Kromer, Austrian Institute for Youth Research, Maria Theresien-Straße 24/10, A-1010 Vienna, ingrid.kromer@oeij.at

Veli Liikanen

research associate in the Finnish locality study

works as a researcher at Mikkeli University of Applied Science. He studied both natural (Ecology) and social (Sociology) sciences at the University of Jyväskylä, participating actively in the Finnish youth environmental movement at the same time. His main research interests are the political participation of young people, civic activity in non-governmental organizations, youth cultures and environmental policy.

Contact: Veli Liikanen, Campus of Culture and Youth Work, Mikkeli University of Applied Sciences, Paukkulantie 22, PL 181, 50101 Mikkeli, veli.liikanen@mamk.fi

Jennifer Maher

research associate in the Welsh locality study

is a research associate and lecturer in the Centre for Criminology at the University of Glamorgan, Wales (UK). She was awarded her PhD in 2007 for her postgraduate study *Angels with Dirty Faces: Youth gangs and troublesome youth groups in South Wales*. Her current research areas include youth violence, youth gangs and the link between animal abuse and human violence.

Contact: Jennifer Maher, Centre for Criminology, University of Glamorgan, Mid Glamorgan, CF45 4LY, UK, jmaher@glam.ac.uk

Youra Petrova

project evaluator

is a research associate and a lecturer in the National Centre for Scientific Research (CNRS) and the Research Institute on Contemporary Societies (IRESCO-GSRL), in Paris (France). She did her postgraduate studies at the High School for Social Sciences (EHESS-CADIS) and is a sociologist working principally in the field of youth cultural studies and youth violence studies. Her other topics of academic interest are identity, racism and masculinity as well as methodology and youth policies linked to them. Current research and publications focus on young people's riots and protesting activism on the street. Recently, she also has been taking an active part in the work of ULISS (International Link Research Unit of CNRS-IRESCO).

Contact: Youra Petrova, Research Institute on Contemporary Societies: IRESCO/ CNRS, Paris, 75017, France, yourapetrova@hotmail.fr

Barbara Riepl

project co-ordinator

works as social researcher at the Austrian Institute for Youth Research. Before joining the Institute in 2005 she was research fellow in the Childhood Programme at the European Centre for Social Welfare Policy and Research for nine years. Her main research interests are disadvantaged children and young people, the civic and political participation of young people, and childhood and youth policies. She has been co-ordinator of a range of national studies on different issues as well as of an international study on political participation of young people below voting age.

Contact: Barbara Riepl, Austrian Institute for Youth Research, Maria Theresienstr. 24/10, A-1010 Vienna, barbara.riepl@oeij.at

Judit Strömpl

co-ordinator of the Estonian locality study

is associate professor at the University of Tartu, Estonia. Her main fields of interest are juvenile delinquency, the residential care of troublesome young people, and sensitive topics such as violence and discrimination. She carried out several qualitative and mixed-method studies with participation of vulnerable people (children and young people in trouble, LGBT-people, Russian and Estonian prostitutes in Helsinki). The goal of her studies is to understand and give voice to those people who are in silence.

Contact: Judit Strömpl, Institute of Sociology and Social Policy of Tartu University, Tiigi Str. 78, 50410 Tartu, Estonia, judit.strompl@ut.ee

Howard Williamson

co-ordinator of the Welsh locality study

is professor of European Youth Policy at the University of Glamorgan. He has worked on a range of 'youth issues' such as formal and non-formal learning, justice, substance misuse, exclusion and citizenship at European and national levels. Currently he co-ordinates the Council of Europe's international reviews of national youth policies. One of his more recent books is *The Milltown Boys Revisited*, a follow-up study of a group of men who were young offenders in the 1970s. He was appointed CBE (Commander of the Order of the British Empire) in 2002 for services to young people. During 2008 he was a member of *The Street Weapons Commission*, looking at the issue of knife and gun crime in the United Kingdom.

Contact: Howard Williamson, Faculty of Humanities and Social Sciences, University of Glamorgan, Pontypridd, Wales, UK CF37 1DL, howardw@glam.ac.uk

from left: Helena Helve, Howard Williamson, Kadi Ilves, Barbara Riepl, Judit Strömpl, Veli Liikanen, Johanna Blum, Jennifer Maher, Ingrid Kromer